Mastering Unity Scripting

Learn advanced C# tips and techniques to make
professional-grade games with Unity

Alan Thorn

PUBLISHING

BIRMINGHAM - MUMBAI

Mastering Unity Scripting

First published: January 2015

Production reference: 1230115

Published by Packt Publishing Ltd.
Livery Place
35 Livery Street
Birmingham B3 2PB, UK.

ISBN 978-1-78439-065-5

www.packtpub.com

Credits

Author
Alan Thorn

Reviewers
Dylan Agis
John P. Doran
Alessandro Mochi
Ryan Watkins

Commissioning Editor
Dipika Gaonkar

Acquisition Editor
Subho Gupta

Content Development Editors
Melita Lobo
Rikshith Shetty

Technical Editors
Shashank Desai
Pankaj Kadam

Copy Editors
Karuna Narayanan
Laxmi Subramanian

Project Coordinator
Kinjal Bari

Proofreaders
Samuel Redman Birch
Ameesha Green

Indexer
Rekha Nair

Production Coordinator
Shantanu N. Zagade

Cover Work
Shantanu N. Zagade

About the Author

Alan Thorn is a London-based game developer, freelance programmer, and author with over 13 years of industry experience. He founded Wax Lyrical Games in 2010, and is the creator of the award-winning game, *Baron Wittard: Nemesis of Ragnarok*. He is the author of 10 video-training courses and 11 books on game development, including *Unity 4 Fundamentals: Get Started at Making Games with Unity*, *Focal Press*, *UDK Game Development*, and *Pro Unity Game Development with C#*, *Apress*. He is also a visiting lecturer on the Game Design & Development Masters Program at the National Film and Television School.

Alan has worked as a freelancer on over 500 projects, including games, simulators, kiosks, serious games, and augmented reality software for game studios, museums, and theme parks worldwide. He is currently working on an upcoming adventure game, *Mega Bad Code*, for desktop computers and mobile devices. Alan enjoys graphics. He is fond of philosophy, yoga, and also likes to walk in the countryside. His e-mail ID is `directx_user_interfaces@hotmail.com`.

About the Reviewers

Dylan Agis is a programmer and game designer, currently doing freelance work on a few projects while also developing a few projects of his own. He has a strong background in C++ and C# as well as Unity, and loves to solve problems.

I would like to thank Packt Publishing for giving me the chance to review the book, and the author for making it an interesting read.

John P. Doran is a technical game designer who has been creating games for over 10 years. He has worked on an assortment of games in teams with members ranging from just himself to over 70 in student, mod, and professional projects.

He previously worked at LucasArts on *Star Wars: 1313* as a game design intern—the only junior designer on a team of seniors. He was also the lead instructor of DigiPen®-Ubisoft® Campus Game Programming Program, instructing graduate-level students in an intensive, advanced-level game programming curriculum.

John is currently a technical designer in DigiPen's Research & Development department. In addition to that, he also tutors and assists students on various subjects while giving lectures on game development, including C++, Unreal, Flash, Unity, and more.

He has been a technical reviewer for nine game development titles, and is the author of *Unity Game Development Blueprints*, *Getting Started with UDK*, *UDK Game Development [Video]*, and *Mastering UDK Game Development HOTSHOT*, all by Packt Publishing. He has also co-authored *UDK iOS Game Development Beginner's Guide*, *Packt Publishing*.

Alessandro Mochi has been playing video games since the Amstrad and NES era, tackling all the possible fields: PC, console, and mobile. Large or small video games are his love and passion. RPGs, strategy, action platformers… nothing can escape his grasp.

With a professional field degree in IT, a distinction in project management diploma, and fluent in Spanish, Italian, and English, he gained sound knowledge of many programs. New challenges are always welcome.

Currently a freelance designer and programmer, he helps young developers turn their concepts into reality. Always traveling all over the world, he is still easy to find on his portfolio at `www.amochi-portfolio.com`.

Ryan Watkins likes to party. He can be found on LinkedIn at `www.linkedin.com/in/ryanswatkins/`.

www.PacktPub.com

Support files, eBooks, discount offers, and more

For support files and downloads related to your book, please visit www.PacktPub.com.

Did you know that Packt offers eBook versions of every book published, with PDF and ePub files available? You can upgrade to the eBook version at www.PacktPub.com and as a print book customer, you are entitled to a discount on the eBook copy. Get in touch with us at service@packtpub.com for more details.

At www.PacktPub.com, you can also read a collection of free technical articles, sign up for a range of free newsletters and receive exclusive discounts and offers on Packt books and eBooks.

https://www2.packtpub.com/books/subscription/packtlib

Do you need instant solutions to your IT questions? PacktLib is Packt's online digital book library. Here, you can search, access, and read Packt's entire library of books.

Why subscribe?

- Fully searchable across every book published by Packt
- Copy and paste, print, and bookmark content
- On demand and accessible via a web browser

Free access for Packt account holders

If you have an account with Packt at www.PacktPub.com, you can use this to access PacktLib today and view 9 entirely free books. Simply use your login credentials for immediate access.

Table of Contents

Preface

Mastering Unity Scripting is a concise and dedicated exploration of some advanced, unconventional, and powerful ways to script games with C# in Unity. This makes the book very important right now because, although plenty of "beginner" literature and tutorials exist for Unity, comparatively little has been said of more advanced subjects in a dedicated and structured form. The book assumes you're already familiar with the Unity basics, such as asset importing, level designing, light-mapping, and basic scripting in either C# or JavaScript. From the very beginning, it looks at practical case studies and examples of how scripting can be applied creatively to achieve more complex ends, which include subjects such as Debugging, Artificial Intelligence, Customized Rendering, Editor Extending, Animation and Motion, and lots more. The central purpose is not to demonstrate abstract principles and tips at the level of theory, but to show how theory can be put into practice in real-world examples, helping you get the most from your programming knowledge to build solid games that don't just work but work optimally. To get the most out of this book, read each chapter in sequence, from start to finish, and when reading, use a general and abstract mindset. That is, see each chapter as being simply a particular example and demonstration of more general principles that persist across time and spaces; ones that you can remove from the specific context in which I've used them and redeploy elsewhere to serve your needs. In short, see the knowledge here not just as related to the specific examples and case studies I've chosen, but as being highly relevant for your own projects. So, let's get started.

What this book covers

Chapter 1, Unity C# Refresher, summarizes in very brief terms the basics of C# and scripting in Unity. It's not intended as a complete or comprehensive guide to the basics. Rather, it's intended as a refresher course for those who've previously studied the basics, but perhaps haven't scripted for a while and who'd appreciate a quick recap before getting started with the later chapters. If you're comfortable with the basics of scripting (such as classes, inheritance, properties, and polymorphism), then you can probably skip this chapter.

Chapter 2, Debugging, explores debugging in depth. Being able to write solid and effective code depends partially on your ability to find and successfully fix errors as and when they occur. This makes debugging is critical skill. This chapter will not only look at the basics, but will go deeper into debugging through the MonoDevelop interface, as well as establish a useful error-logging system.

Chapter 3, Singletons, Statics, GameObjects, and the World, explores a wide range of features for accessing, changing, and managing game objects. Specifically, we'll see the singleton design pattern for building global and persistent objects, as well as many other techniques for searching, listing, sorting, and arranging objects. Scripting in Unity relies on manipulating objects in a unified game world, or coordinate space to achieve believable results.

Chapter 4, Event-driven Programming, considers event-driven programming as an important route to re-conceiving the architecture of your game for optimization. By transferring heavy workloads from update and frequent events into an event-driven system, we'll free up lots of valuable processing time for achieving other tasks.

Chapter 5, Cameras, Rendering, and Scenes, dives deep into seeing how cameras work, not just superficially, but how we can dig into their architecture and customize their rendered output. We'll explore frustum testing, culling issues, line of sight, orthographic projection, depth and layers, postprocess effects, and more.

Chapter 6, Working with Mono, surveys the vast Mono library and some of its most useful classes, from dictionaries, lists, and stacks, to other features and concepts, such as strings, regular expressions and Linq. By the end of this chapter, you'll be better positioned to work with large quantities of data quickly and effectively.

Chapter 7, Artificial Intelligence, manages to apply pretty much everything covered previously in one single example project that considers Artificial Intelligence: creating a clever enemy that performs a range of behaviors, from wandering, chasing, patrolling, attacking, fleeing and searching for health-power ups. In creating this character, we'll cover line-of-sight issues, proximity detection, and pathfinding.

Chapter 8, Customizing the Unity Editor, focuses on the Unity Editor, which is feature filled in many respects, but sometimes you need or want it to do more. This chapter examines how to create editor classes for customizing the editor itself, to behave differently and work better. We'll create customized inspector properties, and even a fully functional localization system for switching your game seamlessly across multiple languages.

Chapter 9, Working with Textures, Models, and 2D, explores many things you can do with 2D elements, such as sprites, textures, and GUI elements. Even for 3D games, 2D elements play an important role, and here we'll look at a range of 2D problems and also explore effective and powerful solutions.

Chapter 10, Source Control and Other Tips, closes the book on a general note. It considers a wide range of miscellaneous tips and tricks (useful concepts and applications) that don't fit into any specific category but are critically important when taken as a whole. We'll see good coding practices, tips for writing clear code, data serialization, source and version control integration, and more.

What you need for this book

This book is a Unity-focused title, which means you only need a copy of Unity. Unity comes with everything you need to follow along with the book, including a code editor. Unity can be downloaded from `http://unity3d.com/`. Unity is a single application that supports two main licenses, free and pro. The free license restricts access to certain features, but nonetheless still gives you access to a powerful feature set. In general, most chapters and examples in this book are compliant with the free version, meaning that you can usually follow along with the free version. Some chapters and examples will, however, require the professional version.

Who this book is for

This is an advanced book intended for students, educators, and professionals familiar with Unity basics as well as the basics of scripting. Whether you've been using Unity for a short time, or are an experienced user, this book has something important and valuable to offer to help you improve your game development workflow.

Conventions

In this book, you will find a number of text styles that distinguish between different kinds of information. Here are some examples of these styles and an explanation of their meaning.

Code words in text, database table names, folder names, filenames, file extensions, pathnames, dummy URLs, user input, and Twitter handles are shown as follows: "Once created, a new script file will be generated inside the `Project` folder with a `.cs` file extension."

A block of code is set as follows:

```
01  using UnityEngine;
02  using System.Collections;
03
04  public class MyNewScript : MonoBehaviour
05  {
```

When we wish to draw your attention to a particular part of a code block, the relevant lines or items are set in bold:

```
//We should hide this object if its Y position is above 100 units
bool ShouldHideObject = (transform.position.y > 100) ? true :
false;

//Update object visibility
gameObject.SetActive(!ShouldHideObject);
```

New terms and **important words** are shown in bold. Words that you see on the screen, for example, in menus or dialog boxes, appear in the text like this: "One way is to go to **Assets | Create | C# Script** from the application menu."

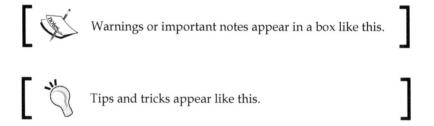

> Warnings or important notes appear in a box like this.

> Tips and tricks appear like this.

Reader feedback

Feedback from our readers is always welcome. Let us know what you think about this book—what you liked or disliked. Reader feedback is important for us as it helps us develop titles that you will really get the most out of.

To send us general feedback, simply e-mail `feedback@packtpub.com`, and mention the book's title in the subject of your message.

If there is a topic that you have expertise in and you are interested in either writing or contributing to a book, see our author guide at www.packtpub.com/authors.

Customer support

Now that you are the proud owner of a Packt book, we have a number of things to help you to get the most from your purchase.

Downloading the example code

You can download the example code files from your account at http://www.packtpub.com for all the Packt Publishing books you have purchased. If you purchased this book elsewhere, you can visit http://www.packtpub.com/support and register to have the files e-mailed directly to you.

Downloading the color images of this book

We also provide you with a PDF file that has color images of the screenshots/diagrams used in this book. The color images will help you better understand the changes in the output. You can download this file from: https://www.packtpub.com/sites/default/files/downloads/0655OT_ColoredImages.pdf.

Errata

Although we have taken every care to ensure the accuracy of our content, mistakes do happen. If you find a mistake in one of our books—maybe a mistake in the text or the code—we would be grateful if you could report this to us. By doing so, you can save other readers from frustration and help us improve subsequent versions of this book. If you find any errata, please report them by visiting http://www.packtpub.com/submit-errata, selecting your book, clicking on the **Errata Submission Form** link, and entering the details of your errata. Once your errata are verified, your submission will be accepted and the errata will be uploaded to our website or added to any list of existing errata under the Errata section of that title.

To view the previously submitted errata, go to https://www.packtpub.com/books/content/support and enter the name of the book in the search field. The required information will appear under the **Errata** section.

Piracy

Piracy of copyrighted material on the Internet is an ongoing problem across all media. At Packt, we take the protection of our copyright and licenses very seriously. If you come across any illegal copies of our works in any form on the Internet, please provide us with the location address or website name immediately so that we can pursue a remedy.

Please contact us at copyright@packtpub.com with a link to the suspected pirated material.

We appreciate your help in protecting our authors and our ability to bring you valuable content.

Questions

If you have a problem with any aspect of this book, you can contact us at questions@packtpub.com, and we will do our best to address the problem.

1
Unity C# Refresher

This book is about mastering scripting for Unity, specifically mastering C# in the context of Unity game development. The concept of mastering needs a definition and qualification, before proceeding further. By mastering, I mean this book will help you transition from having intermediate and theoretical knowledge to having more fluent, practical, and advanced knowledge of scripting. Fluency is the keyword here. From the outset of learning any programming language, the focus invariably turns to language syntax and its rules and laws—the formal parts of a language. This includes concepts such as variables, loops, and functions. However, as a programmer gets experience, the focus shifts from language specifically to the creative ways in which language is applied to solve real-world problems. The focus changes from language-oriented problems to questions of context-sensitive application. Consequently, most of this book will not primarily be about the formal language syntax of C#.

After this chapter, I'll assume that you already know the basics. Instead, the book will be about case studies and real-world examples of the use of C#. However, before turning to that, this chapter will focus on the C# basics generally. This is intentional. It'll cover, quickly and in summary, all the C# foundational knowledge you'll need to follow along productively with subsequent chapters. I strongly recommend that you read it through from start to finish, whatever your experience. It's aimed primarily at readers who are reasonably new to C# but fancy jumping in at the deep end. However, it can also be valuable to experienced developers to consolidate their existing knowledge and, perhaps, pick up new advice and ideas along the way. In this chapter, then, I'll outline the fundamentals of C# from the ground up, in a step-by-step, summarized way. I will speak as though you already understand the very basics of programming generally, perhaps with another language, but have never encountered C#. So, let's go.

Why C#?

When it comes to Unity scripting, an early question when making a new game is which language to choose, because Unity offers a choice. The official choices are C# or JavaScript. However, there's a debate about whether JavaScript should more properly be named "JavaScript" or "UnityScript" due to the Unity-specific adaptations made to the language. This point is not our concern here. The question is which language should be chosen for your project. Now, it initially seems that as we have a choice, we can actually choose all two languages and write some script files in one language and other script files in another language, thus effectively mixing up the languages. This is, of course, technically possible. Unity won't stop you from doing this. However, it's a "bad" practice because it typically leads to confusion as well as compilation conflicts; it's like trying to calculate distances in miles and kilometers at the same time.

The recommended approach, instead, is to choose one of the three languages and apply it consistently across your project as the authoritative language. This is a slicker, more efficient workflow, but it means one language must be chosen at the expense of others. This book chooses C#. Why? First, it's not because C# is "better" than the others. There is no absolute "better" or "worse" in my view. Each and every language has its own merits and uses, and all the Unity languages are equally serviceable for making games. The main reason is that C# is, perhaps, the most widely used and supported Unity language, because it connects most readily to the existing knowledge that most developers already have when they approach Unity. Most Unity tutorials are written with C# in mind, as it has a strong presence in other fields of application development. C# is historically tied to the .NET framework, which is also used in Unity (known as Mono there), and C# most closely resembles C++, which generally has a strong presence in game development. Further, by learning C#, you're more likely to find that your skill set aligns with the current demand for Unity programmers in the contemporary games industry. Therefore, I've chosen C# to give this book the widest appeal and one that connects to the extensive body of external tutorials and literature. This allows you to more easily push your knowledge even further after reading this book.

Creating script files

If you need to define a logic or behavior for your game, then you'll need to write a script. Scripting in Unity begins by creating a new script file, which is a standard text file added to the project. This file defines a program that lists all the instructions for Unity to follow. As mentioned, the instructions can be written in either C#, JavaScript, or Boo; for this book, the language will be C#. There are multiple ways to create a script file in Unity.

One way is to go to **Assets | Create | C# Script** from the application menu, as shown in the following screenshot:

Creating a script file via the application menu

Another way is to right-click on the empty space anywhere within the **Project** panel and choose the **C# Script** option in the **Create** menu from the context menu, as shown in the following screenshot. This creates the asset in the currently open folder.

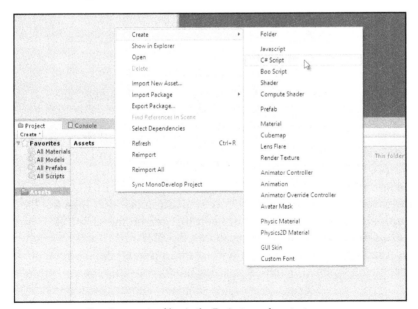

Creating a script file via the Project panel context menu

Once created, a new script file will be generated inside the `Project` folder with a `.cs` file extension (representing C Sharp). The filename is especially important and has serious implications on the validity of your script files because Unity uses the filename to determine the name of a C# class to be created inside the file. Classes are considered in more depth later in this chapter. In short, be sure to give your file a unique and meaningful name.

By unique, we mean that no other script file anywhere in your project should have the same name, whether it is located in a different folder or not. All the script files should have a unique name across the project. The name should also be meaningful by expressing clearly what your script intends to do. Further, there are rules of validity governing filenames as well as class names in C#. The formal definition of these rules can be found online at `http://msdn.microsoft.com/en-us/library/aa664670%28VS.71%29.aspx`. In short, the filename should start with a letter or underscore character only (numbers are not permitted for the first character), and the name should include no spaces, although underscores (_) are allowed:

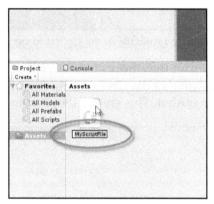

Name your script files in a unique way and according
to the C# class naming conventions

Unity script files can be opened and examined in any text editor or IDE, including Visual Studio and Notepad++, but Unity provides the free and open source editor, **MonoDevelop**. This software is part of the main Unity package included in the installation and doesn't need to be downloaded separately. By double-clicking on the script file from the **Project** panel, Unity will automatically open the file inside MonoDevelop. If you later decide to, or need to, rename the script file, you also need to rename the C# class inside the file to match the filename exactly, as shown in the following screenshot. Failure to do so will result in invalid code and compilation errors or problems when attaching the script file to your objects.

File Edit View Search Project Build Run Version Control Tools Window Help

▶ [   ] ▾ [   ] ▾   ⦿ MonoDevelop-Unity

MyScriptFile.cs   ◉

⊆ MyNewScript ▸ No selection

```
1 ⊟ using UnityEngine;
2 ┕ using System.Collections;
3
4 ⊟ public class MyNewScript : MonoBehaviour
5 │ {
6 │       // Use this for initialization
7 ⊟      void Start () {
8 │
9 ┝      }
10 │
11 │      // Update is called once per frame
12 ⊟     void Update () {
13 │
14 ┝      }
15 ┕ }
16
```

Renaming classes to match the renamed script files

Compiling code

To compile code in Unity, you just need to save your script file in MonoDevelop by choosing the **Save** option in the **File** menu from the application menu (or by pressing *Ctrl + S* on the keyboard) and then return to the main Unity Editor. On refocusing on the Unity window, Unity automatically detects code changes in the files and then compiles your code in response. If there are errors, the game cannot be run, and the errors are printed to the **Console** window. If the compile was successful, you don't need to do anything else, except press **Play** on the **Editor** toolbar and test run your game. Take care here; if you forget to save your file in MonoDevelop after making code changes, then Unity will still use the older, compiled version of your code. For this reason as well as for the purpose of backup, it's really important to save your work regularly, so be sure to press *Ctrl + S* to save in MonoDevelop.

Instantiating scripts

Each script file in Unity defines one main class that is like a blueprint or design that can be instantiated. It is a collection of related variables, functions, and events (as we'll see soon). By default, a script file is like any other kind of Unity asset, such as meshes and audio files. Specifically, it remains dormant in the `Project` folder and does nothing until it's added to a specific scene (by being added to an object as a component), where it comes alive at runtime. Now, scripts, being logical and mathematical in nature, are not added to the scene as tangible, independent objects as meshes are. You cannot see or hear them directly, because they have no visible or audible presence. Instead, they're added onto existing game objects as components, where they define the behavior of those objects. This process of bringing scripts to life as a specific component on a specific object is known as instantiation. Of course, a single script file can be instantiated on multiple objects to replicate the behavior for them all, saving us from making multiple script files for each object, such as when multiple enemy characters must use the same artificial intelligence. The point of the script file, ideally, is to define an abstract formula or behavior pattern for an object that can be reused successfully across many similar objects in all possible scenarios. To add a script file onto an object, simply drag-and-drop the script from the **Project** panel onto the destination object in the scene. The script will be instantiated as a component, and its public variables will be visible in the **Object Inspector** whenever the object is selected, as shown in the following screenshot:

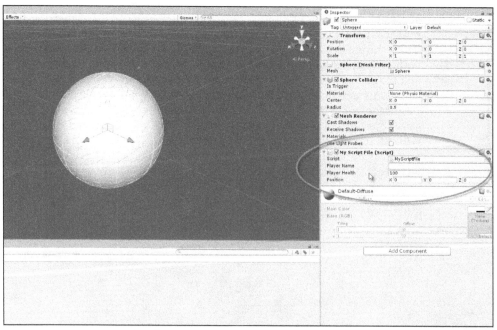

Attaching scripts onto game objects as components

Variables are considered in more depth in the next section.

 More information on creating and using scripts in Unity can be found online at `http://docs.unity3d.com/412/Documentation/Manual/Scripting.html`.

Variables

Perhaps, the core concept in programming and in C# is the variable. Variables often correspond to the letters used in algebra and stand in for numerical quantities, such as *X*, *Y*, and *Z* and *a*, *b*, and *c*. If you need to keep track of information, such as the player name, score, position, orientation, ammo, health, and a multitude of other types of quantifiable data (expressed by nouns), then a variable will be your friend. A variable represents a single unit of information. This means that multiple variables are needed to hold multiple units, one variable for each. Further, each unit will be of a specific type or kind. For example, the player's name represents a sequence of letters, such as "John", "Tom", and "David". In contrast, the player's health refers to numerical data, such as 100 percent (1) or 50 percent (0.5), depending on whether the player has sustained damage. So, each variable necessarily has a data type. In C#, variables are created using a specific kind of syntax or grammar. Consider the following code sample 1-1 that defines a new script file and class called `MyNewScript`, which declares three different variables with class scope, each of a unique type. The word "declare" means that we, as programmers, are telling the C# compiler about the variables required:

```
01 using UnityEngine;
02 using System.Collections;
03
04 public class MyNewScript : MonoBehaviour
05 {
06     public string PlayerName = "";
07     public int PlayerHealth = 100;
08     public Vector3 Position = Vector3.zero;
09
10     // Use this for initialization
11     void Start () {
12
13     }
14
15     // Update is called once per frame
16     void Update () {
17
18     }
19 }
```

Variable data types

Each variable has a data type. A few of the most common ones include
`int`, `float`, `bool`, `string`, and `Vector3`. Here, are a few examples
of these types:

- `int` (integer or whole number) = -3, -2, -1, 0, 1, 2, 3...
- `float` (floating point number or decimal) = -3.0, -2.5, 0.0, 1.7, 3.9...
- `bool` (Boolean or `true`/`false`) = `true` or `false` (1 or 0)
- `string` (string of characters) = "hello world", "a", "another word..."
- `Vector3` (a position value) = (0, 0, 0), (10, 5, 0)...

Notice from lines 06-08 of code sample 1-1 that each variable is assigned a starting
value, and its data type is explicitly stated as `int` (integer), `string`, and `Vector3`,
which represent the points in a 3D space (as well as directions, as we'll see). There's no
full list of possible data types, as this will vary extensively, depending on your project
(and you'll also create your own!). Throughout this book, we'll work with the most
common types, so you'll see plenty of examples. Finally, each variable declaration line
begins with the keyword public. Usually, variables can be either `public` or `private`
(and there is another one called `protected`, which is not covered here).The `public`
variables will be accessible and editable in Unity's Object Inspector (as we'll see soon,
you can also refer to the preceding screenshot), and they can also be accessed by
other classes.

Variables are so named because their values might vary (or change) over time.
Of course, they don't change in arbitrary and unpredictable ways. Rather, they
change whenever we explicitly change them, either through direct assignment in
code, from the Object Inspector, or through methods and function calls. They can
be changed both directly and indirectly. Variables can be assigned values directly,
such as the following one:

```
PlayerName = "NewName";
```

They can also be assigned indirectly using expressions, that is, statements whose
final value must be evaluated before the assignment can be finally made to the
variable as follows:

```
//Variable will result to 50, because: 100 x 0.5 = 50
PlayerHealth = 100 * 0.5;
```

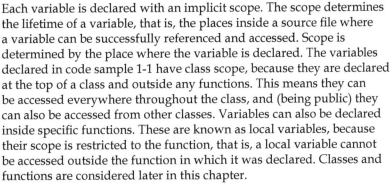

Variable scope

Each variable is declared with an implicit scope. The scope determines the lifetime of a variable, that is, the places inside a source file where a variable can be successfully referenced and accessed. Scope is determined by the place where the variable is declared. The variables declared in code sample 1-1 have class scope, because they are declared at the top of a class and outside any functions. This means they can be accessed everywhere throughout the class, and (being public) they can also be accessed from other classes. Variables can also be declared inside specific functions. These are known as local variables, because their scope is restricted to the function, that is, a local variable cannot be accessed outside the function in which it was declared. Classes and functions are considered later in this chapter.

More information on variables and their usage in C# can be found at http://msdn.microsoft.com/en-us/library/aa691160%28v=vs.71%29.aspx.

Conditional statements

Variables change in potentially many different circumstances: when the player changes their position, when enemies are destroyed, when the level changes, and so on. Consequently, you'll frequently need to check the value of a variable to branch the execution of your scripts that perform different sets of actions, depending on the value. For example, if PlayerHealth reaches 0 percent, you'll perform a death sequence, but if PlayerHealth is at 20 percent, you might only display a warning message. In this specific example, the PlayerHealth variable drives the script in a specified direction. C# offers two main conditional statements to achieve a program branching like this. These are the if statement and the switch statement. Both are highly useful.

The if statement

The if statement has various forms. The most basic form checks for a condition and will perform a subsequent block of code if, and only if, that condition is true. Consider the following code sample 1-2:

```
01 using UnityEngine;
02 using System.Collections;
03
```

```
04 public class MyScriptFile : MonoBehaviour
05 {
06     public string PlayerName = "";
07     public int PlayerHealth = 100;
08     public Vector3 Position = Vector3.zero;
09
10     // Use this for initialization
11     void Start () {
12     }
13
14     // Update is called once per frame
15     void Update ()
16     {
17         //Check player health - the braces symbol {} are option
           for one-line if-statements
18         if(PlayerHealth == 100)
19         {
20         Debug.Log ("Player has full health");
21         }
22     }
23 }
```

The preceding code is executed like all other types of code in Unity, by pressing the **Play** button from the toolbar, as long as the script file has previously been instantiated on an object in the active scene. The if statement at line 18 continually checks the PlayerHealth class variable for its current value. If the PlayerHealth variable is exactly equal to (==) 100, then the code inside the {} braces (in lines 19–21) will be executed. This works because all conditional checks result in a Boolean value of either true or false; the conditional statement is really checked to see whether the queried condition (PlayerHealth == 100) is true. The code inside the braces can, in theory, span across multiple lines and expressions. However, here, there is just a single line in line 20: the Debug.Log Unity function outputs the **Player has full health** string to the console, as shown in the following screenshot. Of course, the if statement could potentially have gone the other way, that is, if PlayerHealth was not equal to 100 (perhaps, it was 99 or 101), then no message would be printed. Its execution always depends on the previous if statement evaluating to true.

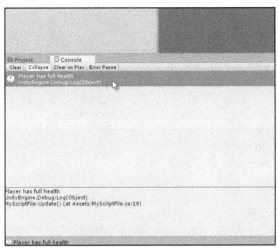

The Unity Console is useful for printing and viewing debug messages

More information on the if statements, the if-else statement, and their usage in C# can be found online at http://msdn.microsoft.com/en-GB/library/5011f09h. aspx.

Unity Console

As you can see in the preceding screenshot, the console is a debugging tool in Unity. It's a place where messages can be printed from the code using the Debug.Log statement (or the Print function) to be viewed by developers. They are helpful to diagnose issues at runtime and compile time. If you get a compile time or runtime error, it should be listed in the **Console** tab. The **Console** tab should be visible in the Unity Editor by default, but it can be displayed manually by selecting **Console** in the **Window** menu from the Unity application file menu. More information on the Debug.Log function can be found at http://docs.unity3d. com/ScriptReference/Debug.Log.html.

You can, of course, check for more conditions than just equality (==), as we did in code sample 1-2. You can use the > and < operators to check whether a variable is greater than or less than another value, respectively. You can also use the != operator to check whether a variable is not equal to another value. Further, you can even combine multiple conditional checks into the same if statement using the && (AND) operator and the || (OR) operator. For example, check out the following if statement. It performs the code block between the { } braces only if the PlayerHealth variable is between 0 and 100 and is not equal to 50, as shown here:

```
if(PlayerHealth >= 0 && PlayerHealth <= 100 && PlayerHealth !=50)
{
```

```
Debug.Log ("Player has full health");
}
```

The if-else statement

One variation of the if statement is the if-else statement. The if statement performs a code block if its condition evaluates to true. However, the if-else statement extends this. It would perform an X code block if its condition is true and a Y code block if its condition is false:

```
if(MyCondition)
{
//X - perform my code if MyCondition is true
}
else
{
//Y - perform my code if MyCondition is false
}
```

The switch statement

As we've seen, the if statement is useful to determine whether a single and specific condition is true or false and to perform a specific code block on the basis of this. The switch statement, in contrast, lets you check a variable for multiple possible conditions or states, and then lets you branch the program in one of many possible directions, not just one or two as is the case with if statements. For example, if you're creating an enemy character that can be in one of the many possible states of action (CHASE, FLEE, FIGHT, HIDE, and so on), you'll probably need to branch your code appropriately to handle each state specifically. The break keyword is used to exit from a state returning to the end of the switch statement. The following code sample 1-3 handles a sample enemy using enumerations:

```
01 using UnityEngine;
02 using System.Collections;
03
04 public class MyScriptFile : MonoBehaviour
05 {
06     //Define possible states for enemy using an enum
07     public enum EnemyState {CHASE, FLEE, FIGHT, HIDE};
08
```

```
09      //The current state of enemy
10      public EnemyState ActiveState = EnemyState.CHASE;
11
12      // Use this for initialization
13      void Start () {
14      }
15
16      // Update is called once per frame
17      void Update ()
18      {
19          //Check the ActiveState variable
20          switch(ActiveState)
21          {
22          case EnemyState.FIGHT:
23          {
24              //Perform fight code here
25              Debug.Log ("Entered fight state");
26          }
27              break;
28
29
30          case EnemyState.FLEE:
31          case EnemyState.HIDE:
32          {
33              //Flee and hide performs the same behaviour
34              Debug.Log ("Entered flee or hide state");
35          }
36              break;
37
38          default:
39          {
40              //Default case when all other states fail
41              //This is used for the chase state
42              Debug.Log ("Entered chase state");
43          }
44              break;
45          }
46      }
47 }
```

Enumerations

This line 07 in code sample 1-3 declares an enumeration (enum) named EnemyState. An enum is a special structure used to store a range of potential values for one or more other variables. It's not a variable itself per se, but a way of specifying the limits of values that a variable might have. In code sample 1-3, the ActiveState variable declared in line 10 makes use of EnemyState. Its value can be any valid value from the ActiveState enumeration. Enums are a great way of helping you validate your variables, limiting their values within a specific range and series of options.

Another great benefit of enums is that variables based on them have their values appear as selectable options from drop-down boxes in the Object Inspector, as shown in the following screenshot:

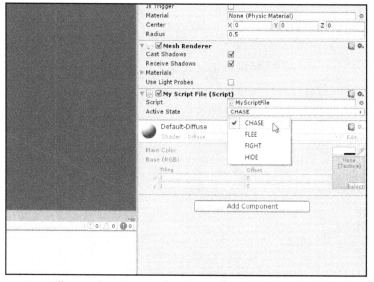

Enumerations offer you drop-down options for your variables from the Object Inspector

More information on enums and their usage in C# can be found online at http://msdn.microsoft.com/en-us/library/sbbt4032.aspx.

The following are the comments for code sample 1-3:

- **Line 20**: The switch statement begins. Parentheses, (), are used to select the variable whose value or state must be checked. In this case, the ActiveState variable is being queried.

- **Line 22**: The first case statement is made inside the switch statement. The following block of code (lines 24 and 25) will be executed if the ActiveState variable is set to EnemyState.Fight. Otherwise, the code will be ignored.

- **Lines 30 and 31**: Here, two case statements follow one another. The code block in lines 33 and 34 will be executed if, and only if, `ActiveState` is either `EnemyState.Flee` or `EnemyState.Hide`.

- **Line 38**: The default statement is optional for a `switch` statement. When included, it will be entered if no other case statements are `true`. In this case, it would apply if `ActiveState` is `EnemyState.Chase`.

- **Lines 27, 36, and 44**: The `break` statement should occur at the end of a case statement. When it is reached, it will exit the complete `switch` statement to which it belongs, resuming program execution in the line after the `switch` statement, in this case, line 45.

 More information on the `switch` statement and its usage in C# can be found at `http://msdn.microsoft.com/en-GB/library/06tc147t.aspx`.

Arrays

Lists and sequences are everywhere in games. For this reason, you'll frequently need to keep track of lists of data of the same type: all enemies in the level, all weapons that have been collected, all power ups that could be collected, all spells and items in the inventory, and so on. One type of list is the array. Each item in the array is, essentially, a unit of information that has the potential to change during gameplay, and so a variable is suitable to store each item. However, it's useful to collect together all the related variables (all enemies, all weapons, and so on) into a single, linear, and traversable list structure. This is what an array achieves. In C#, there are two kinds of arrays: static and dynamic. Static arrays might hold a fixed and maximum number of possible entries in memory, decided in advance, and this capacity remains unchanged throughout program execution, even if you only need to store fewer items than the capacity. This means some slots or entries could be wasted. Dynamic arrays might grow and shrink in capacity, on demand, to accommodate exactly the number of items required. Static arrays typically perform better and faster, but dynamic arrays feel cleaner and avoid memory wastage. This chapter considers only static arrays, and dynamic arrays are considered later, as shown in the following code sample 1-4:

```
01 using UnityEngine;
02 using System.Collections;
03
04 public class MyScriptFile : MonoBehaviour
05 {
06     //Array of game objects in the scene
07     public GameObject[] MyObjects;
08
```

```
09        // Use this for initialization
10        void Start ()
11        {
12        }
13
14        // Update is called once per frame
15        void Update ()
16        {
17        }
18 }
```

In code sample 1-4, line 07 declares a completely empty array of GameObjects, named MyObjects. To create this, it uses the [] syntax after the data type GameObject to designate an array, that is, to signify that a list of GameObjects is being declared as opposed to a single GameObject. Here, the declared array will be a list of all objects in the scene. It begins empty, but you can use the Object Inspector in the Unity Editor to build the array manually by setting its maximum capacity and populating it with any objects you need. To do this, select the object to which the script is attached in the scene and type in a **Size** value for the **My Objects** field to specify the capacity of the array. This should be the total number of objects you want to hold. Then, simply drag-and-drop objects individually from the scene hierarchy panel into the array slots in the Object Inspector to populate the list with items, as shown here:

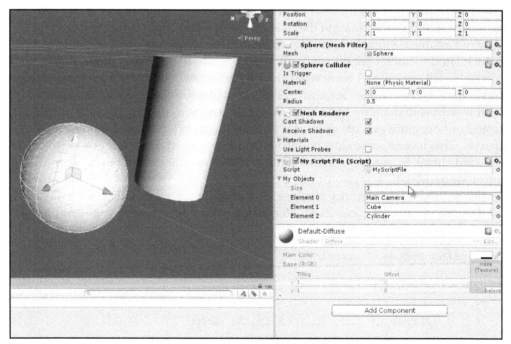

Building arrays from the Unity Object Inspector

You can also build the array manually in code via the Start function instead of using the Object Inspector. This ensures that the array is constructed as the level begins. Either method works fine, as shown in the following code sample 1-5:

```
01 using UnityEngine;
02 using System.Collections;
03
04 public class MyScriptFile : MonoBehaviour
05 {
06     //Array of game objects in the scene
07     public GameObject[] MyObjects;
08
09     // Use this for initialization
10     void Start ()
11     {
12         //Build the array manually in code
13         MyObjects = new GameObject[3];
14         //Scene must have a camera tagged as MainCamera
15         MyObjects[0] = Camera.main.gameObject;

16       //Use GameObject.Find function to
17       //find objects in scene by name
18       MyObjects[1] = GameObject.Find("Cube");
19       MyObjects[2] = GameObject.Find("Cylinder");
20     }
21
22     // Update is called once per frame
23     void Update ()
24     {
25     }
26 }
```

The following are the comments for code sample 1-5:

- **Line 10**: The Start function is executed at level startup. Functions are considered in more depth later in this chapter.

- **Line 13**: The new keyword is used to create a new array with a capacity of three. This means that the list can hold no more than three elements at any one time. By default, all elements are set to the starting value of null (meaning nothing). They are empty.

- **Line 15**: Here, the first element in the array is set to the main camera object in the scene. Two important points should be noted here. First, elements in the array can be accessed using the array subscript operator []. Thus, the first element of MyObjects can be accessed with MyObjects[0]. Second, C# arrays are "zero indexed". This means the first element is always at position 0, the next is at 1, the next at 2, and so on. For the MyObjects three-element array, each element can be accessed with MyObjects[0], MyObjects[1], and MyObjects[2]. Notice that the last element is 2 and not 3.

- **Lines 18 and 19**: Elements 1 and 2 of the MyObjects array are populated with objects using the function GameObject.Find. This searches the active scene for game objects with a specified name (case sensitive), inserting a reference to them at the specified element in the MyObjects array. If no object of a matching name is found, then null is inserted instead.

 More information on arrays and their usage in C# can be found online at http://msdn.microsoft.com/en-GB/library/9b9dty7d.aspx.

Loops

Loops are one of the most powerful tools in programming. Imagine a game where the entire level can be nuked. When this happens, you'll want to destroy almost everything in the scene. Now, you can do this by deleting each and every object individually in code, one line at a time. If you did this, then a small scene with only a few objects would take just a few lines of code, and this wouldn't be problematic. However, for larger scenes with potentially hundreds of objects, you'd have to write a lot of code, and this code would need to be changed if you altered the contents of the scene. This would be tedious. Loops can simplify the process to just a few lines, regardless of scene complexity or object number. They allow you to repeatedly perform operations on potentially many objects. There are several kinds of loops in C#. Let's see some examples.

The foreach loop

Perhaps, the simplest loop type in C# is the foreach loop. Using foreach, you can cycle through every element in an array, sequentially from start to end, processing each item as required. Consider the following code sample 1-6; it destroys all GameObjects from a GameObject array:

```
01 using UnityEngine;
```

```
02 using System.Collections;
03
04 public class MyScriptFile : MonoBehaviour
05 {
06     //Array of game objects in the scene
07     public GameObject[] MyObjects;
08
09     // Use this for initialization
10     void Start ()
11     {
12         //Repeat code for all objects in array, one by one
13         foreach(GameObject Obj in MyObjects)
14         {
15             //Destroy object
16             Destroy (Obj);
17         }
18     }
19
20     // Update is called once per frame
21     void Update ()
22     {
23     }
24 }
```

Downloading the example code

You can download the example code files from your account at http://www. packtpub.com for all the Packt Publishing books you have purchased. If you purchased this book elsewhere, you can visit http://www.packtpub.com/support and register to have the files e-mailed directly to you.

The foreach loop repeats the code block { } between lines 14–17, once for each element in the array MyObjects. Each pass or cycle in the loop is known as an iteration. The loop depends on array size; this means that larger arrays require more iterations and more processing time. The loop also features a local variable obj. This is declared in the foreach statement in line 13. This variable stands in for the selected or active element in the array as the loop passes each iteration, so obj represents the first element in the loop on the first iteration, the second element on the second iteration, and so on.

More information on the foreach loop and its usage in C# can be found at http://msdn.microsoft.com/en-GB/library/ttw7t8t6.aspx.

The for loop

The `foreach` loop is handy when you need to iterate through a single array sequentially from start to end, processing each element one at a time. But sometimes you need more control over the iterations. You might need to process a loop backwards from the end to the start, you might need to process two arrays of equal length simultaneously, or you might need to process every alternate array element as opposed to every element. You can achieve this using the `for` loop, as shown here:

```
//Repeat code backwards for all objects in array, one by one
for(int i = MyObjects.Length-1; i >= 0; i--)
{
    //Destroy object
    DestroyMyObjects[i]);
}
```

The following are the comments for the preceding code snippet:

- Here, the `for` loop traverses the `MyObjects` array backwards from the end to the start, deleting each `GameObject` in the scene. It does this using a local variable `i`. This is sometimes known as an `Iterator` variable, because it controls how the loop progresses.

- The `for` loop line has the following three main parts, each separated by a semicolon character:

    ○ `i`: This is initialized to `MyObjects.Length` - 1 (the last element in the array). Remember that arrays are zero-indexed, so the last element is always `Array Length -1`. This ensures that loop iteration begins at the array end.

    ○ `i >= 0`: This expression indicates the condition when the loop should terminate. The `i` variable acts like a countdown variable, decrementing backwards through the array. In this case, the loop should end when `i` is no longer greater than or equal to `0`, because `0` represents the start of the array.

    ○ `i--`: This expression controls how the variable `i` changes on each iteration of the loop moving from the array end to the beginning. Here, `i` will be decremented by one on each iteration, that is, a value of `1` will be subtracted from `i` on each pass of the loop. In contrast, the statement `++` will add `1`.

- During the loop, the expression `MyObjects[i]` is used to access array elements.

More information on the `for` loop and its usage in C# can be found at
`http://msdn.microsoft.com/en-gb/library/ch45axte.aspx`.

The while loop

Both the `for` and `foreach` loops were especially useful when cycling through an array,
performing specific operations on each iteration. The `while` loop, in contrast, is useful
to continually repeat a specific behavior until a specified condition evaluates to `false`.
For example, if you must deal damage to the player as long as they're standing on
hot lava or continually move a vehicle until the breaks are applied, then a `while`
loop could be just what you need, as shown in the following code sample 1-7:

```
01 using UnityEngine;
02 using System.Collections;
03
04 public class MyScriptFile : MonoBehaviour
05 {
06     // Use this for initialization
07     void Start ()
08     {
09         //Will count how many messages have been printed
10         int NumberOfMessages = 0;
11
12         //Loop until 5 messages have been printed to the console
13         while(NumberOfMessages < 5)
14         {
15             //Print message

16             Debug.Log ("This is Message: " +
                 NumberOfMessages.ToString());

17
18             //Increment counter
19             ++NumberOfMessages;
20         }
21     }
22
23     // Update is called once per frame
24     void Update ()
25     {
26     }
27 }
```

ToString

Many classes and objects in Unity have a ToString function (see line 16 of code sample 1-7). This function converts the object, such as an integer (whole number), to a human-readable word or statement that can be printed to the **Console** or **Debugging** window. This is useful for printing objects and data to the console when debugging. Note that converting numerical objects to strings requires an implicit conversion.

The following are the comments for code sample 1-7:

- Line 13 begins the while loop with the condition that it repeats until the integer variable NumberOfMessages exceeds or equals 5

- The code block between lines 15 and 19 is repeated as the body of the while loop

- Line 19 increments the variable NumberOfMessages on each iteration

The result of code sample 1-7, when executed in the game mode, will be to print five text messages to the Unity Console when the level begins, as shown in the following screenshot:

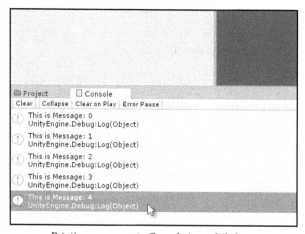

Printing messages to Console in a while loop

More information on the while loop and its usage in C# can be found at http://msdn.microsoft.com/en-gb/library/2aeyhxcd.aspx.

Infinite loops

One danger of using loops, especially `while` loops, is to accidentally create an infinite loop, that is, a loop that cannot end. If your game enters an infinite loop, it will normally freeze, perhaps permanently, requiring you to force a quit by terminating the application or even worse, causing a complete system crash! Often, Unity will catch the problem and exit but don't rely on this. For example, removing line 19 of the code sample 1-7 would create an infinite loop because the `NumberOfMessages` variable will never increment to a level that satisfies the `while` loop condition, thereby causing an exit. The message of this section, then, is first and foremost, "Take care when writing and planning loops to avoid infinite loops." The following is another classic example of an infinite loop that will certainly cause problems for your game, so be sure to avoid them:

```
//Loop forever
while(true)
{
}
```

However, believe it or not, there are times when infinite loops are technically what you need for your game under the right conditions! If you need a moving platform to travel up and down endlessly, a magical orb to continually spin round and round, or a day-night cycle to perpetually repeat, then an infinite loop can be serviceable, provided it's implemented appropriately. Later in this book, we'll see examples where infinite loops can be put to good use. Loops are powerful, fun structures, but when coded inappropriately, whether infinite or not, they can be the source of crashes, stalls, and performance issues, so take care. In this book, we'll see good practices for creating loops.

Functions

We already used functions in this chapter, such as the `Start` and `Update` functions. However, now, it's time to consider them more formally and precisely. In essence, a function is a collection of statements bundled together as a single, identifiable block, which is given a collective name and can be executed on demand, each line of the function being executed in sequence. When you think about the logic of your game, there are times when you need to perform some operations repeatedly on your objects, such as, firing a weapon, jumping in the air, killing enemies, updating the score, and playing a sound. You can copy and paste your code throughout the source file, wherever you need to reuse it; this is not a good habit to cultivate. It's easier to consolidate the recyclable code into a function that can be executed by a name when you need it, as shown in the following code sample 1-8:

```
01 using UnityEngine;
```

```
02  using System.Collections;
03
04  public class MyScriptFile : MonoBehaviour
05  {
06      //Private variable for score
07      //Accessible only within this class
08      private int Score = 0;
09
10      // Use this for initialization
11      void Start ()
12      {
13        //Call update score
14        UpdateScore(5, false); //Add five points
15        UpdateScore (10, false); //Add ten points

16        int CurrentScore = UpdateScore (15, false); //Add fifteen
          points and store result

17
18        //Now double score
19         UpdateScore(CurrentScore);
20      }
21
22      // Update is called once per frame
23      void Update ()
24      {
25      }
26
27      //Update game score

28      public int UpdateScore (int AmountToAdd, bool
        PrintToConsole = true)

29      {
30        //Add points to score
31        Score += AmountToAdd;
32
33        //Should we print to console?

34        if(PrintToConsole){Debug.Log ("Score is: " +
          Score.ToString());}

35
```

```
36          //Output current score and exit function
37          return Score;
38      }
39 }
```

The following is the breakdown of the code present for code sample 1-8:

- **Line 08**: A private, integer class variable Score is declared to keep track of a sample score value. This variable will be used later in the function UpdateScore.

- **Lines 11, 23, and 28**: The class MyScriptFile has three functions (sometimes called methods or member functions). These are Start, Update, and UpdateScore. Start and Update are special functions that Unity provides, as we'll see shortly. UpdateScore is a custom function for MyScriptFile.

- **Line 28**: The UpdateScore function represents a complete block of code between lines 29 and 38. This specific function should be invoked every time the game score must change. When called, the code block (lines 29–38) will be executed sequentially. In this way, functions offer us code recyclability.

- **Lines 14-19**: The UpdateScore function is called several times during the Start function. For each call, the execution of the Start function pauses until the UpdateScore function completes. At this point, the execution resumes in the next line.

- **Line 28**: UpdateScore accepts two parameters or arguments. These are an integer AmountToAdd and a Boolean PrintToConsole. Arguments act like inputs we can plug in to the function to affect how they operate. The AmountToAdd variable expresses how much should be added to the current Score variable, and PrintToConsole determines whether the Score variable should be shown in the **Console** window when the function is executed. There is theoretically no limit to the number of arguments a function can have, and a function can also have no arguments at all, such as the Start and Update functions.

- **Lines 31–34**: Here, the score is actually updated and printed to **Console**, if required. Notice that the PrintToConsole argument has a default value of true already assigned to the function declaration in line 28. This makes the argument optional whenever the function is called. Lines 14, 15, and 16 explicitly override the default value by passing a value of false. Line 19, in contrast, omits a second value and thereby accepts the default of true.

- **Lines 28 and 37**: The UpdateScore function has a return value, which is a data type specified in line 28 before the function name. Here, the value is an int. This means on exiting or completion, the function will output an integer. The integer, in this case, will be the current Score. This is actually output in line 37 using the return statement. Functions don't have to return a value, it's not essential. If no return value is needed, the return type should be void as with Start and Update.

More information on functions and their usage in C# can be found at http://csharp.net-tutorials.com/basics/functions/.

Events

Events are essentially functions used in a distinctive way. Both the Start and Update functions, which we have already seen, would more accurately be described as Unity-specific events. Events are functions called to notify an object that something significant has happened: the level has begun, a new frame has started, an enemy has died, the player has jumped, and others. In being called at these critical times, they offer objects the chance to respond if necessary. The Start function is called automatically by Unity when the object is first created, typically at level startup. The Update function is also called automatically, once on each frame. The Start function, therefore, gives us an opportunity to perform specific actions when the level begins, and the Update function on each frame many times per second. The Update function is especially useful, therefore, to achieve motion and animation in your games. Refer to code sample 1-9, which rotates an object over time:

```
01 using UnityEngine;
02 using System.Collections;
03
04 public class MyScriptFile : MonoBehaviour
05 {
06     // Use this for initialization
07     void Start ()
08     {
09     }
10
11     // Update is called once per frame
12     void Update ()
13     {
14         //Rotate object by 2 degrees per frame around the Y axis
15         transform.Rotate(new Vector3(0.0f, 2.0f, 0.0f));
16     }
17 }
```

Line 15 in code sample 1-9 is called once per frame. It continually rotates an object 2 degrees around the *y* axis. This code is frame rate dependent, which means that it'll turn objects faster when run on machines with higher frame rates, because `Update` will be called more often. There are techniques to achieve frame rate independence, ensuring that your games perform consistently across all machines, regardless of the frame rate. We'll see these in the next chapter. You can easily check the frame rate for your game directly from the Unity Editor **Game** tab. Select the **Game** tab and click on the **Stats** button in the top-right hand corner of the toolbar. This will show the **Stats** panel, offering a general, statistical overview of the performance of your game. This panels displays the game **frames per second (FPS)**, which indicates both how often `Update` is called on your objects and the general performance of your game on your system. In general, an FPS lower than 15 indicates a significant performance problem. Strive for FPS rates of 30 or above. Refer to the following screenshot to access the **Stats** panel:

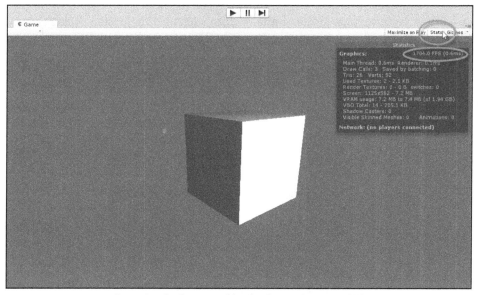

Accessing the Stats panel for the Game tab to view FPS

 There are too many event types to list comprehensively. However, some common events in Unity, such as `Start` and `Update`, can be found in the `MonoBehaviour` class. More information on `MonoBehaviour` is available at `http://docs.unity3d.com/ScriptReference/MonoBehaviour.html`.

Classes and object-oriented programming

A class is an amalgam of many related variables and functions, all brought together into a self-contained unit or "thing". To put it another way, if you think about a game (such as a fantasy RPG), it's filled with many independent things such as wizards, orcs, trees, houses, the player, quests, inventory items, weapons, spells, doorways, bridges, force fields, portals, guards, and so on. Many of these objects parallel objects in the real world too. However, crucially, each of these things is an independent object; a wizard is different and separate from a force field, and a guard is different and separate from a tree. Each of these things, then, can be thought of as an object — a custom type. If we focus our attention on one specific object, an orc enemy, for example, we can identify the properties and behaviors in this object. The orc will have a position, rotation, and scale; these correspond to variables.

The orc might have several kinds of attacks too, such as a melee attack with an axe and a ranged attack with a crossbow. These attacks are performed through functions. In this way, a collection of variables and functions are brought together into a meaningful relationship. The process of bringing these things together is known as encapsulation. In this example, an orc has been encapsulated into a class. The class, in this case, represents the template for a general, abstract orc (the concept of an orc). Objects, in contrast, are particular, concrete instantiations of the Orc class in the level. In Unity, script files define a class. To instantiate the class as an object in the level, add it to GameObject. As we've seen, classes are attached to game objects as components. Components are objects, and multiple components together form a GameObject. Refer to code sample 1-10 for a sample Orc class stub:

```
01 using UnityEngine;
02 using System.Collections;
03
04 public class Orc : MonoBehaviour
05 {
06 //Reference to the transform component of orc (position,
   rotation, scale)
07 private Transform ThisTransform = null;
08
09 //Enum for states of orc
10 public enum OrcStates {NEUTRAL, ATTACK_MELEE, ATTACK_RANGE};
11
12 //Current state of orc
13 public OrcStates CurrentState = OrcStates.NEUTRAL;
14
15 //Movement speed of orc in meters per second
16 public float OrcSpeed = 10.0f;
```

```
17
18 //Is orc friendly to player
19 public bool isFriendly = false;
20
21 //-------------------------------------------------
22 // Use this for initialization
23 void Start ()
24 {
25      //Get transform of orc
26      ThisTransform = transform;
27 }
28 //-------------------------------------------------
29 // Update is called once per frame
30 void Update ()
31 {
32 }
33 //-------------------------------------------------
34 //State actions for orc
35 public void AttackMelee()
36 {
37      //Do melee attack here
38 }
39 //-------------------------------------------------
40 public void AttackRange()
41 {
42      //Do range attack here
43 }
44 //-------------------------------------------------
45 }
```

The following are the comments for code sample 1-10:

- **Line 04**: Here, the class keyword is used to define a class named Orc. This class derives from MonoBehaviour. The next section of this chapter will consider inheritance and derived classes further.

- **Lines 09-19**: Several variables and an enum are added to the Orc class. The variables are of different types, but all are related to the concept of an orc.

- **Lines 35-45**: The orc has two methods: AttackMelee and AttackRange.

 More information on classes and their usage in C# can be found at http://msdn.microsoft.com/en-gb/library/x9afc042.aspx.

Classes and inheritance

Imagine a scenario where you create an `Orc` class to encode an orc object in the game. Having done so, you then decide to make two upgraded types. One is an Orc Warlord, with better armor and weapons, and the other is an Orc Mage who, as the name implies, is a spell caster. Both can do everything that the ordinary orc can do, but more besides. Now, to implement this, you can create three separate classes, `Orc`, `OrcWarlord`, and `OrcMage`, by copying and pasting common code between them.

The problem is that as Orc Warlord and Orc Mage share a lot of common ground and behaviors with orc, a lot of code will be wastefully copied and pasted to replicate the common behaviors. Furthermore, if you discovered a bug in the shared code of one class, you'd need to copy and paste the fix to the other classes to propagate it. This is both tedious and technically dangerous, as it risks wasting time, introducing bugs, and causing needless confusion. Instead, the object-oriented concept of inheritance can help us. Inheritance allows you to create a completely new class that implicitly absorbs or contains the functionality of another class, that is, it allows you to build a new class that extends an existing class without affecting the original one. When inheritance happens, two classes are brought into a relationship with each other. The original class (such as the `Orc` class) is known as the case class or ancestor class. The new class (such as the Orc Warlord or Orc Mage), which extends on the ancestor class, is called a super class or derived class.

 More information on inheritance in C# can be found at `http://msdn.microsoft.com/en-gb/library/ms173149%28v=vs.80%29.aspx`.

By default, every new Unity script file creates a new class derived from `MonoBehaviour`. This means every new script contains all the `MonoBehaviour` functionality and has the potential to go beyond, based on the additional code that you add. To prove this, refer to the following code sample 1-11:

```
01 using UnityEngine;
02 using System.Collections;
03
04 public class NewScript : MonoBehaviour
05 {
06 //------------------------------------------------
07     // Use this for initialization
08     void Start ()
09     {
10         name = "NewObject";
11 }
```

```
12    //---------------------------------------------------
13    // Update is called once per frame
14    void Update ()
15    {
16    }
17 }
```

The following are the comments for code sample 1-11:

- **Line 04**: The class `NewScript` is derived from `MonoBehaviour`. You can, however, substitute `MonoBehaviour` for almost any valid class name from which you want to derive.

- **Line 10**: Here, the variable name is assigned a string during the `Start` event. However, notice that the name is not explicitly declared as a variable anywhere in the `NewScript` source file. If `NewScript` were a completely new class with no ancestor defined in line 04, then line 10 would be invalid. However, because `NewScript` derives from `MonoBehaviour`, it automatically inherits all of its variables, allowing us to access and edit them from `NewScript`.

When to inherit

Only use inheritance where it's really appropriate; otherwise, you'll make your classes large, heavy, and confusing. If you're creating a class that shares a lot of common functionality with another and it makes sense to establish connection between them, then use inheritance. Another use of inheritance, as we'll see next, is when you want to override specific functions.

Classes and polymorphism

To illustrate polymorphism in C#, let's start by considering the following code sample 1-12. This sample doesn't demonstrate polymorphism immediately but represents the start of a scenario where polymorphism will be useful, as we'll see. Here, a basic skeleton class is defined for a potential **non-player character** (**NPC**) in a generic RPG game. The class is intentionally not comprehensive and features basic variables that only mark the starting point for a character. The most important thing here is that the class features a `SayGreeting` function, which should be invoked when the player engages the NPC in conversation. It displays a generic welcome message to **Console** as follows:

```
01 using UnityEngine;
02 using System.Collections;
```

```
03
04 public class MyCharacter
05 {
06 public string CharName = "";
07 public int Health = 100;
08 public int Strength = 100;
09 public float Speed = 10.0f;
10 public bool isAwake = true;
11
12     //Offer greeting to the player when entering conversation
13     public virtual void SayGreeting()
14     {
15         Debug.Log ("Hello, my friend");
16     }
17 }
```

The first problem to arise relates to the diversity and believability of the MyCharacter class if we try imagining how it'd really work in a game. Specifically, every character instantiated from MyCharacter will offer exactly the same greeting when SayGreeting is invoked: men, women, orcs, and everybody. They'll all say the same thing, namely, "Hello, my friend". This is neither believable nor desirable. Perhaps, the most elegant solution would be to just add a public string variable to the class, thus allowing customization over the message printed. However, to illustrate polymorphism clearly, let's try a different solution. We could create several additional classes instead, all derived from MyCharacter, one for each new NPC type and each offering a unique greeting from a SayGreeting function. This is possible with MyCharacter, because SayGreeting has been declared using the virtual keyword (line 13). This allows derived classes to override the behavior of SayGreeting in the MyCharacter class. This means the SayGreeting function in derived classes will replace the behavior of the original function in the base class. Such a solution might look similar to the code sample 1-13:

```
01 using UnityEngine;
02 using System.Collections;
03 //-------------------------------------------
04 public class MyCharacter
05     {
06     public string CharName = "";
```

```
07    public int Health = 100;
08 public int Strength = 100;
09 public float Speed = 10.0f;
10 public bool isAwake = true;
11
12 //Offer greeting to the player when entering conversation
13 public virtual void SayGreeting()
14 {
15        Debug.Log ("Hello, my friend");
16 }
17 }
18 //---------------------------------------------
19 public class ManCharacter: MyCharacter
20 {
21 public override void SayGreeting()
22 {
23        Debug.Log ("Hello, I'm a man");
24 }
25 }
26 //---------------------------------------------
27 public class WomanCharacter: MyCharacter
28 {
29 public override void SayGreeting()
30 {
31        Debug.Log ("Hello, I'm a woman");
32 }
33 }
34 //---------------------------------------------
35 public class OrcCharacter: MyCharacter
36 {
37 public override void SayGreeting()
38 {
39        Debug.Log ("Hello, I'm an Orc");
40 }
41 }
42 //---------------------------------------------
```

With this code, some improvement is made, that is, different classes are created for each NPC type, namely, `ManCharacter`, `WomanCharacter`, and `OrcCharacter`. Each offers a different greeting in the `SayGreeting` function. Further, each NPC inherits all the common behaviors from the shared base class `MyCharacter`. However, a technical problem regarding type specificity arises. Now, imagine creating a tavern location inside which there are many NPCs of the different types defined, so far, all enjoying a tankard of grog. As the player enters the tavern, all NPCs should offer their unique greeting. To achieve this functionality, it'd be great if we could have a single array of all NPCs and simply call their `SayGreeting` function from a loop, each offering their own greeting. However, it seems, initially, that we cannot do this. This is because all elements in a single array must be of the same data type, such as `MyCharacter[]` or `OrcCharacter[]`. We cannot mix types for the same array. We could, of course, declare multiple arrays for each NPC type, but this feels awkward and doesn't easily allow for the seamless creation of more NPC types after the array code has been written. To solve this problem, we'll need a specific and dedicated solution. This is where polymorphism comes to the rescue. Refer to the following sample 1-14, which defines a new `Tavern` class in a completely separate script file:

```
01 using UnityEngine;
02 using System.Collections;
03
04 public class Tavern : MonoBehaviour
05 {
06 //Array of NPCs in tavern
07 public MyCharacter[] Characters = null;
08 //-----------------------------------------------------
09 // Use this for initialization
10 void Start () {
11
12        //New array - 5 NPCs in tavern
13        Characters = new MyCharacter[5];
14
15        //Add characters of different types to array MyCharacter
16        Characters[0] = new ManCharacter();
17        Characters[1] = new WomanCharacter();
18        Characters[2] = new OrcCharacter();
19        Characters[3] = new ManCharacter();
20        Characters[4] = new WomanCharacter();
21
22        //Now run enter tavern functionality
23        EnterTavern();
24 }
25 //-----------------------------------------------------
```

```
26 //Function when player enters Tavern
27 public void EnterTavern()
28 {
29      //Everybody say greeting
30      foreach(MyCharacter C in Characters)
31      {
32              //call SayGreeting in derived class
33              //Derived class is accessible via base class
34              C.SayGreeting();
35      }
36 }
37 //-------------------------------------------------------
38 }
```

The following are the comments for code sample 1-14:

- **Line 07**: To keep track of all NPCs in the tavern, regardless of the NPC type, a single array (Characters) of type MyCharacter is declared.

- **Lines 16-20**: The Characters array is populated with multiple NPCs of different types. This works because, though they are of different types, each NPC derives from the same base class.

- **Line 27**: The EnterTavern function is called at level startup.

- **Line 34**: A foreach loop cycles through all NPCs in the Characters array, calling the SayGreeting function. The result is shown in the following screenshot. The unique messages for each NPC are printed instead of the generic message defined in the base class. Polymorphism allows the overridden method in the derived classes to be called instead.

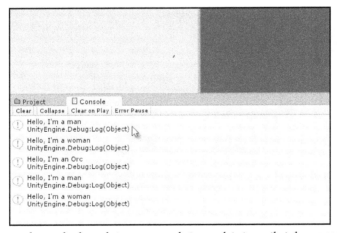

Polymorphism produces a backwards transparency between data types that share a common lineage

More information on polymorphism in C# can be found at `http://msdn.microsoft.com/en-GB/library/ms173152.aspx`.

C# properties

When assigning values to class variables, such as `MyClass.x = 10;`, there are a couple of important things to take care of. First, you'll typically want to validate the value being assigned, ensuring that the variable is always valid. Typical cases include clamping an integer between a minimum and maximum range or allowing only a limited set of strings for a string variable. Second, you might need to detect when a variable changes, initiating other dependent functions and behaviors. C# properties let you achieve both these features. Refer to the following code sample 1-15, which limits an integer between `1` and `10` and prints a message to the console whenever it changes:

```
01 using UnityEngine;
02 using System.Collections;
03 //--------------------------------------------------------
04 //Sample class - can be attached to object as a component
05 public class Database : MonoBehaviour
06 {
07 //--------------------------------------------------------
08 //Public property for private variable iMyNumber
09 //This is a public property to the variable iMyNumber
10 public int MyNumber
11 {
12         //Called when retrieving value
13         get
14         {
15                 return iMyNumber; //Output iMyNumber
16         }
17
18         //Called when setting value
19         set
20         {
21                 //If value is within 1-10, set number else ignore
22                 if(value >= 1 && value <= 10)
23                 {
24                         //Update private variable
25                         iMyNumber = value;
26
```

```
27                      //Call event
28                      NumberChanged();
29              }
30          }
31 }
32 //---------------------------------------------------------
33 //Internal reference a number between 1-10
34 private int iMyNumber = 0;
35 //---------------------------------------------------------
36 // Use this for initialization
37 void Start ()
38 {
39          //Set MyNumber
40          MyNumber = 11; //Will fail because number is > 10
41
42          //Set MyNumber
43           MyNumber = 7; //Will succeed because number is between 1-10
44 }
45 //---------------------------------------------------------
46 //Event called when iMyNumber is changed
47 void NumberChanged()
48 {
49          Debug.Log("Variable iMyNumber changed to : " +
          iMyNumber.ToString());

50 }
51 //---------------------------------------------------------
52 }
53 //---------------------------------------------------------
```

The following are the comments for code sample 1-15:

- **Line 10**: A public integer property is declared. This property is not an independent variable but simply a wrapper and accessor interface for the private variable iMyNumber, declared in line 34.

- **Line 13**: When MyNumber is used or referenced, the internal get function is called.

- **Line 14**: When MyNumber is assigned a value, the internal set function is called.

- **Line 25**: The set function features an implicit argument value that represents the value to be assigned.

- **Line 28**: The event NumberChanged is called when the iMyNumber variable is assigned a value.

Properties and Unity

Properties are useful to validate and control the assignment of values to variables. The main problem with using them in Unity concerns their visibility in the Object Inspector. Specifically, C# properties are not shown in the Object Inspector. You can neither get nor set their values in the editor. However, community-made scripts and solutions are available that can change this default behavior, for example exposing C# properties. These scripts and solutions can be found at `http://wiki.unity3d.com/index.php?title=Expose_properties_in_inspector`.

More information on **Properties** in C# can be found at `http://msdn.microsoft.com/en-GB/library/x9fsa0sw.aspx`.

Commenting

Commenting is the practice of inserting human readable messages into your code, purely for annotation, description, and to make things clearer to the reader. In C#, one-line comments are prefixed with the `//` symbol, and multiline comments begin with `/*` and end with `*/`. Comments are used throughout the code samples in this book. Comments are important, and I recommend that you get into the habit of using them if you're not already in the habit. They benefit not only other developers in your team (if you work with others), but you too! They help remind you of what your code is doing when you return to it weeks or months later, and they even help you get clear and straight about the code you're writing right now. Of course, all these benefits depend on you writing concise and meaningful comments and not long essays filled with irrelevance. However, MonoDevelop offers XML-based comments too to describe functions and arguments specifically and which integrates with code completion. It can significantly boost your workflow, especially when working in teams. Let's see how to use this. Start by writing your function or any function, as shown in the following screenshot:

```
SampleClass.cs
SampleClass ▶ No selection
1  using UnityEngine;
2  using System.Collections;
3
4  public class SampleClass : MonoBehaviour
5  {
6      int AddNumbers(int Num1, int Num2)
7      {
8          return Num1 + Num2;
9      }
10 }
11
```

Writing a function (AddNumbers) in MonoDevelop (preparing for code commenting)

Then insert three forward-slash characters on the line above the function title (///), as shown in the following screenshot:

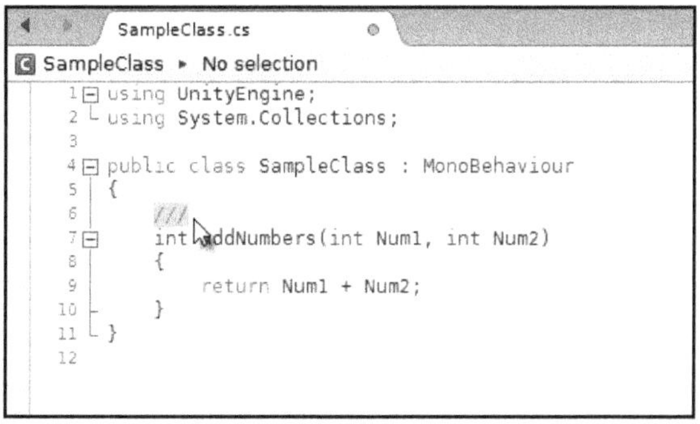

Inserting /// above the function title to create an XML comment

When you do this, MonoDevelop automatically inserts a template XML comment ready for you to complete with appropriate descriptions. It creates a summary section that describes the function generally and param entries for each argument in the function, as shown in the following screenshot:

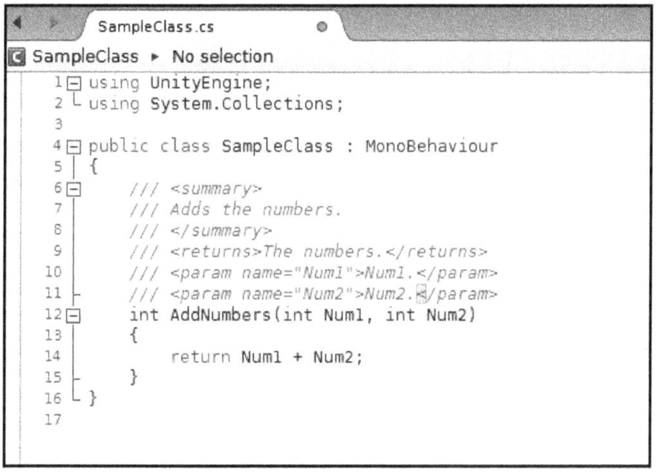

Inserting /// above the function title will autogenerate an XML comment

Next, fill in the XML template completely with comments for your function. Be sure to give each parameter an appropriate comment too, as shown in the following screenshot:

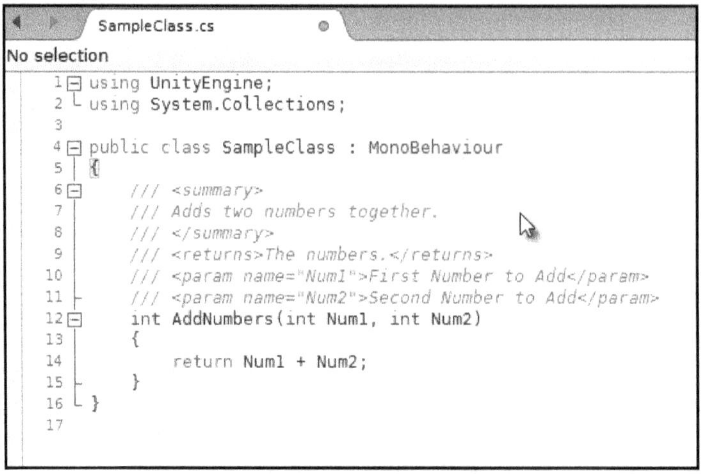

Commenting your functions using XML comments

Now, when calling the AddNumbers function elsewhere in code, the code-completion pop-up helper will display both the summary comment for the function as well as the parameter comments' context sensitively, as shown here:

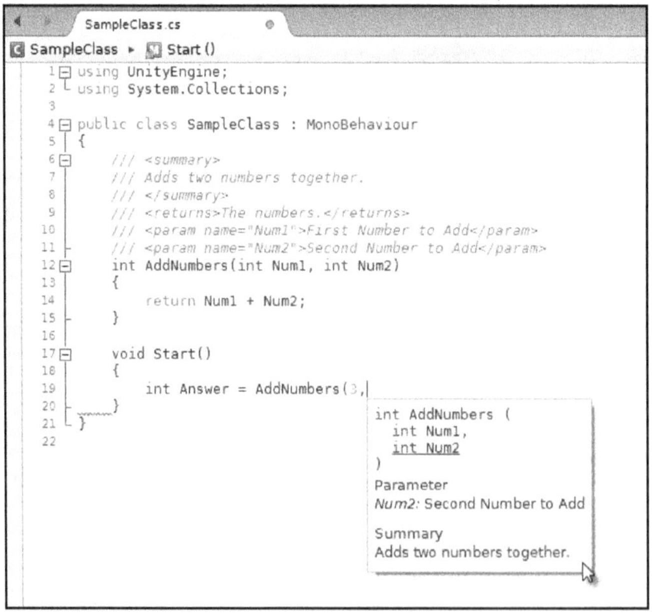

Viewing comments when making function calls

Variable visibility

One excellent feature of Unity specifically is that it exposes (shows) public class variables inside the Object Inspector in the Unity Editor, allowing you to edit and preview variables, even at runtime. This is especially convenient for debugging. However, by default, the Object Inspector doesn't expose private variables. They are typically hidden from the inspector. This isn't always a good thing because there are many cases where you'll want to debug or, at least, monitor private variables from the inspector without having to change their scope to public. There are two main ways to overcome this problem easily.

The first solution would be useful if you want to view all public and private variables in a class. You can toggle the Object Inspector in the **Debug** mode. To do this, click on the context menu icon in the top-right corner of the **Inspector** window and select **Debug** from the context menu, as shown in the following screenshot. When **Debug** is selected, all the public and private variables for a class will show.

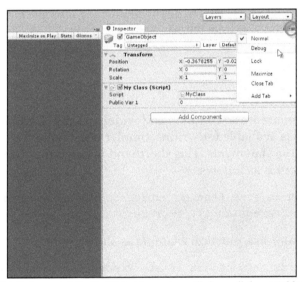

Enabling the Debug mode in the Object Inspector will show all the variables in a class

The second solution is useful for displaying specific private variables, variables that you mark explicitly as wanting to display in the Object Inspector. These will show in both the **Normal** and **Debug** modes. To achieve this, declare the private variable with the attribute `[SerializeField]`. C# attributes are considered later in this book, as shown here:

```
01 using UnityEngine;
02 using System.Collections;
03
```

```
04 public class MyClass : MonoBehaviour
05 {
06 //Will always show
07 public int PublicVar1;
08
09 //Will always show
10 [SerializeField]
11 private int PrivateVar1;
12
13 //Will show only in Debug Mode
14 private int PrivateVar2;
15
16 //Will show only in Debug Mode
17 private int PrivateVar3;
18 }
```

 You can also use the [HideInInspector] attribute to hide a global variable from the inspector.

The ? operator

The if-else statements are so common and widely used in C# that a specialized shorthand notation is available for writing simpler ones, without resorting to the full multiline if-else statements. This shorthand is called the ? operator. The basic form of this statement is as follows:

```
//If condition is true then do expression 1, else do expression 2
(condition) ? expression_1 : expression_2;
```

Let's see the ? operator in a practical example as shown here:

```
//We should hide this object if its Y position is above 100 units
bool ShouldHideObject = (transform.position.y > 100) ? true :
false;

//Update object visibility
gameObject.SetActive(!ShouldHideObject);
```

 The ? operator is useful for shorter statements, but for long and more intricate statements, it can make your code harder to read.

SendMessage and BroadcastMessage

The MonoBehaviour class included in the Unity API, which acts as the base class for most new scripts, offers the SendMessage and BroadcastMessage methods. Using these, you can easily execute functions by name on all components attached to an object. To invoke a method of a class, you typically need a local reference to that class to access and run its functions as well as to access its variables. However, the SendMessage and BroadcastMessage functions let you run functions using string values by simply specifying the name of a function to run. This is very convenient and makes your code look a lot simpler and shorter at the cost of efficiency, as we'll see later. Refer to the following code sample 1-16:

```
01 using UnityEngine;
02 using System.Collections;
03
04 public class MyClass : MonoBehaviour
05 {
06 void start()
07 {
08         //Will invoke MyFunction on ALL components/scripts
           attached to this object (where the function is present)

09         SendMessage("MyFunction",
           SendMessageOptions.DontRequireReceiver);

10 }
11
12 //Runs when SendMessage is called
13 void MyFunction()
14 {
15         Debug.Log ("hello");
16 }
17 }
```

The following are the comments for code sample 1-16:

- **Line 09**: SendMessage is called to invoke the function MyFunction. MyFunction will be invoked not only on this class but on all other components attached to GameObject, if they have a MyFunction member, including the Transform component as well as others.

- **Line 09**: The parameter SendMessageOptions.DontRequireReceiver defines what happens if MyFunction is not present on a component. Here, it specifies that Unity should ignore the component and move on to the next calling MyFunction wherever it is found.

> The term function and member function mean the same thing when the function belongs to a class. A function that belongs to a class is said to be a member function.

We've seen that SendMessage invokes a specified function across all components attached to a single GameObject. BroadcastMessage incorporates the SendMessage behavior and goes a stage further, that is, it invokes a specified function for all components on GameObject and then repeats this process recursively for all child objects in the scene hierarchy, cascading downwards to all children.

More information on SendMessage and BroadcastMessage can be found at http://docs.unity3d.com/ScriptReference/GameObject.SendMessage. html and http://docs.unity3d.com/ScriptReference/Component. BroadcastMessage.html.

Reflection

SendMessage and BroadcastMessage are effective ways to facilitate inter-object communication and inter-component communication, that is, it's a great way to make components talk to one another if they need to, to synchronize behavior and recycle functionality. However, both SendMessage and BroadcastMessage rely internally on a C# feature known as **reflection**. By invoking a function using a string, your application is required to look at itself at runtime (to reflect), searching its code for the intended function to run. This process is computationally expensive compared to running a function in the normal way. For this reason, seek to minimize the usage of SendMessage and BroadcastMessage, especially during Update events or other frame-based scenarios, as the impact on performance can be significant. This doesn't mean you should never use them. There might be times when their use is rare, infrequent, and convenient and has practically no appreciable impact. However, later chapters in this book will demonstrate alternative and faster techniques using delegates and interfaces.

If you'd like more information on C# and its usage before proceeding further with this book, then I recommend the following sources:

- *Learning C# by Developing Games with Unity 3D Beginner's Guide*, Terry *Norton, Packt Publishing*

- *Intro to C# Programming and Scripting for Games in Unity, Alan Thorn* (3DMotive video course found at `https://www.udemy.com/3dmotive-intro-to-c-programming-and-scripting-for-games-in-unity/`)

- *Pro Unity Game Development with C#, Alan Thorn, Apress*

The following are a few online resources:

- `http://msdn.microsoft.com/en-gb/library/aa288436%28v=vs.71%29.aspx`

- `http://www.csharp-station.com/tutorial.aspx`

- `http://docs.unity3d.com/ScriptReference/`

Summary

This chapter offered a general, Unity-specific overview of Unity's C#, exploring the most common and widely-used language features for game development. Later chapters will revisit some of these subjects in a more advanced way, but everything covered here will be critical for understanding and writing the code featured in subsequent chapters.

2
Debugging

Debugging is the process of finding, identifying, and fixing bugs (errors or mistakes) in your code, and there are many ways to achieve this. To script effectively, you'll need to be aware of the most common workflows and toolsets available to you for debugging in Unity. Before considering them further, however, it's important to be aware of the general limitations of debugging and what it cannot achieve. Debugging is not a magical cure-all to remove all bugs and guarantee an error-free application. The computer scientist Edsger W. Dijkstra said, *"Program testing can be used to show the presence of bugs, but never to show their absence"*. The crucial point is that during testing, you might encounter one or more errors. These errors can be identified, tested, and repaired through debugging. Yet, your tests — though perhaps extensive and careful — will never cover every possible case or scenario on every hardware platform under all conditions, as these combinations could be practically infinite. So, you can never be absolutely certain to have found all the possible bugs. Even on the release day, there could still be bugs in your game, which your testing couldn't detect. Of course, there might actually be no bugs remaining at all, but you cannot know this with absolute certainty. So, debugging is not about achieving an error-free application. Its aims are more modest. It's about systematically testing your game in many common and reasonable situations to find and correct as many errors as you encounter or, at least, as many severe errors as your time and budget permits. In any case, debugging is a critical part of scripting, because without it, you will have no way of tracing and fixing errors. Debugging techniques range from simple to complex, and in this chapter, we'll cover a broad spectrum of them.

Compilation errors and the console

Debugging typically refers to error-busting techniques for runtime use; that is, it refers to the things you can do to find and correct errors when your game is running. This understanding of debugging, of course, presupposes that your code is already valid and compiled. The implicit assumption is that you can write valid statements in C# and compile code, and you just want to find runtime errors that occur as a result of program logic. Thus, the focus is not on syntax but on logic, and this is indeed true. However, in this section, I'll speak very briefly about code compilation, about writing valid code, and using the console to find and correct errors of validity. This is important, both to introduce the **Console** window generally and also to establish a firm basis of thinking about debugging in more depth. Consider the following code sample 2-1 script file (`ErrorScript.cs`):

```
01 using UnityEngine;
02 using System.Collections;
03
04 public class ErrorScript : MonoBehaviour
05 {
06 int MyNumber = 5;
07
08 // Use this for initialization
09 void Start () {
10
11        mynumber = 7;
12 }
13
14 // Update is called once per frame
15 void Update () {
16        mynumber = 10;
17 }
18 }
```

To compile the preceding code sample 2-1, simply save the script file in MonoDevelop (*Ctrl* + *S*) and then refocus the Unity Editor window. From here, compilation will happen automatically. If it doesn't, you can also right-click on the script file from the **Project** panel and choose **Reimport** from the context menu. For the code sample 2-1, two errors are generated, and these will be shown in the **Console** window. If you don't already have the **Console** window open, it could be shown by selecting the **Console** option from **Window** from the application menu. The **Console** window is highly important, and you'll almost always want it open somewhere in the interface. This is where Unity as an engine communicates with you as a developer. Thus, if your code has compile errors, Unity would list them to **Console**, letting you know what they are.

The code sample 2-1 generates two compile-time errors, as shown in the following screenshot. These happen because lines 11 and 16 refer to the variable `mynumber` that doesn't exist, although `MyNumber` does (case sensitivity). Compile-time errors such as these are critical because they render your code invalid. This means you cannot compile your code and run your game until the errors are corrected.

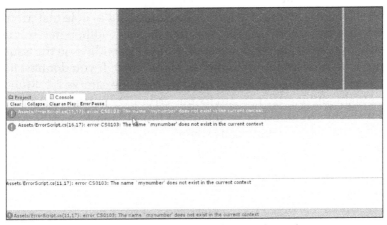

Viewing compilation errors in the Console window

If compilation errors are not shown in **Console** as expected, then make sure that the errors filter is enabled. To enable this, click on the error filter icon (a red exclamation mark icon) in the top-right corner of the **Console** window. The **Console** window features three filters, comments (**A**), warnings (**B**), and errors (**C**), as shown in the following screenshot, to hide and show specific messages. These toggle the visibility of each message type in the **Console** window. Comments refer to the messages that you, as a programmer, explicitly print to the **Console** window from your code using the `Debug.Log` statement. We'll see examples of this shortly (you can also use the `Print` function). Warnings refer to potential issues or wastages detected in your code. These are syntactically valid and will compile even if ignored by you, but they might cause problems or have unintended and wasteful results. Errors refer to any compile-time errors found in your code that affect its compilation validity, such as with code sample 2-1.

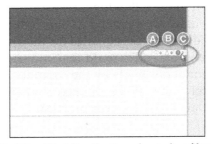

Enabling/disabling the Console window filters

When the console fills with more than one error, the errors are typically listed in the order in which they were detected by the compiler, that is, from top to bottom. It's considered best practice to tackle errors in order, because earlier errors can cause later ones. Thus, resolving earlier errors can, potentially, resolve later ones. To resolve an error, start by double-clicking on the error from the **Console** window, and MonoDevelop will open automatically, highlighting the line where the error itself was found or where the error was first detected. It is important to note that MonoDevelop will take you to the line where the error was first detected, although resolving the error will not always involve editing that line specifically. Depending on the issue, you will need to change to a different line than theone highlighted. If you double-click on the top error (first error) in **Console**, as generated by the code sample 2-1, MonoDevelop will open and highlight line 11. You can fix this error in two ways: either by renaming mynumber to MyNumber in line 11 or by renaming the variable MyNumber to mynumber in line 6. Now, consider the following code sample 2-2:

```
01 using UnityEngine;
02 using System.Collections;
03
04 public class ErrorScript : MonoBehaviour
05 {
06 int MyNumber = 5;
07
08 // Use this for initialization
09 void Start () {
10
11       MyNumber = 7;
12 }
13
14 // Update is called once per frame
15 void Update () {
16       MyNumber = 10;
17 }
18 }
```

Code sample 2-2 fixes the errors in code sample 2-1. However, it leaves us with a warning instead (as shown in the following screenshot). This indicates that the variable MyNumber is never used. It's assigned a value in lines 11 and 16, but this assignment is never of any ultimate consequence for the application. Here, this warning could be ignored and the code would remain valid. Warnings should be seen primarily as recommendations made by the compiler about your code. How you handle them is ultimately your choice, but I recommend that you try to eliminate both errors and warnings wherever practical.

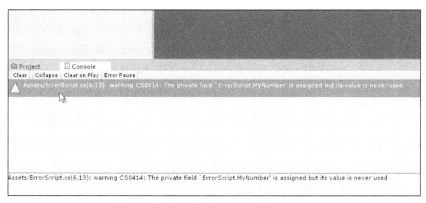

Try to eliminate both errors and warnings

Debugging with Debug.Log – custom messages

Perhaps, the oldest and most well-known debugging technique in Unity is to use Debug.Log statements to print diagnostic messages to **Console**, thus illustrating program flow and object properties. This technique is versatile and appealing because it can be used in practically every **Integrated Development Environment** (**IDE**) and not just MonoDevelop. Further, all the Unity objects, including vector and color objects, have a convenient ToString function that allows their internal members (such as X, Y, and Z) to be printed to a human-readable string—one that can be easily sent to the console for debugging purposes. For example, consider the following code sample 2-3. This code sample demonstrates an important debugging workflow, namely, printing a status message about an object at its instantiation. This script, when attached to a scene object, prints its world position to **Console**, along with a descriptive message:

```
01 using UnityEngine;
02 using System.Collections;
03
04 public class CubeScript : MonoBehaviour
05 {
06 // Use this for initialization
07 void Start () {

08         Debug.Log ("Object created in scene at position: " +
          transform.position.ToString());transform.position.
          ToString());

09 }
10 }
```

The following screenshot demonstrates the output of this code in **Console** when attached to a cube GameObject. The Debug.Log message is printed in the main console message list. If the message is selected with the mouse, **Console** will also indicate a script file and line associated with the statement.

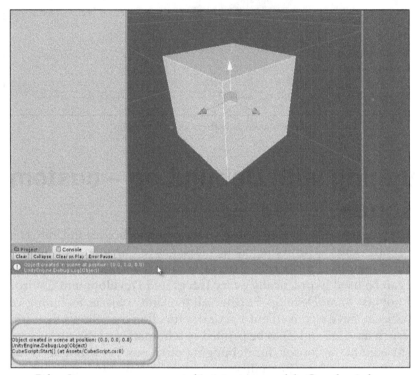

Debug.Log messages can convert objects to strings, and the Console window
also indicates an associated script file and line

The main limitations of Debug.Log as a debugging technique relate to code cleanliness and program complexity. First, the Debug.Log statements require you to explicitly add code to your source files. When you're done debugging, you'll need to either remove the Debug.Log statements manually or leave them there, which is wasteful and results in confusion, especially if you have to add the additional Debug.Log statements in many other places. Second, though Debug.Log is useful to target specific problems or monitor specific variables over time, it's ultimately awkward to get a higher-level picture of your code and its execution to trace errors whose presence you detect but whose location is entirely unknown. These criticisms, however, shouldn't be regarded as advice to avoid using the Debug.Log statements entirely. They should be considered only to use them appropriately. Debug.Log works best when an error or problem can be traced to a prime suspect object, and you want to observe or monitor its values to see how they change or update, especially during events such as OnStart.

Removing the Debug.Log statements

When your game is ready to build and ship, remember to remove or comment away any `Debug.Log` statements for extra cleanliness.

Overriding the ToString method

The following code sample 2-3 demonstrates the convenience of the `ToString` method when used in conjunction with the `Debug.Log` debugging. `ToString` lets you convert an object to a human-readable string that can be output to **Console**. In C#, every class inherits the `ToString` method by default. This means that using inheritance and polymorphism, you can override the `ToString` method of your class that customizes it as required and produce a more readable and accurate debug string that represents your class members. Consider the following code sample 2-4 that overrides `ToString`. If you get into the habit of overriding `ToString` for every class you make, your classes will become easier to debug:

```
using UnityEngine;
using System.Collections;
//---------------------------------------------
//Sample enemy Ogre class
public class EnemyOgre : MonoBehaviour
{
//---------------------------------------------
//Attack types for OGRE
public enum AttackType {PUNCH, MAGIC, SWORD, SPEAR};

//Current attack type being used
public AttackType CurrentAttack = AttackType.PUNCH;

//Health
public int Health = 100;

//Recovery Delay (after attacking)
public float RecoveryTime = 1.0f;

//Movement speed of Ogre - metres per second
```

```
public float Speed = 1.0f;

//Name of Ogre
public string OgreName = "Harry";
//------------------------------------------
//Override ToString method
public override string ToString ()
{
    //Return a string representing the class

        return string.Format ("***Class EnemyOgre*** OgreName:
        {0} | Health: {1} | Speed: {2} | CurrentAttack: {3} |
        RecoveryTime: {4}",
        OgreName, Health, Speed, CurrentAttack, RecoveryTime);
}

//----------------------------------------------
void Start()
{

        Debug.Log (ToString());
}
    //-------------------------------------------
}
//------------------------------------------
```

The output of the preceding code can be seen in the **Console** window, as shown here:

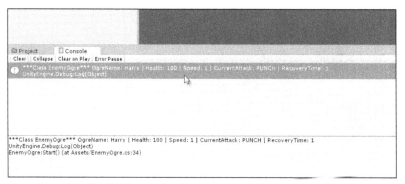

Overriding the ToString method to customize debug messages for a class

String.Format

Line 30 of the code sample 2-3 uses the `String.Format` function to build a complete string. This function is useful when you need to make one long string that includes both literal statements and variable values, which could be different types. By inserting the tokens `{0}`, `{1}`, `{2}`... inside the string argument, the `Format` function will substitute them for the subsequent function arguments in the order in which they are provided; that is, `String.Format` will concatenate your string argument at the location of the tokens, with string versions of your function arguments. Thus, the string `{0}` will be replaced with `OgreName.ToString()`. For more information on `String.Format`, see the online documentation at `http://msdn.microsoft.com/en-us/library/system.string.format%28v=vs.110%29.aspx`.

You can section off and isolate blocks of code between the release and debug versions that allow you to run debug-specific code when specific flags are enabled. When debugging games, for example, you'll frequently develop two sets or variations of code: the release code and the debug code. Imagine a common scenario where to find and resolve a bug in the code, you resort to inserting the `Debug.Log` statements that print out the values of variables and states of classes. You might even insert additional lines, such as `if` statements and loops, to test out alternative scenarios and explore how objects react. After amending the code for a while, the problem seems repaired, so you remove the additional debug code and continue testing as you did earlier. However, later, you discover that the problem has returned, or a similar one has arisen. So now you wish you'd kept the debug code after all, because it'd be useful again. You might promise yourself that next time, you'll simply comment out the debug code as opposed to deleting it entirely. This will let you simply remove the commenting should the code be needed again. However, of course, having to comment and uncomment code is also tedious, especially if there're many lines, and they are scattered across multiple files and parts of files. You can, however, resolve this problem and similar ones using custom global defines. In essence, a global define is a special preprocessor flag that you can enable or disable to conditionally compile or exclude blocks of your code. By setting the flag to `true`, Unity will automatically compile one version of your code, and by setting it to `false`, Unity will compile the other version. This will allow you to maintain two versions or variations of your code in only one set of source files: one for debug and one for release. Let's see this in practice in Unity. Consider the following code sample 2-5:

```
01 using UnityEngine;
```

```
02 using System.Collections;
03
04 public class CubeScript : MonoBehaviour
05 {
06 // Use this for initialization
07 void Start ()
08 {
09       #if SHOW_DEBUG_MESSAGES
10       //runs ONLY if the Define SHOW_DEBUG_MESSAGES is active
11       Debug.Log ("Pos: " + transform.position.ToString());
12       #endif
13
14       //runs because it's outside the #if #endif block
15       Debug.Log ("Start function called");
16 }
17 }
```

Lines 09–12 feature the core functionality using the preprocessor directives `#if` and `#endif` conditional. This conditional is not executed at runtime like a regular `if` statement, but at compile time. At compile time, Unity will decide whether the global define SHOW_DEBUG_MESSAGES is specified or active. If, and only if, it is, then lines 10 and 11 will be compiled, otherwise the compiler will ignore these lines, treating them as comments. Using this feature, you can isolate all debug code within an `#if` `#endif` block that checks for a debug define and activates and deactivates the code on the basis of the SHOW_DEBUG_MESSAGES define, which applies project-wide to all source files. The question that then remains is how is the define set. To set the global define, navigate to **Edit** | **Project Settings** | **Player** from the application menu. Then, enter the define name in the **Scripting Define Symbols** field, making sure that you press the *Enter* key after entering the name to confirm the change, as shown in the following screenshot:

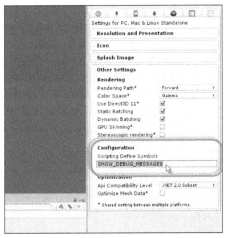

Adding global custom defines from the Unity Editor, which lets you conditionally compile code

Removing defines and adding multiple defines

Simply entering the name of your global define in the **Scripting Define Symbols** field is enough for it to take effect and apply across your code. You can delete the name to remove the define, but you can also prefix the name with / (for example, /SHOW_DEBUG_MESSAGE) to disable the define, thus making it easier to re-enable it later. You can also add multiple defines, separating each with the semicolon symbol (for example, DEFINE1;DEFINE2;DEFINE3...).

Visual debugging

Debugging with abstract or textual representations of data (such as Debug.Log) is often adequate but not always optimal. Sometimes, a picture is worth a thousand words. So, for example, when coding the line-of-sight functionality for enemies and other characters that allow them to see the player and other objects whenever they come in range, it's useful to get a live and graphical representation of where the line of sight actually is in the viewport. This line of functionality is drawn in terms of lines or as a wireframe cube. Similarly, if an object is following a path, it'd be great to draw this path in the viewport that displays it as a colored line. The purpose of this is not to create visual aids that will really show in the final game but simply to ease the debugging process that lets us get a better idea of how the game is working. These kinds of helpers or gizmos are a part of visual debugging. Unity already provides us with many gizmos automatically, such as the wireframe bounding box for colliders and frustum for cameras. However, we also have the ability to create our own gizmos for our own objects. This section explores gizmos further.

As mentioned earlier, many Unity objects, such as colliders, trigger volumes, NavMesh Agents, cameras, and lights, already offer their own visual aids and gizmos when they are selected. These are shown by default in the **Scene** viewport unless you switch them off or reduce their size to zero. So, if you've added a native Unity object and don't see a gizmo in the **Scene** viewport, then be sure to check the **Gizmo** panel that is accessible from the **Scene** toolbar via the **Gizmo** button. Enable all the gizmos you want to see and adjust the **Size** slider that increases or decreases the gizmo size (choose a size that is best for you), as shown here:

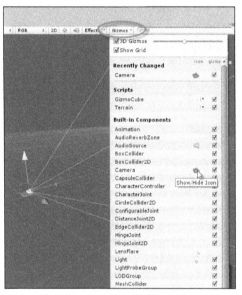

Enabling gizmos in the Scene view

Gizmos in the Game tab

Gizmos don't show by default in the **Game** tab. You can, however, change this behavior easily using the **Gizmo** button in the top-right corner of the **Game** tab toolbar. This menu works just like the **Gizmos** menu for the **Scene** tab, as shown in the preceding screenshot.

Consider the following code sample 2-6. This is a sample class that can be attached to an object and it relies on the Unity gizmo class to draw a custom range of helper gizmos. More information can be found online at http://docs.unity3d.com/ScriptReference/Gizmos.html. Here, this sample class draws a bounding wireframe sphere of a specified radius centered on the object that represents its range of attack. In addition, it draws a line-of-sight vector that represents the object's forward direction, providing a visual indication of the way the object is facing. All of these gizmos are drawn inside the OnDrawGizmos event of MonoBehaviour on the condition that the variable DrawGizmos is true:

```
using UnityEngine;
using System.Collections;

public class GizmoCube : MonoBehaviour
{
//Show debugging info?
    public bool DrawGizmos = true;

    //Called to draw gizmos. Will always draw.
    //If you want to draw gizmos for only selected object, then call

    //OnDrawGizmosSelected
    void OnDrawGizmos()
    {
        if(!DrawGizmos) return;

         //Set gizmo color
         Gizmos.color = Color.blue;

        //Draw front vector - show the direction I'm facing
        Gizmos.DrawRay(transform.position,
        transform.forward.normalized *  4.0f);

          //Set gizmo color
          //Show proximity radius around cube
          //If cube were an enemy, they would detect the player
          within this radius

Gizmos.color = Color.red;
        Gizmos.DrawWireSphere(transform.position, 4.0f);

        //Restore color back to white
        Gizmos.color = Color.white;
    }
}
```

The following screenshot shows how to draw gizmos that helps with debugging:

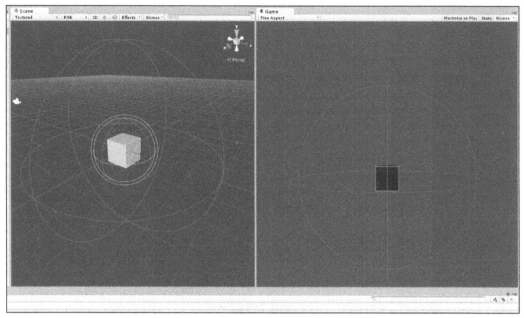

Drawing gizmos

Error logging

When you compile and build your game to distribute to testers, whether they're collected together in an office or scattered across the globe, you'll need a way to record errors and exceptions as and when they happen during gameplay. One way to do this is through logfiles. Logfiles are human-readable text files that are generated on the local computer by the game at runtime, and they record the details of errors as they occur, if any occur at all. The amount of information you record is a matter for careful consideration, as logging too much detail can obfuscate the file and too little can render the file useless. However, once a balance is reached the tester will be able to send you the log for inspection, and this will, hopefully, allow you to quickly pin-point errors in your code and repair them effectively, that is without introducing new errors! There are many ways to implement logging behavior in Unity. One way is using the native `Application` class to receive exception notifications by way of delegates. Consider the following code sample 2-7:

```
01 //-------------------------------------------------
02 using UnityEngine;
03 using System.Collections;
```

```
04 using System.IO;
05 //-----------------------------------------------
06 public class ExceptionLogger : MonoBehaviour
07 {
08       //Internal reference to stream writer object
09       private System.IO.StreamWriter SW;
10
11       //Filename to assign log
12       public string LogFileName = "log.txt";
13
14       //-------------------------------------------------
15       // Use this for initialization
16       void Start ()
17       {
18             //Make persistent
19             DontDestroyOnLoad(gameObject);
20
21       //Create string writer object

22        SW = new
         System.IO.StreamWriter(Application.persistentDataPath + "/" +
         LogFileName);

23
24       Debug.Log(Application.persistentDataPath + "/" +
         LogFileName);

25       }
26       //-------------------------------------------------
27       //Register for exception listening, and log exceptions
28       void OnEnable()
29       {
30             Application.RegisterLogCallback(HandleLog);
31       }
32       //-------------------------------------------------
33       //Unregister for exception listening
34       void OnDisable()
35       {
36             Application.RegisterLogCallback(null);
37       }
```

```
38          //----------------------------------------------
39          //Log exception to a text file

40          void HandleLog(string logString, string stackTrace,
            LogType type)

41          {
42          //If an exception or error, then log to file
43          if(type == LogType.Exception || type == LogType.Error)
44              {

45                      SW.WriteLine("Logged at: " +
                        System.DateTime.Now.ToString() +
                        " - Log Desc: " + logString + " -
                        Trace: " + stackTrace + " - Type: " +
                        type.ToString());

46              }
47          }
48          //----------------------------------------------
49          //Called when object is destroyed
50          void OnDestroy()
51          {
52                  //Close file
53                  SW.Close();
54          }
55          //----------------------------------------------
56 }
57 //----------------------------------------------
```

The following are the comments for code sample 2-7:

- **Line 22**: A new `StreamWriter` object is created to write debug strings
  to a file on the computer. The file is created inside `Application.
  persistentDataPath`; this points to a system location that is always writable.

- **Line 30**: The `Application.RegisterLogCallBack` method is invoked with a
  function reference to `HandleLog` as an argument. This relies on delegates. In
  short, a reference to the `HandleLog` function is passed, and this will be called
  when an error or exception occurs that allows us to write details to a logfile.

- **Line 45**: The `WriteLine` method of `StreamWriter` is called to print textual data to the logfile when an error occurs. The error information is provided by Unity through the `HandleLog` arguments: `logString`, `stackTrace`, and `LogType`. The `StreamWriter` class is part of the Mono Framework, which is an open source implementation of the Microsoft NET Framework. More information on `StreamWriter` can be found at `http://msdn.microsoft.com/en-us/library/system.io.streamwriter%28v=vs.110%29.aspx`.

> One of the quickest ways to test out your error logger is to create a divide by zero error. Don't forget to insert a `Debug.Log (Application.persistentDataPath);` line somewhere in your code to print the logfile path to the **Console** window. This can help you quickly find the logfile on your system via Windows Explorer or Mac Finder. Note that the `persistentDataPath` variable is used as opposed to an absolute path, because it varies from operating system to operating system.

The following screenshot shows how to print errors to a text-based logfile:

Printing errors to a text-based logfile can make debugging and bug fixing easier

What are delegates in C#? Imagine that you're able to create a variable and assign it a function reference instead of a regular value. Having done this, you can invoke the variable just like a function to call the referenced function at a later time. You can even reassign the variable to reference a new and different function later. This, in essence, is how delegates work. If you're familiar with C++, delegates are practically equivalent to the function pointers. Thus, delegates are special types that can reference and invoke functions. They're ideal to create extensible callback systems and event notifications. For example, by keeping a list or array of delegate types, potentially, many different classes can register themselves as listeners for callbacks by adding themselves to the list. More information on C# can be found at http://msdn.microsoft.com/en-gb/library/ms173171.aspx. Consider the following code sample 2-8 for an example of the delegate usage in C# with Unity:

```
using UnityEngine;
using System.Collections;
//------------------------------------------------------
public class DelegateUsage : MonoBehaviour
{
  //Defines delegate type: param list
  public delegate void EventHandler(int Param1, int Param2);
//------------------------------------------------------
//Declare array of references to functions from Delegate type -
max 10 events

public EventHandler[] EH = new EventHandler[10];
//------------------------------------------------------
/// <summary>
/// Awake is called before start. Will add my Delegate
HandleMyEvent to list
/// </summary>
void Awake()
{
    //Add my event (HandleMyEvent) to delegate list
    EH[0] = HandleMyEvent;
}
//------------------------------------------------------
/// <summary>
/// Will cycle through delegate list and call all events
/// </summary>
 void Start()
  {
    //Loop through all delegates in list
    foreach(EventHandler e in EH)
    {
        //Call event here, if not null
        if(e!=null)
```

```
          e(0,0); //This calls the event
     }
  }
//------------------------------------------------------
/// <summary>
/// This is a sample delegate event. Can be referenced by Delegate
Type EventHandler
/// </summary>
/// <param name="Param1">Example param</param>
/// <param name="Param2">Example param</param>
 void HandleMyEvent (int Param1, int Param2)
 {
     Debug.Log ("Event Called");
 }
//------------------------------------------------------
```

Editor debugging

It's sometimes claimed that Unity has no debugging tools built into the editor, but this is not quite true. With Unity, you can play your game and edit the scene at the same time while the game is running. You can even observe and edit properties in the Object Inspector, both private and public, as we saw earlier. This can give you a complete and graphical picture of your game at runtime; and allow you to detect and observe a wide range of potential errors. This form of debugging should not be underestimated. To get the most from in-editor debugging, activate the **Debug** mode from the Object Inspector by clicking on the context menu icon in the top-right corner of the inspector and then choose **Debug** from the menu, as shown here:

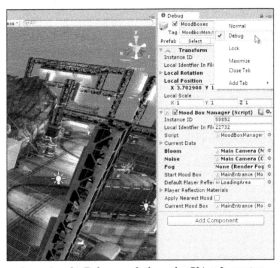

Accessing the Debug mode from the Object Inspector

Next, make sure that your viewports are configured appropriately so that they allow you to see both the **Scene** and **Game** views simultaneously during the **Play** mode, along with the **Stats** panel. To achieve this, disable the **Maximize on Play** button from the **Game** tab toolbar if it's activated. Then, arrange the **Scene** and **Game** tabs side-by-side in the interface, or else arrange them across multiple monitors if you have more than one. Multiple monitors are strongly recommended if your budget allows, but a single monitor can work well too, provided you invest extra time arranging and sizing each window to best meet your needs. In addition, you'll generally want the **Console** window visible and the **Project** panel hidden to prevent accidental selection and movement of assets, as shown in the following screenshot. Remember that you can also customize the Unity GUI Layout. For more information see `http://docs.unity3d.com/Manual/CustomizingYourWorkspace.html`.

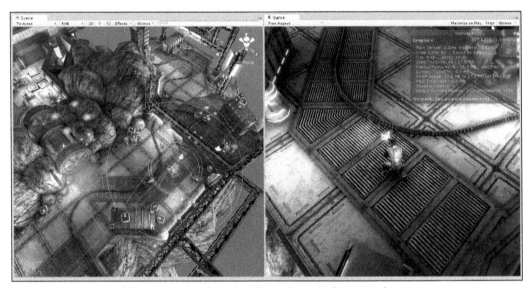

Debugging games from the editor using a single monitor layout

Once you're ready for in-editor debugging, click on the play button on the toolbar and use pause if you ever need to stop game events to inspect a specific object and its values from the Object Inspector. Remember that you can still use the transform (position, rotation, and scale) tools in-game to reposition the player or enemies, thus trying out new values and seeing which ones work and which ones do not. Most importantly, however, all edits to the scene in the **Game** mode, via the Object Inspector or transform tools, are temporary and will revert back after the **Play** mode ends. For this reason, if you need to make permanent changes to settings, then you would need to make them in the **Edit** mode. You can, of course, copy and paste values between the **Play** and **Edit** modes using the **Component** context menu at any time, as shown in the following screenshot. Remember that the hot key (*Ctrl + P*) toggles between the **Play** mode and (*Ctrl + Shift + P* between paused and unpaused). A full list of Unity hot keys is listed at `http://docs.unity3d.com/Manual/UnityHotkeys.html`.

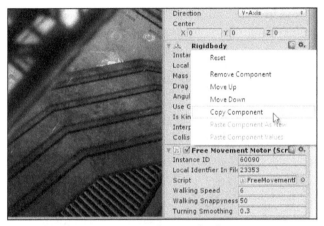

Copying and pasting component values via the Component context menu

Using the profiler

One additional tool that's used partly for debugging and partly for optimization is the **Profiler** window, which is available only in Unity Pro by clicking on the **Profiler** tab in **Window** in the application menu, as shown in the following screenshot. In short, the profiler gives you a statistical top-down view of how time and workload is distributed across the different parts of your game and across system hardware components, such as the CPU and graphics card. Using profiler, you can determine, for example, how much time is consumed by camera rendering in the scene compared to physics calculations or to audio functionality, as well as to other categories. It lets you measure performance, compare numbers, and assess where performance can be improved. The profiler is not really a tool that alerts you to the presence of bugs in your code specifically. However, if you're experiencing performance problems in running the game, such as lags and freezes, then it could guide you to where optimizations can be made. For this reason, the profiler is a tool to which you'll turn if you decide that performance is an issue for your game and you need an educated, studied analysis of where to start implementing improvements.

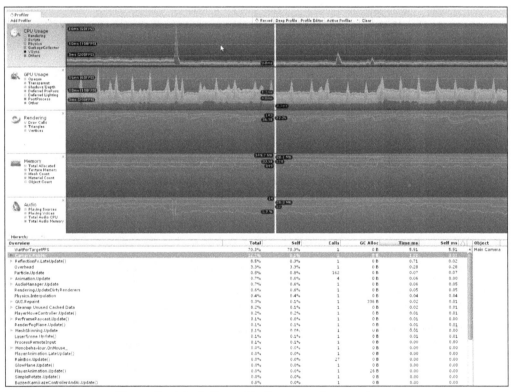

The profiler is typically used to diagnose performance issues

When you run your game with the **Profiler** window open, the graph will populate with statistics about the most recent frames. The profiler doesn't usually record information about all the frames since the game began, but only the most recent ones as will fit into memory sensibly. There is a toggleable "deep profile" method available in the upper toolbar of the **Profiler** window, which allows you (in theory) to get extra information about your game, but I'd recommend that you avoid this mode. It can cause performance issues with the Unity Editor when running asset-heavy and code-heavy games, and it can even freeze the editor altogether. Instead, I'd recommend that you only use the default mode. When using this mode, in most cases, you'll want to disable the visualization of **VSync** from the **CPU Usage** area to get a better view of other performance statistics, including **Rendering** and **Scripts**, as shown in the following screenshot. To do this, simply click on the **VSync** icon in the graph index area:

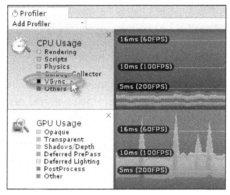

Disabling the VSync display from the CPU usage area in the Profiler window

The horizontal axis of the graph represents frames — the most recent frames added to the memory buffer. This axis keeps populating with new data while the game is running. The vertical axis represents time or computational expense: higher values are expressive of a more demanding and slower frame time. After the graph is filled with some data during the **Play** mode, you can pause the game to examine its state. Select the frames from the graph to view more information on game performance during that frame. When you do this, the **Hierarchy** panel in the bottom half of the **Profile** window fills with function data about the code that is being executed on the selected frame. When viewing the graph, it's good practice to watch for sudden increases (peaks or spikes), as shown in the following screenshot. These indicate frames of sudden and intense activity. Sometimes, they can be one-off occurrences that are either unavoidable due to hardware operations or that happen legitimately and are not the source of performance problems, such as scene transitions or loading screens.

However, they can indicate trouble too, especially if they happen regularly. So, when diagnosing performance issues, looking for spikes is a good place to start your investigation.

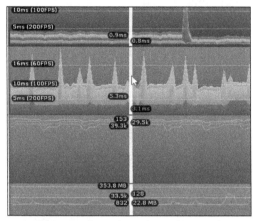

Selecting a frame from the profiler graph

The **Hierarchy** view lists all the main functions and events in code that executes on the selected frame. For each function, there are several crucial properties such as **Total**, **Self**, **Time ms**, and **Self ms**, which are shown here:

Overview	Total	Self
WaitForTargetFPS	49.1%	49.1%
Camera.Render	22.2%	0.2%
Camera.ImageEffects	12.3%	0.0%
▷ Culling	3.9%	0.1%
▷ Drawing	3.6%	0.0%
▷ UpdateDepthTexture	2.0%	1.9%
Camera.GUILayer	0.0%	0.0%
RenderTexture.SetActive	0.0%	0.0%
▷ ReflectionFx.LateUpdate()	10.5%	0.1%
Overhead	4.0%	4.0%
Physics.Simulate	1.9%	1.9%
▷ GUI.Repaint	1.3%	0.2%
▷ RainBox.Update()	1.1%	1.1%
Particle.Update	1.0%	1.0%
▷ PlayerMoveController.Update()	1.0%	0.2%
▷ RenderFogPlane.Update()	1.0%	0.7%
▷ LaserScope.Update()	0.8%	0.5%
▷ AudioManager.Update	0.7%	0.6%
Rendering.UpdateDirtyRenderers	0.7%	0.7%
▷ Animation.Update	0.6%	0.0%
▷ FreeMovementMotor.FixedUpdate()	0.5%	0.3%
▷ KamikazeMovementMotor.FixedUpdate()	0.4%	0.2%
▷ Monobehaviour.OnMouse_	0.3%	0.0%
▷ PerFrameRaycast.Update()	0.3%	0.0%
▷ PlayerAnimation.LateUpdate()	0.2%	0.1%
AudioManager.FixedUpdate	0.2%	0.2%
▷ MeshSkinning.Update	0.1%	0.0%
▷ PlayerAnimation.FixedUpdate()	0.1%	0.1%
▷ SimpleRotate.Update()	0.1%	0.0%
▷ GlowPlane.Update()	0.1%	0.1%
▷ MoodBoxManager.Update()	0.1%	0.0%
▷ PlayerAnimation.Update()	0.1%	0.0%
Physics.Interpolation	0.1%	0.1%

Examining function calls during selected frames

Let's discuss these crucial properties in more detail:

- **Total and Time ms**: The **Total** column represents the proportion of frame time consumed by the function. The value of **49.1**%, for example, means that 49.1 percent of the total time required for the selected frame was consumed by the function, including any time taken to call subfunctions (functions called within the function). The **Time ms** column expresses the frame consumption time in absolute terms, measured in milliseconds. Together, these two values give you both a relative and absolute measure of how expensive calling the function is on each frame and in total.

- **Self and Self ms**: The **Total** and **Total ms** settings measure the expense of the function for the selected frame, but they include the total time spent inside other functions that were invoked from within the function. Both **Self** and **Self ms** exclude this time and express only the total time spent within the function, minus any additional time waiting for other functions to complete. These values are often the most important when seeking to pinpoint a specific function that causes performance problems.

More information on the Unity Profiler can be found at `http://docs.unity3d.com/Manual/ProfilerWindow.html`.

Debugging with MonoDevelop – getting started

Earlier, we encountered the `Debug.Log` method of debugging to print helper messages to the console at critical moments in the code to help us see how the program executes. This method, while functional, however, suffers some significant drawbacks. First off, when writing larger programs with many `Debug.Log` statements it's easy to effectively "spam" the console with excessive messages. This makes it difficult to differentiate between the ones you need and the ones you don't. Second, it's generally a bad practice to change your code by inserting the `Debug.Log` statements simply to monitor program flow and find errors. Ideally, we should be able to debug without changing our code. Therefore, we have compelling reasons to find alternative ways to debug. MonoDevelop can help us here. Specifically, in the latest releases of Unity, MonoDevelop can natively attach itself to a running Unity process. In doing this, we get access to a range of common debugging tools, the kind encountered when developing other types of software, such as breakpoints and traces. Presently, the connectivity between MonoDevelop and Unity can be buggy however, for some users on some systems. However, when working as intended, MonoDevelop can offer a rich and useful debugging experience that allows us to move beyond simply writing the `Debug.Log` statements.

To start debugging with MonoDevelop, let's consider breakpoints. When debugging code, you'll likely need to observe the program flow when it reaches a specified line. A breakpoint lets you mark one or more lines in a source file from MonoDevelop, and when the program runs in Unity, its execution will pause at the first breakpoint. At this pause, you get the opportunity to examine the code and the status of variables as well as to inspect and edit their values. You can also continue execution with stepping. This lets you push execution forward to the next line, following the normal program logic line-by-line. You get the opportunity of inspecting your code in each line as it passes. Let's see an example case. The following code sample 2-9 shows a simple script file. When attached to an object, it retrieves a list of all objects in the scene (including itself) and then sets their position to the world origin (0, 0, 0) when the **Start** function is executed, which occurs at level startup:

```
using UnityEngine;
using System.Collections;

public class DebugTest : MonoBehaviour
{
    // Use this for initialization
void Start ()
    {
        //Get all game objects in scene
        Transform[] Objs = Object.FindObjectsOfType<Transform>();

        //Cycle through all objects
        for(int i=0; i<Objs.Length; i++)
        {
            //Set object to world origin
            Objs[i].position = Vector3.zero;
        }
    }
}
```

Let's set a breakpoint in the highlighted line via MonoDevelop. This will pause the program execution whenever it reaches this line. To set the breakpoint, position your mouse cursor on the highlighted line, right-click on the left-hand gray margin, and choose **New Breakpoint**. Otherwise, use the MonoDevelop application menu to choose the **New Breakpoint** option in **Run**, or you can also press the *F9* key (or you can left-click on the line number), as shown here:

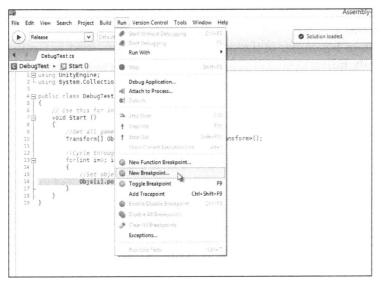

Creating a new breakpoint in MonoDevelop

The breakpoint line will be highlighted in red. To get this breakpoint to work properly with Unity when the game runs, you'll need to attach MonoDevelop to the running Unity process. To do this, make sure that the Unity Editor is running alongside MonoDevelop and then choose the **Attach to Process** option from **Run** from the MonoDevelop application menu, as shown in the following screenshot:

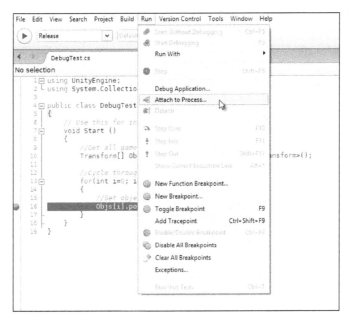

Attach to Process

The **Attach to Process** dialog appears, and the **Unity Editor** should be listed as **Process Name** to which MonoDevelop can be attached. The **Debugger** drop-down list in the bottom-left corner of the window should be specified as **Unity Debugger**. Select the **Unity Editor** option and then choose the **Attach** button, as shown here:

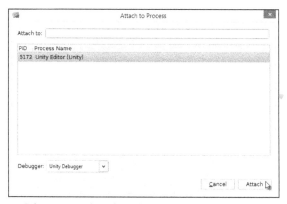

Select Unity Editor from the Attach to Process dialog

When MonoDevelop is attached to Unity as a process, two new bottom-aligned panes will dock themselves to the MonoDevelop interface, and these include the **Watch** window and the **Immediate** window, as shown in the following screenshot. These windows offer additional debugging information and views when your game runs in the Unity Editor, as we'll see in the next section.

Two new panes dock themselves to MonoDevelop when attaching to a Unity process

Next, return to the Unity Editor and make sure that the script file `DebugTest.cs`, as shown in code sample 2-9, is attached to an object in the scene and that the scene includes other objects (any objects, such as cubes or cylinders). Then, run your game using the play button from the Unity toolbar, as shown here:

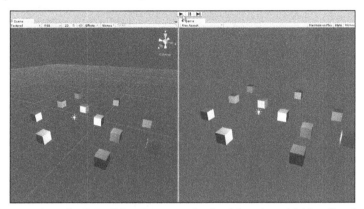

Running from the Unity Editor in preparation for debugging with MonoDevelop

When you press the play button on the Unity toolbar with MonoDevelop attached, the execution of Unity will freeze when the breakpoint is reached (the break mode). The focus will switch to the MonoDevelop window with the breakpoint line highlighted in yellow inside the source file that indicates the current step of execution, as shown in the following screenshot. During this mode, you cannot use the Unity Editor, and you cannot switch between viewports or even edit settings inside the Object Inspector as you can with in-editor debugging. MonoDevelop is waiting exclusively for your input to resume execution. The next few sections will consider some useful debugging tools that you can use in the break mode.

Entering the break mode from within MonoDevelop

Debugging with MonoDevelop – the Watch window

A **Watch** window allows you to view the value of a variable that's active in memory in the current step, and this includes both local and global variables. One way to quickly add a watch for a variable while it is in the break mode is to highlight it in the code editor and then hover your mouse over it. When you do this, leaving the mouse hovered for a few seconds, a pop-up window appears automatically. This window allows the full inspection of a variable, as shown in the following screenshot. You can contract and expand the members of a class and examine the state of all its variables.

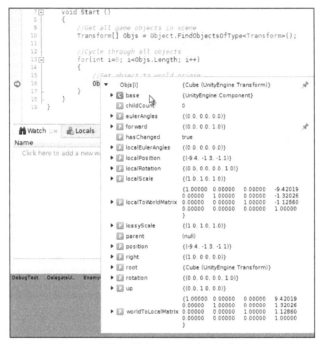

Inspecting a variable with hover watches in the break mode

You can inspect practically all variable values for any active object using this hover method. However, typically, you'll want to place a more permanent watch on a variable and even a group of variables so that you can see their values collated together in a list. For this, you can use the **Watch** window docked in the bottom-left corner of the MonoDevelop interface. To add a new watch in this window, right-click inside the **Watch** list and choose **Add watch** from the context menu, as shown here:

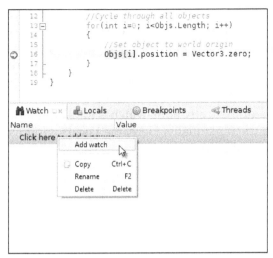

Adding a watch to the Watch window

On adding a new watch, you can enter any valid expression or variable name in the **Name** field, and the resultant value will be shown in the **Value** column, as shown in the following screenshot. The values shown in the **Watch** field are valid for the current line of execution only, and they will change as the program progresses. Remember that you can add a watch for any valid variable that can be referenced in the current scope, including `name`, `tag`, `transform.position`, and so on.

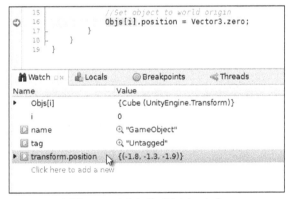

Adding a watch to the Watch window

You can use the **Watch** window to examine any valid variables and expressions, whether they pertain to the active class or line of code. This means you can see the value for global variables and any variables related to other classes or objects, as long as they're valid and in memory. However, if you're only interested in viewing local variables, that is, variables whose scope is relevant to the block of code being executed in the current step, then you could use the **Locals** window instead of **Watch**. This window automatically adds watches for all the local variables. You don't need to add them manually. Here, the **Locals** window is by default tabbed next to the **Watch** window:

Inspecting local variables only with the Locals window

If you don't see any of the relevant **Debug** windows in the MonoDevelop interface, such as the **Watch** window or the **Locals** window, you can show or hide them manually by clicking on the **Debug Windows** option in **View** from the MonoDevelop application menu:

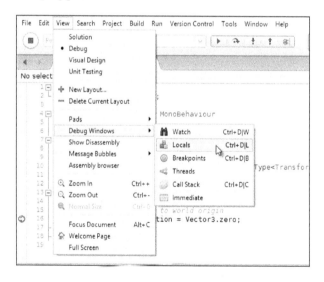

One great thing about the **Watch** and **Locals** windows is that they offer read and write access to variables. This means that you're not restricted to simply viewing variable values, but you can write to them as well, changing the variable from within MonoDevelop. To do this, simply double-click on the **Value** field from either the **Watch** or **Locals** window and then enter a new value for the variable:

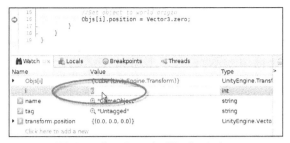

Editing values from the Watch window

Debugging with MonoDevelop – continue and stepping

After reaching a breakpoint and inspecting your code, it's likely that you'll want to exit from the break mode and continue program execution in some way. You might want to continue program execution, which effectively hands program control back to Unity. This allows the execution to continue as normal, until it meets the next breakpoint, if any. This method effectively resumes execution as normal, and it'll never pause again unless a new breakpoint is encountered. To continue in this way from MonoDevelop, press the *F5* key or press the play button from the MonoDevelop toolbar. Otherwise, choose the **Continue Debugging** option in **Run** from the MonoDevelop application menu, as shown here:

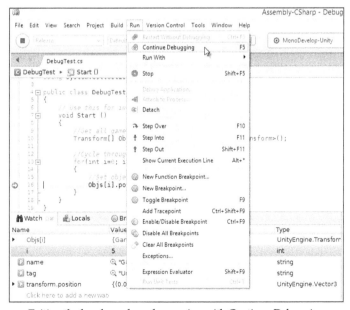

Exiting the break mode and resuming with Continue Debugging

There are many occasions, however, where you don't want to continue execution in this way. Instead, you want to step execution over the lines of code, line by line, evaluating each line as it progresses and examining the program flow to see how variables change and are affected by statements. The step mode effectively lets you observe the program flow as it happens. There are three main kinds of steps in debugging: step over, step into, and step out. Step over instructs the debugger to move to the next line of code and then to pause again, awaiting your inspection as though the next line were a new breakpoint. If an external function call is encountered in the next line, the debugger would invoke the function as usual and then step to the next line without stepping into the function. In this way, the function is "stepped over". The function still happens, but it happens in the continue mode, and the next step or breakpoint is set in the next line after the function. To step over, press *F10*, choose the **Step Over** command in **Run** from the application menu, or press the **Step Over** button in the MonoDevelop toolbar, as shown here:

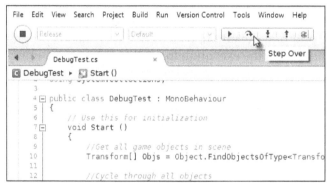

Stepping over code moves execution to the next statement without stepping into an external function

If an external function call is encountered, the **Step Into** (*F11*) command allows debugging to enter this function. This effectively sets the next breakpoint in the first line of the entered function that allows debugging to resume in the next step. This can be useful if you need to observe how many functions are working together. If, at any point, you want to exit the entered function by moving it forward in the continue mode, you could use the **Step Out** (*Shift + F11*) command, and the execution would resume in the next line in the outer function.

Debugging with MonoDevelop – call stack

More complex programs typically involve lots of functions and function calls. During execution, functions can invoke other functions, and these functions can go on to invoke yet more functions in an intricate chain of functions within functions. This means that when setting breakpoints inside functions, you can never know how the function was invoked initially when it's actually called at runtime. The breakpoint tells you that program execution has reached the specified line, but it doesn't tell you how execution arrived there in the first place. Sometimes, it might be easy to deduce, but at other times it can be much harder, especially when functions are invoked within loops, conditionals, and nested loops and conditionals. Consider the following code sample 2-10, which has been amended from the earlier code sample 2-9. This class contains several functions that invoke other functions:

```
using UnityEngine;
using System.Collections;

public class DebugTest : MonoBehaviour
{
    // Use this for initialization
    void Start ()
    {
        //Get all game objects in scene
        Transform[] Objs =
Object.FindObjectsOfType<Transform>();

        //Cycle through all objects
        for(int i=0; i<Objs.Length; i++)
        {
            //Set object to world origin
            Objs[i].position = Vector3.zero;
        }

        //Enter Function 01
        Func01();
    }
    //-------------------------------------
    //Function calls func2
    void Func01()
    {
        Func02();
    }
```

```
//----------------------------------------
//Function calls func3
void Func02()
{
        Func03();
}
//----------------------------------------
//Function prints message
void Func03()
{
        Debug.Log ("Entered Function 3");
}
//----------------------------------------
}
```

If a breakpoint is set in line 38 of code sample 2-10 (highlighted), execution will pause when this line is reached. By reading this sample, we can see that one route to that function is by the `Start` function calling `Func01`, `Func01` calling `Func02`, and then `Func02` finally calling `Func03`. But how do we know that this is the only route? It's technically possible, for example, for another class and function elsewhere in the project to invoke `Func03` directly. So, how can we know the route by which we've reached this function in this step while debugging? Based on the tools examined so far, we can't. However, we can use the **Call Stack** window. This window, displayed by default in the bottom-right corner of the MonoDevelop interface, lists all the function calls that were made to reach the active function for the current step that leads back to the first or initial function call. It gives us a breadcrumb trail of function names that leads from the active function to the first or initial function. Thus, **Call Stack** lists function names upside down, the active or most recent function being at the top of the stack that leads downwards to the earliest or first function at the bottom of the stack. You can also access the functions at their locations to assess the variables in their scope, as shown here:

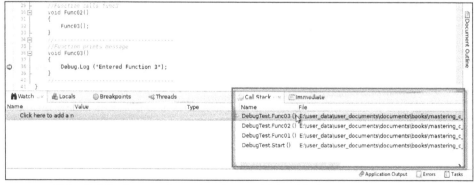

Using Call Stack to trace how a function was initiated during program execution

Debugging with MonoDevelop – the Immediate window

For games, the **Immediate** window acts like the **Console** window, as found in many first-person shooter games such as *Unreal, Half Life*, or *Call of Duty*. The **Immediate** window is docked by default in the bottom-right corner of the MonoDevelop interface. It becomes active in the break mode. Using it, we can enter expressions and statements that are evaluated immediately as though they were part of the source code for this step. We can get and set the values for active variables as well as perform additional operations. We can write any valid expression, such as 2+2 and 10*5. The result of these expressions is output in the next line in the **Immediate** window, as shown here:

Evaluating expressions inside the Immediate window

Of course, you're not simply restricted to writing isolated statements that involve basic arithmetical operations, such as addition and subtraction. You can write full expressions that include active variables:

```
Call Stack        Immediate    x
> i+5 * Objs[i].position.x
1.942265
>
```

Writing more advanced expressions in the Immediate window

Overall, the **Immediate** window is especially useful to test code, write alternative scenarios in the **Immediate** window, and see how they evaluate.

Debugging with MonoDevelop – conditional breakpoints

Breakpoints are critical for debugging, and represents the starting point at which application execution pauses into a debug state. Often, they'll be just what you need to set a breakpoint and start debugging! However, there are times when breakpoints, in their default configuration, can become annoying. One example is when a breakpoint is set inside a loop. Sometimes, you only want the breakpoint to take effect or pause execution after a loop has exceeded a specified number of iterations, as opposed to taking effect from the beginning and on every iteration afterwards. By default, a breakpoint inside a loop will pause the execution on every iteration, and if the loop is long, such pausing behavior can quickly become tiresome. To resolve this, you can set breakpoint conditions that specify the states that must be true for the breakpoint to take effect. To set a breakpoint condition, right-click on the breakpoint and choose **Breakpoint Properties** from the context menu, as shown here:

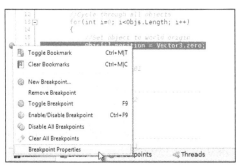

Accessing Breakpoint Properties to set a condition

Selecting **Breakpoint Properties** will display the **Breakpoint Properties** dialog where conditions for the breakpoint can be specified. In the **Condition** section, choose the **Break when condition is true** option and then use the **Condition expression** field to specify the condition that determines the breakpoint. For loop conditions, the expression $i>5$ will trigger the breakpoint when the loop iterator has exceeded 5. Of course, the variable i should be substituted for your own variable names.

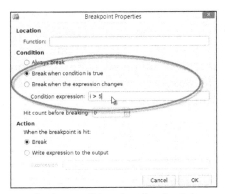

Setting conditions for a breakpoint

Debugging with MonoDevelop – tracepoints

Tracepoints can offer you a neater alternative to using `Debug.Log` statements that, as we've seen, force us to amend the code we're debugging. Tracepoints work like breakpoints, in that they mark lines within your source file. They don't change the code itself, but (unlike breakpoints) they don't pause the program execution when encountered by the debugger. Instead, they perform a specified instruction automatically. Typically, they print a debug statement to the **Application Output** window in MonoDevelop, though not to the Unity's **Console**. To set a breakpoint in line 16 of code sample 2-10, position your cursor on line 16 and select **Add Tracepoint** in **Run** from the application menu (or press *Ctrl + Shift + F9*), as shown here:

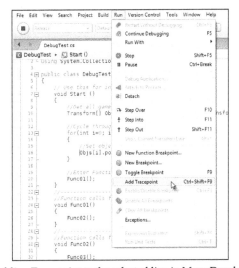

Adding Tracepoint to the selected line in MonoDevelop

On selecting the **Add Tracepoint** option, MonoDevelop will show the **Add Tracepoint** dialog. The **Trace Text** field allows you to input the text to be printed to the **Application Output** window when the tracepoint is encountered at runtime. You can also insert the curly braces opening and closing symbols to define the regions in the string where expressions should be evaluated. This lets you print the values of variables into the debug string, such as `"Loop counter is {i}"`, as shown here:

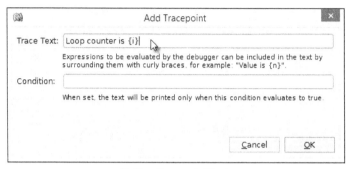

Setting Tracepoint Text

After clicking on **OK**, the tracepoint is added to the selected line. Inside MonoDevelop, the line will be marked with a diamond shape as opposed to a circle; this diamond shape indicates a breakpoint:

```
8        {
9            //Get all game objects in scene
10           Transform[] Objs = Object.FindObjectsOfType<Trans
11
12           //Cycle through all objects
13           for(int i=0; i<Objs.Length; i++)
14           {
15               //Set object to world origin
16               Objs[i].position = Vector3.zero;
17           }
18
19           //Enter Function 01
20           Func01();
21       }
```

Inserting a tracepoint

After setting the tracepoint in the selected line in the code editor and running the application via the attachment with MonoDevelop, the game will run as normal, directly from the Unity Editor. However, when the tracepoint is encountered, the application will not pause or enter the break mode as it would with breakpoints. Instead, the tracepoint will automatically output its printed statements to MonoDevelop's **Application Output** window, without causing a pause.
By default, this window is docked at the bottom of the MonoDevelop interface:

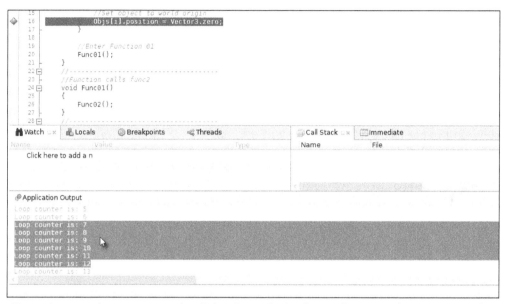

Tracepoints can print statements such as Debug.Log to the Application Output window in MonoDevelop

Tracepoints are an effective and helpful alternative to using the Debug.Log statements inside Unity, and you don't need to amend your code in any way to use them as you do with Debug.Log. Unfortunately, they don't print directly to Unity's **Console**. Instead, they appear inside the **Application Output** window in MonoDevelop. However, as long as you recognize this, working with tracepoints can be a powerful and useful method to find and remove bugs.

Summary

This chapter considered the process of debugging, which is centrally about finding and removing errors from your game. There are many methods to achieve this end, especially in Unity. Specifically, the methods considered here included the `Debug.Log` statement, perhaps the simplest of all debugging methods. Using this technique, `Debug.Log` statements are inserted into your code in critical lines, and these print diagnostic messages to Unity's **Console**. Next, we looked at is custom defines: using them, you can section off and isolate blocks of your code between the release and debug versions; this allows you to run debug-specific code when specific flags are enabled. Then, we looked at error logging. This chapter demonstrated how to create an error logger class that integrates with native Unity's application class, using delegates. We also saw the profiler; the Unity profiler is a pro-only feature that gives us a high-level statistical insight into how processing is distributed over time and system resources. In addition, we explored in-editor debugging and visual debugging to gain a clearer visual insight into our scene, and factors that affect object behavior. Finally, we saw MonoDevelop debugging, which does not require us to edit our code. These include breakpoints, tracepoints, steps, and watches. Next up, we'll explore how to work with `GameObjects`.

3
Singletons, Statics, GameObjects, and the World

Every level or game world in Unity is represented by a scene, and a scene is a collection of game objects situated inside a Cartesian 3D coordinate system with x, y and z axes. Units in a scene are measured in Unity units, and these correspond (for practical purposes) to meters. In order to script masterfully with Unity, it's critical to understand the anatomy of both scenes and objects and how interobject communication happens; that is, it's important to know how separate and independent objects in a scene can communicate with each other to make things happen as you expect. Consequently, this chapter focuses on the native Unity methods available to optimally search, reference, and access objects in a scene. It also focuses on additional concepts such as statics and singletons for the creation of objects that travel between scenes, retaining their data as they move. Of course, this chapter will not only consider these methods individually, but it'll try to appraise them in practical contexts, with performance and efficiency in mind.

The GameObject

The GameObject is, in many senses, the fundamental unit or entity inside a scene. It corresponds most naturally to what we'd call a *thing* in the everyday sense. It doesn't really matter what kind of context-specific behaviors or things you'll actually need inside your own games, because in all cases, you'll need GameObjects to implement them. GameObjects don't need to be visible to the gamer; they can be, and often are, invisible. Sounds, colliders, and manager classes are some examples of invisible GameObjects. On the other hand, many GameObjects will be visible: meshes, animated meshes, sprites, and so on. In all cases, however, whether visible or invisible, the GameObject is instantiated inside a scene as a collection of related components. A **component** is essentially a class derived from MonoBehaviour, and it can be attached to a GameObject in the scene to change its behavior. Every GameObject has at least one minimal component in common, and it's impossible to remove it, namely, the **Transform** component (or the RectTransform for GUI objects). This component keeps track of an object's position, rotation, and scale. For example, if you create a blank, empty game object in the scene by going to **GameObject | Create Empty** from the application menu, as shown in the following screenshot, you would end up with a new game object in the scene, featuring only a Transform component. Thus, even a new and empty GameObject is not, strictly speaking, empty, but it's as empty as a GameObject ever gets. The object still needs a Transform component to maintain its physical location in a scene.

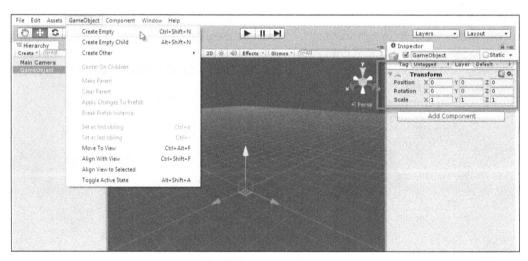

All GameObjects feature a Transform component

Of course, a `GameObject` can have many components, and the behavior of an object arises from the combination and interaction of its components. You can add more premade components to an object using the **Component** menu, and you can add your own custom components by dragging-and-dropping your scripts onto an object.

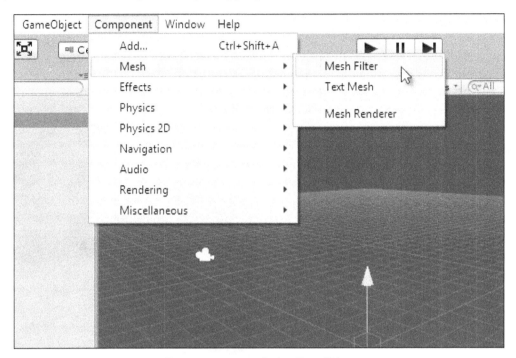

Components are attached to GameObjects

So, GameObjects are composed of components. At a higher level, scenes are composed of a collection of GameObjects inside a single world space. Furthermore, objects themselves exist in an important relationship with each other, as defined by the scene hierarchy. Objects can be the children of others, who are in turn their parents (transform.parent). This relationship has important implications for how objects move and transform. In short, values for an object's Transform component will cascade downwards and be added to the transform of all its children. In this way, a child GameObject is always offset and transformed relative to its parent; the parent position is the origin of the child position. However, if an object has no parent, then it would be transformed away from the world origin at (0, 0, 0). The following screenshot shows the **Hierarchy** panel:

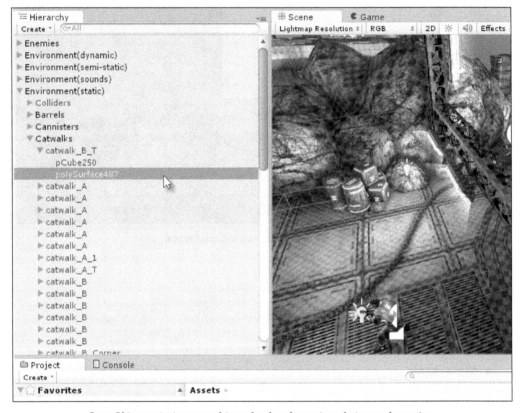

GameObjects exist in a scene hierarchy that determines their transformations

Component interactions

We've seen the anatomy of a GameObject as a collection of components and nothing more. This raises logistical issues about how components should interact and communicate with each other. Each component is effectively implemented as a self-contained script file, separate from any other component, yet a component must often interact with others. Specifically, you'll often need to access variables and call functions on other components on the same GameObject, and you might even need to do this on every frame. This section explores such intercomponent communication.

One way to call functions on other components is to use SendMessage and BroadcastMessage, as shown in *Chapter 1, Unity C# Refresher*. These functions are type agnostic. Specifically, they're functions we might call anywhere in the script to invoke methods by names on *all* other components attached to the same object, regardless of their type. These functions don't care about the component type at all. This makes both SendMessage and BroadcastMessage convenient to use. However, the problem with them is twofold. First, they're an all or nothing affair; we might call a function by name on all components or on none at all. We can't pick and choose which component the message is dispatched to, because it's always dispatched to them all. Second, both methods (SendMessage and BroadcastMessage) rely internally on reflection, which can cause performance issues when used often, such as by calling these functions in Update events or, even worse, in OnGUI events. For these reasons, seek to use alternative methods wherever practically possible. Let's consider these in the following sections.

GetComponent

If you need direct access to a specific and single component on an object and you know its data type, try using GetComponent as shown in the following code sample 3-1. This function gives you access to the first component of a matching type attached to a GameObject. Once you get a reference to it, you can access the component like any regular object, setting and getting its public variables and invoking its methods:

```
01 using UnityEngine;
02 using System.Collections;
03 //---------------------------------------------------------
04 public class MyCustomComponent : MonoBehaviour
05 {
06   //Reference to transform of object
07   private Transform ThisTransform = null;
08 //---------------------------------------------------------
09   // Use this for initialization
10   void Start ()
```

```
11   {
12       //Get cached reference to transform
13       ThisTransform = GetComponent<Transform>();
14   }
15 //-------------------------------------------------------
16   // Update is called once per frame
17   void Update ()
18   {
19       //Update position

20       if(ThisTransform !=null) {ThisTransform.localPosition +=
            Time.deltaTime * 10.0f * ThisTransform.forward;}

21   }
22 //-------------------------------------------------------
23 }
24 //-------------------------------------------------------
```

The following are the comments on the code sample 3-1:

- **Lines 07 and 13**: The variable `ThisTransform` is declared as private. This variable is assigned a reference to the Transform component attached to the `GameObject`, and it achieves this inside the `Start` event using the `GetComponent` function. In the case of accessing the Transform component specifically, we could also have used an inherited `transform` property, such as `ThisTransform= transform;`.

- **Line 20**: Here, the `ThisTransform` variable is used directly to set the `localPosition` of the `GameObject`. Again, for the Transform component specifically, we could also have used `transform.localPosition`. However, this approach internally invokes an extra function call, because the member `transform` is a C# property and not a standard variable. More on properties can be found in *Chapter 1, Unity C# Refresher*. For this reason, using `GetComponent` inside a `Start` or `Awake` event to retrieve a component reference to a private class variable is typically one of the most efficient ways to access external components, especially if the component must be accessed regularly, such as inside an `Update` function.

localPosition versus position

The Transform component exposes two main position members: `position` and `localPosition`. Setting either of these will change an object's position in specific and distinct ways. The position member always defines an object's position in world space as a measure from the world origin. Setting this variable in script, therefore, might not correspond to the numbers you actually see for the Transform component in the Object Inspector when the object is selected. If your object is a child of another object that's not positioned to the world origin, for example, then Unity would offset the object's local position away from its parent, by however much is necessary, to position it at the world space location that is specified. The `localPosition` member, in contrast, corresponds directly to the `position` value shown for the Transform component in the Object Inspector. Specifically, it specifies the position of an object as a measured offset away from its parent location or else from the world origin if the object has no parent. In the latter case, both the `position` and `localPosition` members will be identical.

More information on the `GetComponent` function can be found in the online Unity documentation at `http://docs.unity3d.com/ScriptReference/GameObject.GetComponent.html`.

You can also access the Unity documentation from the MonoDevelop **Help** menu, by navigating to **Help | Unity API Reference**.

Getting multiple components

Occasionally, you'll want to retrieve multiple components in a list: sometimes, a list of all components and sometimes, a list matching only a specific type. You can get this using the `GetComponents` function. See the following code sample 3-2. As with the `GetComponent` function, it's good practice to call `GetComponents` during one-off events such as `Start` and `Awake` as opposed to frequent events such as `Update`:

```
01 using UnityEngine;
02 using System.Collections;
03 //------------------------------------------------------
04 public class MyCustomComponent : MonoBehaviour
05 {
```

```
06    //Reference to all components as array
07    private Component[] AllComponents = null;
08    //------------------------------------------------------
09    // Use this for initialization
10    void Start ()
11    {
12      //Gets a list of all components attached to this object
13      AllComponents = GetComponents<Component>();
14
15      //Loops through each and list it to the console
16      foreach(Component C in AllComponents)
17      {
18        //Print to console
19        Debug.Log (C.ToString());
20      }
21    }
22 }
23 //------------------------------------------------------
```

More on Components

Unity offers additional variations on the GetComponent and GetComponents functions that facilitate interobject communication and not just communication between components in the same object. These functions include GetComponentsInChildren to retrieve an accumulative list of all components in all children and also GetComponentsInParent to retrieve all components in an object's parent.

More information on the GetComponents function can be found in the online Unity documentation at http://docs.unity3d.com/ScriptReference/Component.GetComponents.html.

Components and messages

The GetComponent family of functions work well and should meet almost all your needs for intercomponent communication. They certainly perform better than either SendMessage or BroadcastMessage when used appropriately. Yet, there are situations where it'd be ideal if, given a GameObject, you could invoke a method with SendMessage on *only one* component as opposed to all, without having to know anything about the component type in advance. Now, you could achieve this behavior to some extent using delegates and interfaces (covered in the next chapter). However, here we'll consider the SendMessage approach. One scenario where this would be especially useful is for the creation of extendable behaviors. For example, perhaps your game has many enemy types and you need to leave open the possibility of adding more, all of which could be implemented in different ways. Yet, despite their differences, all enemies will need to save their data to a persistent file when the game is saved. It'd then be useful for the enemy to handle an OnSave function, which will be implemented by a specific component. This is fine, but you want the OnSave function on that component alone to be called by the SendMessage system. You don't want the method invoked for other components on the object, in case they too handle a function OnSave that you don't want called inadvertently. In short, you can achieve this using the Invoke method. Consider the following code sample 3-3:

```
01 using UnityEngine;
02 using System.Collections;
03 //---------------------------------------------------------
04 public class MyCustomComponent : MonoBehaviour
05 {
06    //Reference to component on which function must be called
07    public MonoBehaviour Handler = null;
08
09    //----------------------------------------------------
10    // Use this for initialization
11    void Start ()
12    {
13       //Call function immediately
14       Handler.Invoke("OnSave",0.0f);
15    }
16 }
17 //---------------------------------------------------------
```

The following are the comments on the code sample 3-3:

- **Line 07**: This class features a public reference variable `Handler`. Using this field, you can drag-and-drop any component via the Object Inspector into the `Handler` slot. This represents the component to which a message will be dispatched. Notice that its class type is `MonoBehaviour` or any class derived from this. This means type agnosticism is achieved and we don't need to know the object type in advance.

- **Line 14**: The `Invoke` method of `MonoBehaviour` is called to run any method of matching name. The second floating point argument specifies the time in seconds, after which the function should be invoked. A time of 0 specifies immediate invoking.

> More information on the `Invoke` function can be found in the online Unity documentation at `http://docs.unity3d.com/ScriptReference/MonoBehaviour.Invoke.html`.

GameObjects and the world

Another pivotal task in Unity involves searching for objects in the scene from script, especially if objects are instantiated at runtime. Tasks such as "get me the player object" and "get me all enemies in the scene" are important for many operations, from respawning enemies and power-ups to repositioning the player and checking collisions between objects. To retrieve references to specific `GameObjects`, Unity offers a set of functions associated with the `GameObject` class. These functions can be useful but expensive, so be sure to call them during one-off events, such as `Start` and `Awake`, wherever possible. Let's explore these further, in addition to other techniques and methods to work with found objects.

Finding GameObjects

Finding an object in the scene can be achieved through either the `GameObject.Find` or `GameObject.FindObjectWithTag` function. Of these two, the latter should almost always be preferred for performance reasons. However, let's consider `GameObject.Find` first. This function searches the scene for the first occurrence of an object with an exactly matching name (case-sensitive) and then returns that object. The name that's searched should match the object name as it appears in the **Hierarchy** panel. Unfortunately, the function performs string comparisons to determine the match, so it's a slow and cumbersome option. Besides, it's only truly effective for objects guaranteed to have unique names, and many times, objects won't have. However, that said, `GameObject.Find` is still highly useful when objects are appropriately named:

```
//Find Object with the name of player
ObjPlayer = GameObject.Find ("Player");
```

GameObject Finding

If you notice the `GameObject`, you would realize that the `Find` function is static. This means that you don't need an instantiation of any specific `GameObject` to call the function. You can call it directly from any source file via `GameObject.Find`. The concept of static and global scope is considered later in this chapter.

More information on the `GameObject.Find` function can be found in the online Unity documentation at `http://docs.unity3d.com/ScriptReference/GameObject.Find.html`.

`GameObject.Find` can be a slow function. For this reason, use it only inside one-fire events, such as `Awake` and `Start`.

A more effective search is by tag. Every object in the scene has a tag member that is assigned **Untagged** by default. This member is a unique identifier that can mark a single object or multiple objects bringing them together into a collection. Generally, to search for objects by tag, you'll first need to explicitly assign an object with a tag. You can do this in script, using the GameObject.tag public member. However, you'll use the Unity Editor more commonly. You can assign a tag to a selected object from the Unity Editor by clicking the **Tag** drop-down list in the Object Inspector and picking a tag. In addition, you can create new, custom tags by selecting the **Add Tag** option. Common tags include **Player**, **Enemy**, **Weapon**, **Bonus**, **Prop**, **Environment**, **Light**, **Sound**, and **GameController**, among others. Take a look at the following screenshot:

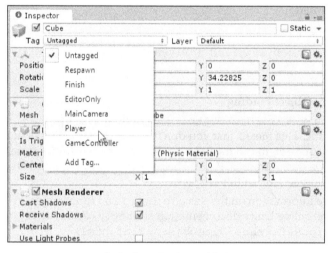

Assigning a tag to an object

After one or more objects are assigned a tag in the scene, you can effectively search for objects by tag in code. The GameObject.FindGameObjectWithTag function searches the scene for an object with a matching tag and returns the first occurrence. The GameObject.FindObjectsWithTag returns an array of all occurrences. See the following code sample 3-4 for an example. Note that although the FindGameObjectsWithTag function requires a string argument, Unity internally converts the string into a numerical form to increase the speed of tag comparisons:

```
using UnityEngine;
using System.Collections;
//-----------------------------------------------------
public class ObjectFinder : MonoBehaviour
{
  //Tag name of objects to find
  public string TagName = "Enemy";
```

```
    //Array of found objects matching tag
    public GameObject[] FoundObjects;


    //-----------------------------------------------------
    // Use this for initialization
    void Start ()
    {
      //Find objects of matching tag

      FoundObjects = GameObject.FindGameObjectsWithTag(TagName);


    }
}
//-----------------------------------------------------
```

 Sometimes, you'd like to assign multiple tags to a single object. Unfortunately, Unity doesn't support this behavior yet. However, you can work around the limitation by parenting empty game objects to your main object and assigning each of the children the tag you need. When searching for objects by tag, though, just remember to get a reference to the parent object, which is actually the object you need.

Comparing objects

The GameObject searching functions are helpful when searching scene-wide for specific objects, but there are times when you'll need to compare two objects that you've found already. Typically, you'll want compare the names or tags of two objects. You can achieve a tag comparison using the CompareTag function:

```
//Compares tag of this object with another Obj_Y
bool bMatch = gameObject.CompareTag(Obj_Y.tag);
```

In addition, you'll sometimes want to compare two objects for equality to determine whether they're the same object and not simply whether they share the same tag. This is especially important when coding decision-making behaviors. For example, in determining whether an enemy character should fight or flee from the player during combat, it'd be helpful to ascertain whether the enemy has supporting units nearby to help him. To answer this, you can find all enemies in the scene with a tag search, as we saw earlier. However, the results will also include the enemy who made the call originally and who is now deciding what to do, so we'll want to exclude him from the results. Code sample 3-4 demonstrates how GetInstanceID can help us:

```
01 //Find objects of matching tag
02 FoundObjects = GameObject.FindGameObjectsWithTag(TagName);
03
04 //Search through all objects and exclude ourselves
05 foreach(GameObject O in FoundObjects)
06 {
07   //If two objects are the same
08   if(O.GetInstanceID() == gameObject.GetInstanceID())
09     continue; //Skip this iteration
10
11   //[...] Do stuff here
12 }
```

Getting the nearest object

Given an array of GameObjects, perhaps returned from a search, how can you find the one nearest to you in the scene in terms of linear distance? The following code sample 3-5 demonstrates how you can find this object using the Vector3.Distance function to retrieve the shortest distance (in meters) between any two points in the scene:

```
//Returns the nearest game object
GameObject GetNearestGameObject(GameObject Source, GameObject[]
  DestObjects)
{
  //Assign first object
  GameObject Nearest = DestObjects[0];

  //Shortest distance
  float ShortestDistance =
    Vector3.Distance(Source.transform.position,
    DestObjects[0].transform.position);

  //Loop through all objects
  foreach(GameObject Obj in DestObjects)
  {
    //Calculate distance
    float Distance = Vector3.Distance(Source.transform.position,
      Obj.transform.position);
```

```
    //If this is shortest, then update
    if(Distance < ShortestDistance)
    {
      //Is shortest, now update
      Nearest = Obj;
      ShortestDistance = Distance;
    }
  }

  //Return nearest
  return Nearest;
}
```

Finding any object of a specified type

Sometimes, you just want a list of all the components of a specified type in the scene, regardless of which game objects they're actually attached to; these components include all enemies, all collectible objects, all transform components, all colliders, and so on. Achieving this from script is simple but expensive, as shown in the following code sample 3-6. Specifically, by calling the Object.FindObjectsOfType function, you can retrieve a complete list of all instances of a specified object in the scene, unless an object is deactivated. Due to the expense of this method, avoid calling it during frame-based events such as Update. Use the Start and Awake events, as well as infrequent functions instead:

```
void Start()
{
  //Get a list of all colliders in the scene
  Collider[] Cols = Object.FindObjectsOfType<Collider>();
}
```

Clearing a path between GameObjects

Given any two `GameObjects` in the scene, such as the **Player** and an **Enemy** character, it's common to test for a clear path between them, that is, to test whether there are any colliders intersecting an imaginary line drawn between the two objects. This can be helpful in line-of-sight systems, as we'll see later, but also more generally for object culling, to determine AI functionality and others.

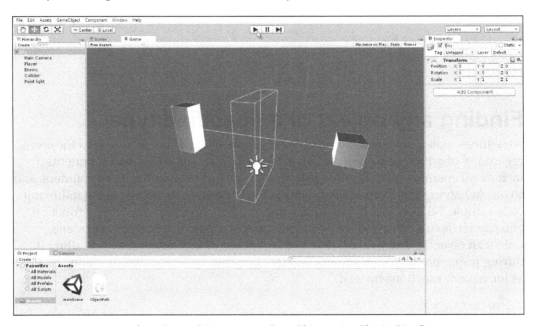

Testing for a clear path between two GameObjects using Physics.LineCast

There are many ways to achieve this behavior. One way is to use the `Physics.LineCast` function, as shown in the following code sample 3-7:

```
01 using UnityEngine;
02 using System.Collections;
03 //Determines if a clear line or path exists between two objects
04 public class ObjectPath : MonoBehaviour
05 {
06   //Reference to sample enemy object
07   public GameObject Enemy = null;
08
09   //Layer mask to limit line detection
10   public LayerMask LM;
11   //-------------------------------------------------
12   // Update is called once per frame
13   void Update ()
14   {
```

```
15      //Check if clear path between objects

16      if(!Physics.Linecast(transform.position,
        Enemy.transform.position, LM))

17      {
18        //There is clear path
19        Debug.Log ("Path clear");
20      }
21    }
22    //------------------------------------------------------
23    //Show helper debug line in viewport
24    void OnDrawGizmos()
25    {
26      Gizmos.DrawLine(transform.position, Enemy.transform.position);
27    }
28    //------------------------------------------------------
29  }
```

The following are the comments on the code sample 3-7:

- **Line 07**: This sample class should be attached to the `Player`; otherwise, another source object accepts a public member variable `Enemy` to whom a clear path should be tested.

- **Line 10**: The `LayerMask` variable specifies a bitmask, indicating which layers in the scene the collision test applies to. More information on bitmasks can be found in the online Unity documentation at `http://docs.unity3d.com/Manual/Layers.html`.

- **Line 16**: The `Physics.Linecast` function is used to determine whether a clear and nonbroken path exists between two objects in the scene. Note that if the two objects themselves have colliders, such as `BoxColliders`, then these will be included in the collision detection; they will not be ignored. In other words, an object's own collider can affect the results of any `LineCast` calls. For this reason, use the `LayerMask` variable to include or exclude specific layers.

 A `Physics.LineCast` project is included in the book's companion files in the `Chapter03/LineCast` folder.

Accessing object hierarchies

The **Hierarchy** panel in Unity offers a graphical illustration of the parent-child relationship that holds among all GameObjects in a scene. This relationship is important because child objects are contained by, and inherit, the transformations of their parents. However, being able to define and edit the hierarchical relationship in the editor is usually not enough. You'll frequently need to parent one object to another in code and also cycle through all children of a specified object to process data or invoke functionality on them. Let's first see how to parent objects. The following code sample 3-8 demonstrates how to attach one object X to another object Y as its child, through the Transform component:

```
using UnityEngine;
using System.Collections;
//----------------------------------------------------
public class Parenter : MonoBehaviour
{
  //Reference to child object in scene
  private GameObject Child;
  //Reference to parent object in scene
  private GameObject Parent;
  //----------------------------------------------------
  // Use this for initialization
  void Start ()
  {
    //Get parent and child objects
    Child = GameObject.Find("Child");
    Parent = GameObject.Find("Parent");

    //Now parent them
    Child.transform.parent = Parent.transform;
  }
  //----------------------------------------------------
}
//----------------------------------------------------
```

Now, let's see how to cycle through all the child objects attached to a parent. Again, this is achieved through the Transform component, as shown in the following code sample 3-9:

```
using UnityEngine;
using System.Collections;
//----------------------------------------
public class CycleChildren : MonoBehaviour
{
  //----------------------------------------
  // Use this for initialization
  void Start ()
  {
    //Cycle though children of this object
    for(int i=0; i<transform.childCount; i++)
    {
      //Print name of child to console
      Debug.Log (transform.GetChild(i).name);
    }
  }
  //----------------------------------------
}
//----------------------------------------
```

The world, time, and updates

A Unity scene represents a collection of finite GameObjects inside the same 3D space and that also share the same timeframe. Every game needs to establish a unified concept of time to achieve synchronized animation and change, because animation means change over time. In Unity, the Time class is available for reading and understanding time and its passing in script. Working with this class is therefore a critical skill for the creation of predictable and consistent motion in your games. More on this shortly.

Every game has a frame rate, which is defined in **frames per second** (**FPS**). This rate is viewable from the **Stats** panel in the **Game** tab. The FPS tells you how many times in 1 second Unity is able to loop or iterate through your game code to draw a new render from the cameras to the screen. Each iteration is called a **frame**. The frame rate varies dramatically over time and across different computers. It's influenced by the power of your computer, other processes that might be running, and by how much content it needs to render in the current frame, among other factors. This means you can never rely on FPS being consistent over time or the same across different computers; there'll often be a different number of FPS. Have a look at the following screenshot:

FPS is important for the creation of time-based behavior and animations

To approximate the concept of a frame, Unity offers three class events that every `MonoBehaviour` class can implement to perform functionality that must continually update or change over time. These events have already been seen, but now, we'll consider them in more depth, specifically `Update`, `FixedUpdate` and `LateUpdate`:

- `Update`: The `Update` event is called *once* per frame for every active component on every active `GameObject` in the scene. If an object is deactivated by the `MonoBehaviour.SetActive` method, then `Update` events will not be called for that object until it is activated. In short, the `Update` event most accurately represents the concept of a frame in Unity, so it's useful for performing repetitive behaviors or functionality that must be updated and monitored over time, such as player input events, keyboard presses, and mouse clicks. Note that the order in which `Update` events are invoked across all components for each frame is not guaranteed; that is, you cannot be sure whether the `Update` function on object X will be called before that on object Y during any one frame.

- FixedUpdate: Like Update, this event is typically called multiple times per frame. However, its calling pattern is regular and normalized, with fixed time intervals between each call. The most common use of FixedUpdate is to work with Unity physics. If you need to update the velocity or properties of a Rigidbody component over time, then FixedUpdate rather than Update would be the place to do it.

- LateUpdate: This is called on each frame, like Update. However, LateUpdate is always called after Update and FixedUpdate. This means that when LateUpdate is called, you can be sure that Update and FixedUpdate have already been called for every object on the current frame. This makes LateUpdate a useful place to update camera movement, especially third-person cameras, ensuring that the camera always follows objects at their latest positions on the current frame.

The details of Update, FixedUpdate and LateUpdate, in combination with the concepts of time and FPS, have significant implications on how you should or should not code your games when creating motion over time. Specifically, two main guidelines emerge, and these are considered over the next two subsections.

Rule #1 – frames are precious

Frames should occur many times per second; if they don't, your game will look laggy and broken. On each frame, an Update event is called once for every active MonoBehaviour in the scene. This means the computational complexity (and performance) of your scenes on each frame depends, in large measure, on what you do inside Update events. More functionality demands more processing time and workload, either for the CPU or GPU. For large scenes with many objects and components, it would be easy then for things to get out of hand if you don't reduce the workload inside Update functions by careful code planning. It's important, therefore, to think of Update events or any regularly called frame-based events as precious. In short, you should only put code inside them when you really need to, such as to read player input or observe cursor movement. It's helpful to start thinking of event-driven programming, as this can help you seriously reduce the workload inserted inside Update functions. The next chapter considers event-driven programming and event systems.

Rule #2 – motion must be relative to time

As you cannot guarantee the frequency of frames (frame rate differs over time and across computers), then you need to code motion and change very carefully to achieve a consistent experience for the gamer. Consider the simple case of moving a cube object in the scene smoothly over time. One way (a bad way) to create motion will be as shown in the following code sample 3-10:

```csharp
using UnityEngine;
using System.Collections;

public class Mover : MonoBehaviour
{
  //Amount to move cube per frame
  public float AmountToMove = 1.0f;

  // Update is called once per frame
  void Update ()
  {
    //Move cube along x axis
    transform.localPosition += new Vector3(AmountToMove,0,0);
  }
}
```

This code is effective insofar as it will move the attached object by the variable AmountToMove on each frame. The problem is that it's frame-rate dependent. Now, because frames are inconsistent over time and across computers, each user will ultimately receive a different experience; specifically, they'll see the cube moving at different speeds. This is bad because we simply cannot predict how the game will run for any specific user. To fix this, we need to map motion to time as opposed to frames. Frames are variable, but time is constant; one second is exactly that. To achieve this, we can use the deltaTime variable, which is part of the Time class. See the following code sample 3-11. This is an amended version of sample 3-10.

```csharp
using UnityEngine;
using System.Collections;

public class Mover : MonoBehaviour
{
  //Speed of cube
  public float Speed = 1.0f;

  // Update is called once per frame
  void Update ()
  {
```

```
//Move cube along forward direction by speed
transform.localPosition += transform.forward * Speed *
    Time.deltaTime;
    }
}
```

The `deltaTime` variable is a floating-point value and always expresses how much time, in seconds, has elapsed since the previous `Update` function was called. A value of 0.5, for example, means half a second has elapsed since the previous frame and so on. This is useful because `deltaTime` can act as a multiplier. By multiplying a speed variable by `deltaTime` on each frame, we can know how far an object should move because *distance = speed x time*. Thus, `deltaTime` gives us frame-rate independence for object motion.

Immortal objects

By default, Unity regards every object as existing within the self-enclosed time and space of a scene. The difference between scenes is like the difference between separate universes. Consequently, objects don't survive outside the scene to which they belong; this means that they die whenever the active scene changes. This is typically how you want objects to behave, because scenes are usually very different and separate from one another. However, even so, there will be objects that you don't want destroyed. There will be objects that you need *carried over* between scenes, such as the **Player** character, a high-score system, or a `GameManager` class. These are normally high-order objects whose existence shouldn't be limited to specific scenes; they should rather span or arc across multiple scenes. You can create object persistence easily using the `DontDestroyOnLoad` function, but it has important consequences worth considering. Take a look at the following code sample 3-12:

```
using UnityEngine;
using System.Collections;
//-------------------------------------------
//This object will survive scene changes
public class PersistentObj : MonoBehaviour
{
  //-------------------------------------------
  // Use this for initialization
  void Start ()
  {
    //Make this object survive
    DontDestroyOnLoad(gameObject);
  }
}
//-------------------------------------------
```

Object persistence between scenes is important, but *travelling objects* take their baggage with them as they move between scenes. This means any and all child objects will survive with the persistent object as well as any assets or resources it uses, such as meshes, textures, sounds, and others. This is not a problem per se, but it is important to be aware of it. For this reason, many persistent objects are created light, that is, as empty game objects with no children, featuring only the basic component makeup they need to work properly. This ensures that only the essential, critical data survives between scene changes.

Scene Changing

To change the active scene in Unity, use the `Application.LoadLevel` function. There are variations on this, including `LoadLevelAsync`, `LoadLevelAdditive`, and `LoadLevelAdditiveAsync`. More information on the level-loading functions can be found online at `http://docs.unity3d.com/ScriptReference/Application.html`.

As we saw earlier, the `DontDestroyOnLoad` function is called on an existing object in the active scene and prevents that object from being destroyed on future scene changes. From this, however, an issue sometimes arises concerning object duplication. Specifically, if you later reload or return to the original scene in which the persistent object first existed, then a persistent duplicate of the object is made, namely, the persistent original that came with you from the previous scene and a newer instantiation of the object created for the newly entered instance of the scene. This problem is, of course, magnified for each occasion you re-enter the scene, as each time a new duplicate will be made. Such duplication is usually not what you want. You typically want only one instance of the object to exist at any one time: one player, one game manager, or one high-score board. To achieve this, you'll need to create a singleton object, as explained in the next section.

Understanding singleton objects and statics

Some classes are fundamentally different from others in the way they should be instantiated. Most classes define a template for a collection of properties and behaviors that might be instantiated many times in a scene as GameObjects. An enemy class can be used to instantiate many enemy objects, a power-up class for many power-up objects, and so on. However, some classes such as GameManager, HighScoreManager, AudioManager, or SaveGameManager are intended to exist as a lone entity, one that consolidates a unified set of behaviors. In short, there should only ever be one instance of the class at any one time and never more than one. To have more than one instance would either be nonsensical or damage the object's authority and usefulness in some way. These kinds of objects are known as singletons. Singletons are often persistent objects that survive across scenes, though they need not be. The only essential ingredient in a singleton (which makes it what it is) is that there cannot be more than one instance of the class in memory at any one time. Let's now create a singleton object in the context of making a sample GameManager class.

Practically, every game has a GameManager or GameController class; and these are almost always singleton objects that persist. The GameManager is essentially responsible for all high-level functionality in a game. It must determine whether a game is paused, whether the win condition has been satisfied, and have a reliable way of knowing what's happening in the game at any one time, among others. Consider the sample beginnings of a GameManager in the following code sample 3-13:

```
using UnityEngine;
using System.Collections;
//----------------------------------------
//Sample Game Manager class
public class GameManager : MonoBehaviour
{
  //----------------------------------------
  //High score
  public int HighScore = 0;

  //Is game paused
  public bool IsPaused = false;

  //Is player input allowed
  public bool InputAllowed = true;
  //----------------------------------------
  // Use this for initialization
```

```
   void Start ()
   {
     //Make game manager persistent
     DontDestroyOnLoad(gameObject);
   }
   //----------------------------------------
}
//----------------------------------------
```

This object will persist across scenes, but how can it (or any class like it) become a singleton object? The following code sample 3-14 demonstrates how:

```
01 using UnityEngine;
02 using System.Collections;
03 //----------------------------------------
04 //Sample Game Manager class - Singleton Object
05 public class GameManager : MonoBehaviour
06 {
07   //----------------------------------------
08   //C# Property to get access to singleton instance
09   //Read only - only has get accessor
10   public static GameManager Instance
11   {
12     //return reference to private instance
13     get
14     {
15       return instance;
16     }
17   }
18
19   //----------------------------------------
20   private static GameManager instance = null;
21   //----------------------------------------
22   //High score
23   public int HighScore = 0;
24
25   //Is game paused
26   public bool IsPaused = false;
```

```
27
28   //Is player input allowed
29   public bool InputAllowed = true;
30   //---------------------------------------
31   // Use this for initialization
32   void Awake ()
33   {
34      //Check if existing instance of class exists in scene
35      //If so, then destroy this instance
36      if(instance)
37      {
38         DestroyImmediate(gameObject);
39         return;
40      }
41
42      //Make this active and only instance
43      instance = this;
44
45      //Make game manager persistent
46      DontDestroyOnLoad(gameObject);
47   }
48   //---------------------------------------
49 }
50 //---------------------------------------
```

The following are the comments on the code sample 3-14:

- **Lines 10-20**: A private member `instance` is added to the `Manager` class, which is declared as `static`. This means the variable is shared across all instances of the class if there are multiple instances, as opposed to being a variable whose value is specific to each instance. This allows each new instance, when created, to determine whether there is any existing instance of the class in memory. This variable is made publically accessible too via the `Instance` property, which only has a `get` member to make it read-only.

- **Lines 36-43**: Here, in the `Awake` event (called at object creation), the instance variable is checked to see whether any valid instance of the class exists in the current scene already. If it does, then the current object is deleted, because only one instance of this class is allowed and already exists. This means the `GameManager` will persist across scene changes, and there will always be only one original instance of the object in the scene.

Awake versus Start

The GameManager class uses the Awake function, as opposed to Start, in code sample 3-12. The difference between Start and Awake is as follows:

Awake is always called before Start.

Awake is always called at object creation. Start is called on the first frame in which the GameObject becomes active. If a GameObject starts the scene deactivated, then Start will not be called until the object is activated. For objects that are activated by default, Start is called at the beginning of the scene, after the Awake event.

If you need to cache component references into local variables of a class, such as the Transform component in ThisTransform, then use the Awake event rather than Start. During the Start event, the assumption should be that all local references to objects are already valid.

The great benefit of having a global, static Instance property for GameManager is that it becomes instantly and directly accessible to any other script file, without the need for any local variables or object references. This means every class has instant access to all GameManager properties and can call upon high-order game functionality. For example, to set the game score variable on the GameManager from a different class, the following code sample 3-15 can be used:

```
using UnityEngine;
using System.Collections;
//-----------------------------------------
public class ScoreSetter : MonoBehaviour
{
  //-----------------------------------------
  // Use this for initialization
  void Start ()
  {
    //Set score on GameManager
    GameManager.Instance.HighScore = 100;
  }
  //-----------------------------------------
}
//-----------------------------------------
```

More information on singleton objects can be found online at http://unitypatterns.com/singletons/.

Summary

This chapter considered GameObjects, scenes, and components, as well as their general usage throughout scenes. These issues might superficially seem simple, but understanding their usage and being able to employ them to manage objects is a powerful skill that's required in almost all Unity game development projects. Specifically, we've seen the GameObject, a collection of components that interact to produce a unified behavior. The Transform component is especially important. We also looked at scenes. A scene is a single time and space inside which GameObjects exist. Typically, a scene is a self-enclosed entity that prevents any objects from existing outside it. Further, every scene works through a concept of time that makes change and animation possible. Time can be measured through deltaTime, which acts like a multiplier and allows us to achieve frame-rate-independent motion. Finally, we explored the singleton design pattern, which uses static members to define classes that, in practice, can only have one instantiation active in memory at any one time. In the next chapter, we'll move on to event-driven programming.

4
Event-driven Programming

The Update events for MonoBehaviour objects seem to offer a convenient place for executing code that should perform regularly over time, spanning multiple frames, and possibly multiple scenes. When creating sustained behaviors over time, such as artificial intelligence for enemies or continuous motion, it may seem that there are almost no alternatives to filling an Update function with many if and switch statements, branching your code in different directions depending on what your objects need to do at the current time. But, when the Update events are seen this way, as a default place to implement prolonged behaviors, it can lead to severe performance problems for larger and more complex games. On deeper analysis, it's not difficult to see why this would be the case. Typically, games are full of so many behaviors, and there are so many things happening at once in any one scene that implementing them all through the Update functions is simply unfeasible. Consider the enemy characters alone, they need to know when the player enters and leaves their line of sight, when their health is low, when their ammo has expired, when they're standing on harmful terrain, when they're taking damage, when they're moving or not, and lots more. On thinking initially about this range of behaviors, it seems that all of them require constant and continuous attention because enemies should always know, instantly, when changes in these properties occur as a result of the player input. That is, perhaps, the main reason why the Update function seems to be the most suitable place in these situations but there are better alternatives, namely, event-driven programming. By seeing your game and your application in terms of events, you can make considerable savings in performance. This chapter then considers the issue of events and how to manage them game wide.

Events

Game worlds are fully deterministic systems; in Unity, the scene represents a shared 3D Cartesian space and timeline inside which finite GameObjects exist. Things only happen within this space when the game logic and code permits them to. For example, objects can only move when there is code somewhere that tells them to do so, and under specific conditions, such as when the player presses specific buttons on the keyboard. Notice from the example that behaviors are not simply random but are interconnected; objects move only when keyboard events occur. There is an important connection established between the actions, where one action entails another. These connections or linkages are referred to as events; each unique connection being a single event. Events are not active but passive; they represent moments of opportunity but not action in themselves, such as a key press, a mouse click, an object entering a collider volume, the player being attacked, and so on. These are examples of events and none of them say what the program should actually do, but only the kind of scenario that just happened. Event-driven programming starts with the recognition of events as a general concept and comes to see almost every circumstance in a game as an instantiation of an event; that is, as an event situated in time, not just an event concept but as a specific event that happens at a specific time. Understanding game events like these is helpful because all actions in a game can then be seen as direct responses to events as and when they happen. Specifically, events are connected to responses; an event happens and triggers a response. Further, the response can go on to become an event that triggers further responses and so on. In other words, the game world is a complete, integrated system of events and responses. Once the world is seen this way, the question then arises as to how it can help us improve performance over simply relying on the Update functions to move behaviors forward on every frame. And the method is simply by finding ways to reduce the frequency of events. Now, stated in this way, it may sound a crude strategy, but it's important. To illustrate, let's consider the example of an enemy character firing a weapon at the player during combat.

Throughout the gameplay, the enemy will need to keep track of many properties. Firstly, their health, because when it runs low the enemy should seek out medical kits and aids to restore their health again. Secondly, their ammo, because when it runs low the enemy should seek to collect more and also the enemy will need to make reasoned judgments about when to fire at the player, such as only when they have a clear line of sight. Now, by simply thinking about this scenario, we've already identified some connections between actions that might be identified as events. But before taking this consideration further, let's see how we might implement this behavior using an Update function, as shown in the following code sample 4-1. Then, we'll look at how events can help us improve on that implementation:

```
// Update is called once per frame
void Update ()
{
```

```
//Check enemy health
//Are we dead?
if(Health <= 0)
{
        //Then perform die behaviour
        Die();
        return;
}

//Check for health low
if(health <= 20)
{
        //Health is low, so find first-aid
        RunAndFindHealthRestore();
        return;
}

//Check ammo

//Have we run out of ammo?
if(Ammo <= 0)
{
        //Then find more
        SearchMore();
        return;
}

//Health and ammo are fine. Can we see player? If so, shoot
if(HaveLineOfSight)
{
        FireAtPlayer();
}
}
```

The preceding code sample 4-1 shows a heavy Update function filled with lots of condition checking and responses. In essence, the Update function attempts to merge event handling and response behaviors into one and the results in an unnecessarily expensive process. If we think about the event connections between these different processes (the health and ammo check), we see how the code could be refactored more neatly. For example, ammo only changes on two occasions: when a weapon is fired or when new ammo is collected. Similarly, health only changes on two occasions: when an enemy is successfully attacked by the player or when an enemy collects a first-aid kit. In the first case, there is a reduction, and in the latter case, an increase.

Since these are the only times when the properties change (the events), these are the only points where their values need to be validated. See the following code sample 4-2 for a refactored enemy, which includes C# properties and a much reduced Update function:

```csharp
using UnityEngine;
using System.Collections;

public class EnemyObject : MonoBehaviour
{
    //-----------------------------------------------------------
    //C# accessors for private variables
    public int Health
    {
        get{return _health;}
        set
        {
            //Clamp health between 0-100
            _health = Mathf.Clamp(value, 0, 100);

            //Check if dead
            if(_health <= 0)
            {
                OnDead();
                return;
            }

            //Check health and raise event if required
            if(_health <= 20)
            {
                OnHealthLow();
                return;
            }
        }
    }
    //-----------------------------------------------------------
    public int Ammo
    {
        get{return _ammo;}
        set
        {
            //Clamp ammo between 0-50
            _ammo = Mathf.Clamp(value,0,50);
```

```
                //Check if ammo empty
                if(_ammo <= 0)
                {
                        //Call expired event
                        OnAmmoExpired();
                        return;
                }
        }
    }
    //----------------------------------------------------------
    //Internal variables for health and ammo
    private int _health = 100;
    private int _ammo = 50;
    //----------------------------------------------------------
    // Update is called once per frame
    void Update ()
    {
    }
    //----------------------------------------------------------
    //This event is called when health is low
    void OnHealthLow()
    {
        //Handle event response here
    }
    //----------------------------------------------------------
    //This event is called when enemy is dead
    void OnDead()
    {
        //Handle event response here
    }
    //----------------------------------------------------------
    //Ammo run out event
    void OnAmmoExpired()
    {
        //Handle event response here
    }
    //----------------------------------------------------------
}
```

The enemy class in the code sample 4-2 has been refactored to an event-driven design, where properties such as `Ammo` and `Health` are validated not inside the `Update` function but on assignment. From here, events are raised wherever appropriate based on the newly assigned values. By adopting an event-driven design, we introduce performance optimization and cleanness into our code; we reduce the excess baggage and value checks as found with the `Update` function in the code sample 4-1, and instead we only allow value-specific events to drive our code, knowing they'll be invoked only at the relevant times.

Event management

Event-driven programming can make our lives a lot easier. But no sooner than we accept events into the design do we come across a string of new problems that require a thoroughgoing resolution. Specifically, we saw in the code sample 4-2 how C# properties for health and ammo are used to validate and detect for relevant changes and then to raise events (such as `OnDead`) where appropriate. This works fine in principle, at least when the enemy must be notified about events that happen to itself. However, what if an enemy needed to know about the death of another enemy or needed to know when a specified number of other enemies had been killed? Now, of course, thinking about this specific case, we could go back to the enemy class in the code sample 4-2 and amend it to call an `OnDead` event not just for the current instance but for all other enemies using functions such as `SendMessage`, as we've seen in the previous chapters. But this doesn't really solve our problem in the general sense. In fact, let's state the ideal case straight away; we want every object to optionally listen for every type of event and to be notified about them as and when they happen, just as easily as if the event had happened to them. So the question that we face now is about how to code an optimized system to allow easy event management like this. In short, we need an `EventManager` class that allows objects to listen to specific events. This system relies on three central concepts, as follows:

- `EventListener`: A listener refers to any object that wants to be notified about an event when it happens, even its own events. In practice, almost every object will be a listener for at least one event. An enemy, for example, may want notifications about low health and low ammo among others. In this case, it's a listener for at least two separate events. Thus, whenever an object expects to be told when an event happens, it becomes a listener.

- `EventPoster`: In contrast to listeners, when an object detects that an event has occurred, it must announce or post a public notification about it that allows all other listeners to be notified. In the code sample 4-2, the enemy class detects the `Ammo` and `Health` events using properties and then calls the internal events, if required. But to be a true poster in this sense, we require that the object must raise events at a global level.

- EventManager: Finally, there's an overarching singleton EventManager object that persists across levels and is globally accessible. This object effectively links listeners to posters. It accepts notifications of events sent by posters and then immediately dispatches the notifications to all appropriate listeners in the form of events.

Starting event management with interfaces

The first or original entity in the event handling system is the listener — the thing that should be notified about specific events as and when they happen. Potentially, a listener could be any kind of object or any kind of class; it simply expects to be notified about specific events. In short, the listener will need to register itself with the EventManager as a listener for one or more specific events. Then, when the event actually occurs, the listener should be notified directly by a function call. So, technically, the listener raises a type-specificity issue for the EventManager about how the manager should invoke an event on the listener if the listener could potentially be an object of any type. Of course, this issue can be worked around, as we've seen, using either SendMessage or BroadcastMessage. Indeed, there are event handling systems freely available online, such as NotificationCenter that rely on these functions. However, in this chapter, we'll avoid them using interfaces and use polymorphism instead, as both SendMessage and BroadcastMessage rely heavily on reflection (information on reflection is covered later in *Chapter 8, Customizing the Unity Editor*). Specifically, we'll create an interface from which all listener objects derive.

More information on the freely available NotificationCenter (C# version) is available from the Unity wiki at http://wiki.unity3d.com/index.php?title=CSharpNotificationCenter.

In C#, an interface is like a hollow abstract base class. Like a class, an interface brings together a collection of methods and functions into a single template-like unit. But, unlike a class, an interface only allows you to define function prototypes such as the name, return type, and arguments for a function. It doesn't let you define a function body. The reason being that an interface simply defines the total set of functions that a derived class will have. The derived class may implement the functions however necessary, and the interface simply exists so that other objects can invoke the functions via polymorphism without knowing the specific type of each derived class. This makes interfaces a suitable candidate to create a Listener object. By defining a Listener interface from which all objects will be derived, every object has the ability to be a listener for events.

The following code sample 4-3 demonstrates a sample Listener interface:

```
01 using UnityEngine;
02 using System.Collections;
03 //-----------------------------------------------------------
04 //Enum defining all possible game events
05 //More events should be added to the list
06 public enum EVENT_TYPE {GAME_INIT,
07                              GAME_END,
08                              AMMO_EMPTY,
09                              HEALTH_CHANGE,
10                              DEAD};
11 //-----------------------------------------------------------
12 //Listener interface to be implemented on Listener classes
13 public interface IListener
14 {
15 //Notification function invoked when events happen
16 void OnEvent(EVENT_TYPE Event_Type, Component Sender, Object Param
   = null);

17 }
18 //-----------------------------------------------------------
```

The following are the comments on the code sample 4-3:

- **Lines 06-10**: This enumeration should define a complete list of all possible game events that could be raised. The sample code lists only five game events: GAME_INIT, GAME_END, AMMO_EMPTY, HEALTH_CHANGE, and DEAD. Your game will presumably have many more. You don't actually need to use enumerations for encoding events; you could just use integers. But I've used enumerations to improve event readability in code.

- **Lines 13-17**: The Listener interface is defined as IListener using the C# interfaces. It supports just one event, namely OnEvent. This function will be inherited by all derived classes and will be invoked by the manager whenever an event occurs for which the listener is registered. Notice that OnEvent is simply a function prototype; it has no body.

 More information on C# interfaces can be found at http://msdn.microsoft.com/en-us/library/ms173156.aspx.

Using the `IListener` interface, we now have the ability to make a listener from any object using only class inheritance; that is, any object can now declare itself as a listener and potentially receive events. For example, a new `MonoBehaviour` component can be turned into a listener with the following code sample 4-4. This code, as in the previous chapters, uses multiple inheritance, that is, it inherits from two classes. More information on multiple inheritance can be found at `http://www.dotnetfunda.com/articles/show/1185/multiple-inheritance-in-csharp`:

```
using UnityEngine;
using System.Collections;

public class MyCustomListener : MonoBehaviour, IListener
{
    // Use this for initialization
    void Start () {}
    // Update is called once per frame
    void Update () {}
    //-------------------------------------
    //Implement OnEvent function to receive Events
    public void OnEvent(EVENT_TYPE Event_Type, Component Sender,
    Object Param = null)
    {
    }
    //-------------------------------------
}
```

Creating an EventManager

Any object can now be turned into a listener, as we've seen. But still the listeners must register themselves with a manager object of some kind. Thus, it is the duty of the manager to call the events on the listeners when the events actually happen. Let's now turn to the manager itself and its implementation details. The manager class will be called `EventManager`, as shown in the following code sample 4-5. This class, being a persistent singleton object, should be attached to an empty `GameObject` in the scene where it will be directly accessible to every other object through a static instance property. More on this class and its usage is considered in the subsequent comments:

```
001 using UnityEngine;
002 using System.Collections;
003 using System.Collections.Generic;
004 //-----------------------------------
005 //Singleton EventManager to send events to listeners
006 //Works with IListener implementations
```

```
007 public class EventManager : MonoBehaviour
008 {
009      #region C# properties
010 //--------------------------------
011     //Public access to instance
012     public static EventManager Instance
013       {
014             get{return instance;}
015             set{}
016       }
017    #endregion
018
019    #region variables
020       // Notifications Manager instance (singleton design pattern)
021    private static EventManager instance = null;
022
023     //Array of listeners (all objects registered for events)
024     private Dictionary<EVENT_TYPE, List<IListener>> Listeners
        = new Dictionary<EVENT_TYPE, List<IListener>>();

025    #endregion
026 //-----------------------------------------------------------
027    #region methods
028     //Called at start-up to initialize
029    void Awake()
030    {
031            //If no instance exists, then assign this instance
032            if(instance == null)
033            {
034                 instance = this;
035                 DontDestroyOnLoad(gameObject);
036            }
037            else
038                 DestroyImmediate(this);
039    }
040//-----------------------------------------------------------
041     /// <summary>
042     /// Function to add listener to array of listeners
043     /// </summary>
044     /// <param name="Event_Type">Event to Listen for</param>
045     /// <param name="Listener">Object to listen for event</param>
```

```
046        public void AddListener(EVENT_TYPE Event_Type, IListener
           Listener)
047        {
048               //List of listeners for this event
049               List<IListener> ListenList = null;
050
051               // Check existing event type key. If exists, add to
list
052               if(Listeners.TryGetValue(Event_Type, out ListenList))
053               {
054                       //List exists, so add new item
055                       ListenList.Add(Listener);
056                       return;
057               }
058
059               //Otherwise create new list as dictionary key
060               ListenList = new List<IListener>();
061               ListenList.Add(Listener);
062               Listeners.Add(Event_Type, ListenList);
063        }
064 //----------------------------------------------------------
065      /// <summary>
066      /// Function to post event to listeners
067      /// </summary>
068      /// <param name="Event_Type">Event to invoke</param>
069      /// <param name="Sender">Object invoking event</param>
070      /// <param name="Param">Optional argument</param>
071        public void PostNotification(EVENT_TYPE Event_Type,
           Component Sender, Object Param = null)

072        {
073               //Notify all listeners of an event
074
075               //List of listeners for this event only
076               List<IListener> ListenList = null;
077
078               //If no event exists, then exit
079               if(!Listeners.TryGetValue(Event_Type, out ListenList))
080                       return;
081
082               //Entry exists. Now notify appropriate listeners
083               for(int i=0; i<ListenList.Count; i++)
```

```
084                 {
085                     if(!ListenList[i].Equals(null))
086                         ListenList[i].OnEvent(Event_Type, Sender, Param);
087                 }
088         }
089 //----------------------------------------------------------
090     //Remove event from dictionary, including all listeners
091     public void RemoveEvent(EVENT_TYPE Event_Type)
092     {
093             //Remove entry from dictionary
094             Listeners.Remove(Event_Type);
095     }
096 //----------------------------------------------------------
097      //Remove all redundant entries from the Dictionary
098     public void RemoveRedundancies()
099     {
100             //Create new dictionary
101             Dictionary<EVENT_TYPE, List<IListener>>
TmpListeners = new Dictionary<EVENT_TYPE, List<IListener>>();

102
103             //Cycle through all dictionary entries
104             foreach(KeyValuePair<EVENT_TYPE, List<IListener>>
                Item in Listeners)

105                 {
106                     //Cycle all listeners, remove null objects
107                     for(int i = Item.Value.Count-1; i>=0; i--)
108                     {
109                         //If null, then remove item
110                         if(Item.Value[i].Equals(null))
111                             Item.Value.RemoveAt(i);
112                     }
113
114             //If items remain in list, then add to tmp dictionary
115                 if(Item.Value.Count > 0)
116                     TmpListeners.Add(Item.Key, Item.Value);
117                 }
118
119             //Replace listeners object with new dictionary
120             Listeners = TmpListeners;
```

```
121          }
122 //------------------------------------------------------------
123          //Called on scene change. Clean up dictionary
124          void OnLevelWasLoaded()
125          {
126                RemoveRedundancies();
127          }
128 //------------------------------------------------------------
129          #endregion
130 }
```

 More information on the OnLevelWasLoaded event can be found at http://docs.unity3d.com/ScriptReference/ MonoBehaviour.OnLevelWasLoaded.html.

The following are the comments on the code sample 4-5:

- **Line 003**: Notice the addition of the System.Collections.Generic namespace giving us access to additional mono classes, including the Dictionary class. This class will be used throughout the EventManager class. More information on mono and its classes are explained later in *Chapter 6, Working with Mono*. In short, the Dictionary class is a special kind of 2D array that allows us to store a database of values based on key-value pairing. More information on the Dictionary class can be found at http:// msdn.microsoft.com/en-us/library/xfhwa508%28v=vs.110%29.aspx.

- **Line 007**: The EventManager class is derived from MonoBehaviour and should be attached to an empty GameObject in the scene where it will exist as a persistent singleton.

- **Line 024**: A private member variable Listeners is declared using a Dictionary class. This structure maintains a hash-table array of key-value pairs, which can be looked up and searched like a database. The key-value pairing for the EventManager class takes the form of EVENT_TYPE and List<Component>. In short, this means that a list of event types can be stored (such as HEALTH_CHANGE), and for each type there could be none, one, or more components that are listening and which should be notified when the event occurs. In effect, the Listeners member is the primary data structure on which the EventManager relies to maintain who is listening for what. For more detailed information on the Mono Framework and common classes within it, refer to *Chapter 6, Working with Mono*.

- **Lines 029-039**: The Awake function is responsible for the singleton functionality, that is, to make the EventManager class into a singleton object that persists across scenes. For more information on persistent singletons, refer to *Chapter 3, Singletons, Statics, GameObjects, and the World*.

- **Lines 046-063**: The AddListener method of EventManager should be called by a Listener object once for each event for which it should listen. The method accepts two arguments: the event to listen for (Event_Type) and a reference to the listener object itself (derived from IListener), which should be notified if and when the event happens. The AddListener function is responsible for accessing the Listeners dictionary and generating a new key-value pair to store the connection between the event and the listener.

- **Lines 071-088**: The PostNotification function can be called by any object, whether a listener or not, whenever an event is detected. When called, the EventManager cycles all matching entries in the dictionary, searching for all listeners connected to the current event, and notifies them by invoking the OnEvent method through the IListener interface.

- **Lines 098-127**: The final methods for the EventManager class are responsible for maintaining data integrity of the Listeners structure when a scene change occurs and the EventManager class persists. Although the EventManager class persists across scenes, the listener objects themselves in the Listeners variable may not do so. They may get destroyed on scene changes. If so, scene changes will invalidate some listeners, leaving the EventManager with invalid entries. Thus, the RemoveRedundancies method is called to find and eliminate all invalid entries. The OnLevelWasLoaded event is invoked automatically by Unity whenever a scene change occurs.

Dictionaries

The great thing about dictionaries is not just their access speed as a dynamic array (which is comparatively fast) but also the way you work with them through object types and the array subscript operator. In a typical array, every element must be accessed by its numerical and integer index, such as MyArray[0] and MyArray[1]. But with dictionaries, the case is different. Specifically, you can access elements using objects of EVENT_TYPE, which represents the key part of the key-value pair, for example, MyArray[EVENT_TYPE.HEALTH_CHANGE]. For more information on dictionaries, see the official Microsoft documentation at http://msdn.microsoft.com/en-us/library/xfhwa508%28v=vs.110%29.aspx.

Code folding in MonoDevelop with #region and #endregion

The two preprocessor directives `#region` and `#endregion` (in combination with the code folding feature) can be highly useful for improving the readability of your code and also for improving the speed with which you can navigate the source file. They add organization and structure to your source code without affecting its validity or execution. Effectively, `#region` marks the top of a code block and `#endregion` marks the end. Once a region is marked, it becomes foldable, that is, it becomes collapsible using the `MonoDevelop` code editor, provided the code folding feature is enabled. Collapsing a region of code is useful for hiding it from view, which allows you to concentrate on reading other areas relevant to your needs, as shown in the following screenshot:

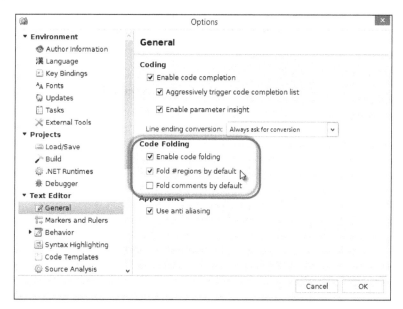

Enabling code folding in MonoDevelop

To enable code folding in `MonoDevelop`, select **Options** in **Tools** from the application menu. This displays the **Options** window. From here, choose the **General** tab in the **Text Editor** option and click on **Enable code folding** as well as **Fold #regions by default**.

Using EventManager

Now, let's see how to put the `EventManager` class to work in a practical context from the perspective of listeners and posters in a single scene. First, to listen for an event (any event) a listener must register itself with the `EventManager` singleton instance. Typically, this will happen once and at the earliest opportunity, such as the `Start` function. Do not use the `Awake` function; this is reserved for an object's internal initialization as opposed to the functionality that reaches out beyond the current object to the states and setup of others. See the following code sample 4-6 and notice that it relies on the `Instance` static property to retrieve a reference to the active `EventManager` singleton:

```
//Called at start-up
void Start()
{
//Add myself as listener for health change events
EventManager.Instance.AddListener(EVENT_TYPE.HEALTH_CHANGE, this);
}
```

Having registered listeners for one or more events, objects can then post notifications to `EventManager` as events are detected, as shown in the following code sample 4-7:

```
public int Health
{
get{return _health;}
set
{
   //Clamp health between 0-100
   _health = Mathf.Clamp(value, 0, 100);

   //Post notification - health has been changed
   EventManager.Instance.PostNotification(EVENT_TYPE.
   HEALTH_CHANGE, this, _health);
}
}
```

Finally, after a notification is posted for an event, all the associated listeners are updated automatically through `EventManager`. Specifically, `EventManager` will call the `OnEvent` function of each listener, giving listeners the opportunity to parse event data and respond where needed, as shown in the following code sample 4-8:

```
//Called when events happen
public void OnEvent(EVENT_TYPE Event_Type, Component Sender,
object Param = null)
{
```

```
//Detect event type
switch(Event_Type)
{
    case EVENT_TYPE.HEALTH_CHANGE:
        OnHealthChange(Sender, (int)Param);
    break;
}
}
```

 For a demonstration on using `EventManager`, see the `events` folder project in the code bundle of this chapter.

Alternative with delegates

Interfaces are an efficient and trim way of implementing an event handling system, but they are not the only way. We can also use a C# feature, known as delegates. Essentially, we can create a function and store a reference to it inside a variable. This variable allows you to treat functions as a reference type variable. That is, with delegates, you can store references to functions, which can then be used later to invoke the function itself. Other languages, such as C++, offer a similar behavior through function pointers. By implementing the event system using delegates, we eliminate the need for interfaces. Consider the following code sample 4-7, which is an alternative implementation of `EventManager` using delegates. Relevant code changes are highlighted to help illustrate the differences between the interface and delegate implementations. Apart from minor changes to accommodate the delegate types, all other functions remained unchanged, as shown here:

```
001 using UnityEngine;
002 using System.Collections;
003 using System.Collections.Generic;
004 //-----------------------------------------------------------
005 //Enum defining all possible game events
006 //More events should be added to the list
007 public enum EVENT_TYPE {GAME_INIT,
008         GAME_END,
009         AMMO_CHANGE,
010         HEALTH_CHANGE,
011         DEAD};
012 //-----------------------------------------------------------
013 //Singleton EventManager to send events to listeners
014 //Works with delegate implementations
```

```
015  public class EventManager : MonoBehaviour
016  {
017       #region C# properties
018  //------------------------------------------------------------
019       //Public access to instance
020       public static EventManager Instance
021       {
022             get{return instance;}
023             set{}
024       }
025       #endregion
026
027       #region variables
028       //Notifications Manager instance (singleton design pattern)
029       private static EventManager instance = null;
030
031       // Declare a delegate type for events
032       public delegate void OnEvent(EVENT_TYPE Event_Type,
             Component Sender, object Param = null);

033
034        //Array of listener objects
035        private Dictionary<EVENT_TYPE, List<OnEvent>> Listeners
             = new Dictionary<EVENT_TYPE, List<OnEvent>>();

036        #endregion
037  //------------------------------------------------------------
038       #region methods
039       //Called at start-up to initialize
040       void Awake()
041       {
042            //If no instance exists, then assign this instance
043            if(instance == null)
044            {
045                   instance = this;
046                   DontDestroyOnLoad(gameObject);
047            }
048            else
049                   DestroyImmediate(this);
050       }
051  //------------------------------------------------------------
052       /// <summary>
```

```
053        /// Add listener-object to array of listeners
054        /// </summary>
055        /// <param name="Event_Type">Event to Listen for</param>
056        /// <param name="Listener">Object to listen for
           event</param>
057    public void AddListener(EVENT_TYPE Event_Type, OnEvent
       Listener)

058        {
059                //List of listeners for this event
060                List<OnEvent> ListenList = null;
061
062            // Check existing event. If one exists, add to list
063            if(Listeners.TryGetValue(Event_Type, out ListenList))
064            {
065                    //List exists, so add new item
066                    ListenList.Add(Listener);
067                    return;
068            }
069
070            //Otherwise create new list as dictionary key
071            ListenList = new List<OnEvent>();
072            ListenList.Add(Listener);
073            Listeners.Add(Event_Type, ListenList);
074        }
075 //------------------------------------------------------------
076        /// <summary>
077        /// Function to post event to listeners
078        /// </summary>
079        /// <param name="Event_Type">Event to invoke</param>
080        /// <param name="Sender">Object invoking event</param>
081        /// <param name="Param">Optional argument</param>
082        public void PostNotification(EVENT_TYPE Event_Type,
           Component Sender, object Param = null)

083        {
084            //Notify all listeners of an event
085
086            //List of listeners for this event only
087            List<OnEvent> ListenList = null;
088
089            //If no entry exists, then exit
```

```
090                 if(!Listeners.TryGetValue(Event_Type, out ListenList))
091                     return;
092
093             //Entry exists. Now notify appropriate listeners
094             for(int i=0; i<ListenList.Count; i++)
095               {
096                   if(!ListenList[i].Equals(null))
097                       ListenList[i](Event_Type, Sender, Param);
098               }
099         }
100 //------------------------------------------------------------
101         //Remove event from dictionary, including all listeners
102         public void RemoveEvent(EVENT_TYPE Event_Type)
103         {
104             //Remove entry from dictionary
105             Listeners.Remove(Event_Type);
106         }
107 //------------------------------------------------------------
108         //Remove all redundant entries from the Dictionary
109         public void RemoveRedundancies()
110         {
111              //Create new dictionary
112              Dictionary<EVENT_TYPE, List<OnEvent>> TmpListeners
                 = new Dictionary<EVENT_TYPE, List<OnEvent>>();

113
114             //Cycle through all dictionary entries
115             foreach(KeyValuePair<EVENT_TYPE, List<OnEvent>>
                Item in Listeners)

116             {
117                 //Cycle through all listeners
118                 for(int i = Item.Value.Count-1; i>=0; i--)
119                 {
120                     //If null, then remove item
121                     if(Item.Value[i].Equals(null))
122                         Item.Value.RemoveAt(i);
123                 }
124
125                 //If items remain, then add to tmp dictionary
126                 if(Item.Value.Count > 0)
127                     TmpListeners.Add(Item.Key, Item.Value);
```

```
128                  }
129
130              //Replace listeners with new dictionary
131              Listeners = TmpListeners;
132          }
133 //-------------------------------------------------------------
134      //Called on scene change. Clean up dictionary
135      void OnLevelWasLoaded()
136      {
137              RemoveRedundancies();
138      }
139 //-------------------------------------------------------------
140          #endregion
141 }
```

 More information on C# delegates can be found in the Microsoft documentation at http://msdn.microsoft.com/en-gb/ library/aa288459%28v=vs.71%29.aspx.

The following are the comments on the code sample 4-7:

- **Lines 005-011**: Here, the event type enumeration has been shifted into the EventManager file from the original IListener class. Since the delegate implementation avoids the need for interfaces and for IListener specifically, the enumeration can be shifted to the manager source file.

- **Line 032**: The public member OnEvent is declared as a delegate type. Notice that the declaration is hybrid insofar as it combines variable declaration style with a function prototype. This specifies the function prototype that may be assigned to the delegate variable; any function with that structure can be assigned from any class or any script file. Thus, the OnEvent function becomes a delegate type, and this is used in the next statement creating the internal dictionary.

- **Line 035**: The private dictionary listeners is declared, and for each event type, an array of delegates (instead of interfaces) is stored; each delegate refers to a function that should be invoked when the event occurs.

- **Line 097**: Critically, the `PostNotification` function is called on `EventManager` to invoke all the delegates (listener functions) when an event occurs. This happens at line 097 with the statement `ListenList[i](Event_ Type, Sender, Param);`. This invokes the delegate just like a function, as shown in the following screenshot:

Exploring the EventManager projects

The preceding screenshot shows the `EventManager` projects.

> To see the `EventManager` delegate implementation in action, see the `events_delgateversion` folder project in code bundle of this chapter.

MonoBehaviour events

To close this chapter, let's consider some of the events Unity offers us already for working with event-driven programming. The MonoBehaviour class already exposes a wide range of events that are called automatically under specific conditions. These functions or events begin with the prefix On and include events such as OnGUI, OnMouseEnter, OnMouseDown, OnParticleCollision, and others. This section considers some details for common event types.

 The full list of MonoBehaviour events can be found in the Unity documentation at http://docs.unity3d.com/ScriptReference/MonoBehaviour.html.

Mouse and tap events

One set of useful events is the mouse-input and touch-input set of events. These include OnMouseDown, OnMouseEnter, and OnMouseExit. In the earlier versions of Unity, these events were only triggered for mouse-specific events and not touch input. But more recently, touch input has been mapped to them; meaning that a tap will now register by default as a mouse event. To clarify, OnMouseDown is called once when a mouse button is pressed down while the cursor is hovering on an object. The event is not, however, called repeatedly until the button is released. Likewise, OnMouseEnter is called once when a cursor first hovers over an object without having exited and OnMouseExit is called when the cursor hovers away from an object it has previously entered. The success of these events depends on an object having a collider component attached to approximate its volume within which mouse events are detected. This means that none of the mouse events will fire without a collider attached to the object.

However, there are occasions when MouseEvents will not fire, even with a collider attached, because other objects (with colliders) are obscuring the objects you need to click on based on the current view from the active camera. That is, the clickable objects are in the background. You can, of course, solve the issue (at least in many cases) by simply assigning the foreground objects to an IgnoreRaycast layer making them immune from physics raycast operations.

To assign an object to an `IgnoreRaycast` layer, just select the object in the scene and then click on the **Layer** dropdown in the Object Inspector, assigning the object to the **Ignore Raycast** layer, as shown in the following screenshot:

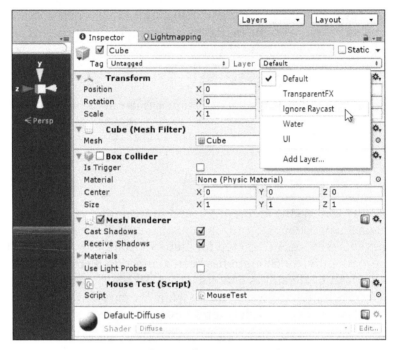

Assigning objects to the Ignore Raycast layer

But even this just isn't feasible sometimes. Often you'll need multiple cameras and many objects with colliders, and they'll sometimes obscure objects you want to select or adjust according to mouse input events. In these cases, you may need to manually handle mouse input events. The following code sample 4-8 achieves these, invoking specific mouse events manually on the basis of input. In essence, this code uses the `Raycast` system to redirect manually detected input events to the `MonoBehaviour` mouse events. This code uses **Coroutines** too; considered after the code sample:

```
using UnityEngine;
using System.Collections;
//---------------------
public class ManualMouse : MonoBehaviour
{
    //---------------------
    //Get collider attached to this object
    private Collider Col = null;
    //---------------------
```

```
//Awake function - called at start up
void Awake()
{
    //Get collider
    Col = GetComponent<Collider>();
}
//--------------------
//Start Coroutine
void Start()
{
    StartCoroutine(UpdateMouse());
}
//--------------------
public IEnumerator UpdateMouse()
{
    //Are we being intersected
    bool bIntersected = false;

    //Is button down or up
    bool bButtonDown = false;

    //Loop forever
    while(true)
    {
    //Get mouse screen position in terms of X and Y
    //You may need to use a different camera
    Ray ray = Camera.main.ScreenPointToRay(Input.mousePosition);
    RaycastHit hit;

            //Test ray for collision against this collider
            if (Col.Raycast(ray, out hit, Mathf.Infinity))
            {
    //Object was interesected
    if(!bIntersected) SendMessage("OnMouseEnter",
    SendMessageOptions.DontRequireReceiver);

                    bIntersected = true;

            //Test for mouse events
            if(!bButtonDown && Input.GetMouseButton(0))
{
bButtonDown = true; SendMessage("OnMouseDown",
SendMessageOptions.DontRequireReceiver);
```

```
            }

                    if(bButtonDown && !Input.GetMouseButton(0))
    {
bButtonDown = false; SendMessage("OnMouseUp", SendMessageOptions.
DontRequireReceiver);
    }
                    }
                    else
                    {
                            //Was previously entered and now leaving
                            if(bIntersected) SendMessage("OnMouseExit",
                            SendMessageOptions.DontRequireReceiver);

                            bIntersected = false;
                            bButtonDown = false;
                    }

                    //Wait until next frame
                    yield return null;
                }
        }
        //--------------------
    }
    //--------------------
```

Coroutines

Coroutines are a special kind of function. They behave like threads insofar as they appear to run in parallel or asynchronously to the main game loop, that is, once you execute them, they seem to run in the background. Execution doesn't pause or wait until the function is completed as it does with traditional functions. This makes Coroutines great for creating asynchronous-looking behaviors. Technically, all Coroutines must return a type of IEnumerator, contain at least one yield statement in their body, and must be launched with the StartCoroutine function. The yield statement is a special statement that suspends execution of the Coroutine until its condition is met. The statement yield return new WaitForSeconds(x) will pause execution for x seconds, resuming after the interval at the next line. In contrast, the statement yield returned null will suspend execution for the current frame, resuming execution at the next line on the next frame. More information on Coroutines and their use can be found in the Unity documentation at http://docs.unity3d.com/Manual/Coroutines.html.

Application focus and pausing

Three additional `MonoBehaviour` events are notable for causing confusion or surprise about their operation. They are: `OnApplicationPause`, `OnApplicationFocus`, and `OnApplicationQuit`.

`OnApplicationQuit` is sent to all objects in the scene just before the game exits but before the scene and its contents are effectively destroyed. If the game is being tested in the editor, then `OnApplicationQuit` is called when playback is stopped. Significantly, however, `OnApplicationQuit` may not be called for iOS devices, which usually don't quit or exit applications but rather suspend them while users do other things, which allows them to return and resume from where they left off. If you need or want to receive `OnApplicationQuit` events on suspension, you'll need to enable the relevant option from the **Player Settings** window. To access this, navigate to **Edit** | **Project Settings** | **Player** from the application menu and then from the Object Inspector, expand the **Other Settings** tab for the iOS builds and enable the **Exit on Suspend** checkbox, as shown in the following screenshot:

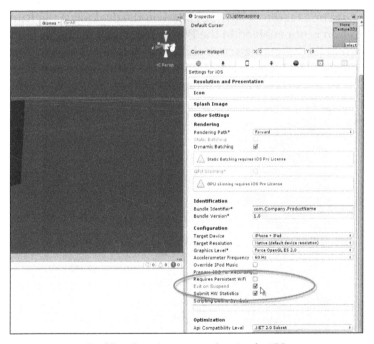

Enabling the exit on suspend option for iOS

OnApplicationFocus is an event sent to all objects in the scene when the game loses focus, typically when the game window is deactivated on desktop computers during multitask operations. This can be a significant in-game event, especially for multiplayer games where action and events in a shared world continue, even when one or more of the players are not actively participating. In these cases, you may need to pause or resume specific behaviors or fade-in or fade-out game music.

OnApplicationPause is an ambiguous event because the concept of a pause in Unity is not clearly defined. There are, I believe, two distinct kinds of pauses, namely, an ultimate and relative pause. The ultimate kind is where every activity and every event in a game is totally suspended; in this state, there is no passing of time and nothing can move forward. The relative kind, in contrast, is the most common. Here, the game is self-conscious or aware of being in a paused state; it halts some events, such as in-world events, but allows other events to continue such as GUI interaction and user input, which can unpause the game. The OnApplicationPause event refers to the first kind of pause and not the latter. This event will be called when several conditions are met. These are considered in the next sections.

First, OnApplicationPause will only be called on the desktop if the **Run In Background** option is not enabled in the **Player Settings** tab, under the **Resolution** group, as shown in the following screenshot. This option, when disabled, will automatically pause a desktop game whenever the window focus is lost. This means OnApplicationPause will follow an OnApplicationFocus event.

Disabling the Run In Background option

In iOS, `OnApplicationPause` will be called whenever the application is minimized or pushed into the background.

 Do not rely on the `OnApplicationPause` event for creating your own relative pause functionality. To achieve this, use the `Time.timeScale` variable or code a more comprehensive system in which you have selective control over which elements are paused.

Summary

This chapter focused on the manifold benefits available for your applications by adopting an event-driven framework consistently through the `EventManager` class. In implementing such a manager, we were able to rely on either interfaces or delegates, and either method is powerful and extensible. Specifically, we saw how it's easy to add more and more functionality into an `Update` function but how doing this can lead to severe performance issues. Better is to analyze the connections between your functionality to refactor it into an event-driven framework. Essentially, events are the raw material of event-driven systems. They represent a necessary connection between one action (the cause) and another (the response). To manage events, we created the `EventManager` class—an integrated class or system that links posters to listeners. It receives notifications from posters about events as and when they happen and then immediately dispatches a function call to all listeners for the event. In the next chapter, we'll examine cameras and rendering.

5
Cameras, Rendering, and Scenes

This chapter focuses on some of the many things you can do with cameras, rendering, and scenes, as well as interesting combinations of them. Generally speaking, the camera is an eye point from which a scene is rendered. It is a point in 3D space from which a view of the scene, from a given perspective and field of view, is captured and rasterized to a texture in the form of pixels. After this, it's rendered to the screen by being blended and composited on top of any previous renders from any other cameras. Thus, cameras, rendering, and scenes are intimately connected processes. In this chapter, we'll see how to animate cameras and build fly-through animations, move cameras along curved paths, and see how objects can know whether they are being seen and when they are being seen by any specific camera. In addition, we'll see how to manually edit and process camera renders to create a postprocess effect, and we'll also see how to configure orthographic cameras to render pixel perfect 2D textures for 2D games and graphic user interfaces. So let's get started.

Camera gizmos

When a camera is selected in the **Scene** tab and the **Gizmo** display is enabled, it displays a frustum gizmo that indicates clearly where the camera is positioned in the scene and what the camera can see from that view, given its other properties such as field of view, as shown in the following screenshot:

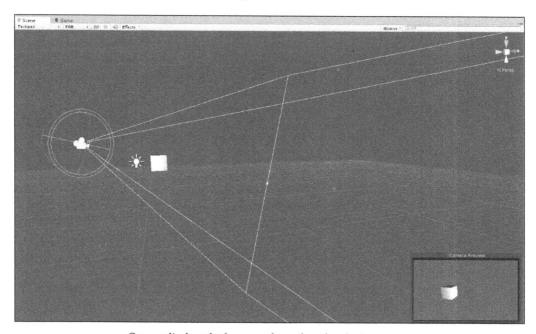

Camera displays the frustum when selected in the Scene view

This gizmo is especially helpful to position selected cameras to get the best possible view of the scene. However, there are times when you want to achieve almost the reverse, that is, to position objects in the view of unselected cameras. Specifically, you'll want to move particular objects in the frustum of a camera and make sure it's visible to that camera. This can be tedious to achieve under normal circumstances, because, by default, cameras don't display their frustum gizmo when deselected. This means that as you move objects around, you'll need to continually select and reselect your cameras to check whether the moved objects are really in the camera frustum, and adjust and tweak their positions if required. To solve this issue, it'd be great if Unity allowed you to view the frustum gizmo permanently, even when the camera was deselected, but it doesn't, at least, not at the time of writing this book. To work around this, however, you can write a script, as shown in the following code sample 5-1:

```
01 using UnityEngine;
02 using System.Collections;
03 //----------------------------------------------------------
04 [ExecuteInEditMode]
05 [RequireComponent(typeof(Camera))]
06 //----------------------------------------------------------
07 public class DrawFrustumRefined : MonoBehaviour
08 {
09 //----------------------------------------------------------
10 private Camera Cam = null;
11 public bool ShowCamGizmo = true;
12 //----------------------------------------------------------
13 void Awake()
14 {
15      Cam = GetComponent<Camera>();
16 }
17 //----------------------------------------------------------
18 void OnDrawGizmos()
19 {
20      //Should we show gizmo?
21      if(!ShowCamGizmo) return;
22      //Get size (dimensions) of Game Tab
23      Vector2 v = DrawFrustumRefined.GetGameViewSize();
24      float GameAspect = v.x/v.y; //Calculate tab aspect ratio
25      float FinalAspect = GameAspect / Cam.aspect;
26
27      Matrix4x4 LocalToWorld = transform.localToWorldMatrix;
28      Matrix4x4 ScaleMatrix = Matrix4x4.Scale(new
         Vector3(Cam.aspect * (Cam.rect.width / Cam.rect.height),
         FinalAspect,1));
29      Gizmos.matrix = LocalToWorld * ScaleMatrix;
30      Gizmos.DrawFrustum(transform.position, Cam.fieldOfView,
         Cam.nearClipPlane, Cam.farClipPlane, FinalAspect);
31      Gizmos.matrix = Matrix4x4.identity; //Reset gizmo matrix
32 }
33 //----------------------------------------------------------
34 //Function to get dimensions of game tab
35 public static Vector2 GetGameViewSize()
36 {
37      System.Type T =
         System.Type.GetType("UnityEditor.GameView,UnityEditor");
```

```
38          System.Reflection.MethodInfo GetSizeOfMainGameView =
            T.GetMethod("GetSizeOfMainGameView",System.Reflection.
            BindingFlags.NonPublic | System.Reflection.BindingFlags.
            Static);

39          return (Vector2)GetSizeOfMainGameView.Invoke(null,null);
40 }
41 //-------------------------------------------------------------
42 }
43 //-------------------------------------------------------------
```

The following are the comments in code sample 5-1:

- **Lines 27-31**: The `Gizmos.DrawFrustum` function accepts arguments such as position and rotation in world space and not local space. This means all positional arguments must first be transformed using a matrix from local space to world space. This is achieved with the `localToWorldMatrix` member of the `Transform` class. Additionally, the aspect argument requires further calculation between the actual viewport height and width, and the size of the game window in width and height.

- **Lines 35-40**: The `GetGameViewSize` function returns a 2D vector that express the actual pixel dimensions of the **Game** tab view. It retrieves these values using undocumented editor features. The "undocumented" nature of the function call should be emphasized; this means that the code can easily be broken or invalidated by future and even minor releases.

The following screenshot shows the frustum:

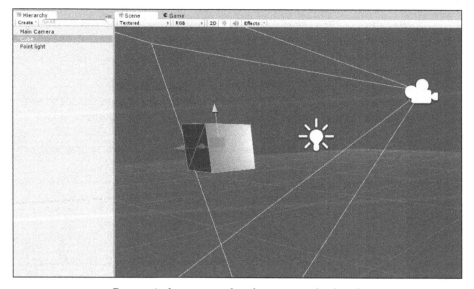

Frustum is shown even when the camera is deselected

Being seen

There are many occasions during gameplay when questions of object visibility arise, some actual and some hypothetical. Concerning the actual occasion, there are several questions we could ask, including whether object X is visible to camera Y right now, whether object X is visible to any camera right now, or when does object X become visible or nonvisible to a specific camera or to any camera. With regard to hypotheticals, we would ask whether object X would be visible if camera Y were moved to position Z. In the actual occasion case, we're concerned with the real visibility of objects for the current frame, based on the positions of all cameras, and concerning hypotheticals, we're concerned with what would be the case if a camera were moved to a specific position. Both these cases are important for games. Knowing whether objects (such as enemy characters) are really visible to the camera is important to define behavior and AI. This is because when objects are not visible, there are many behaviors and calculations we could suspend to save the processing workload. Further, knowing whether an object would become visible if the camera were moved is helpful because it lets us anticipate which objects, if any, will enter visibility for the next frame so that we can prepare them ahead of time. Now, before moving on to consider how these questions can be answered in script, it's worth considering the visibility in its narrowest sense.

In terms of visibility, there are two main concepts: frustum and occlusion. Each perspective camera has a viewing frustum, as we saw earlier; this frustum is a trapezoidal volume extended outwards from the camera lens and contains a region defined by field of view and clipping plane distance properties. The frustum, in essence, mathematically defines the horizons of a camera — the region of a scene that the camera can potentially observe right now. The word, potentially, is significant, because even when an active and visible object is within the camera frustum, it doesn't necessarily mean that it's visible to the camera. This is because objects within the frustum can occlude others also inside the frustum; that is, nearer objects can obscure or conceal objects behind them either fully or partially. For this reason, true visibility tests involve at least two processes: first, determining whether an object is in the frustum, and second, determining whether it is occluded or not. Only if an object passes both tests can it be classified as visible to the camera, and even then, only on the assumption that an object is not concealed or rendered invisible by custom shaders or other postprocess effects. In short, there are many reasons why true visibility testing is an intricate process, but here, I'll take the two-stage test as good enough for most purposes.

Detecting the object visibility

Perhaps, the simplest and more direct visibility test for objects in Unity is determining when an object becomes visible and invisible to any camera. The two companion events, OnBecameVisible and OnBecameInvisible, are called automatically on any object with a renderer component, including MeshRenderer and SkinnedMeshRenderer. It's not, of course, called on empty game objects even if they fall within the view of the camera, as they (technically speaking) contain no visible parts, despite all parts being spatially located. You can handle these events, as shown in the following code sample 5-2:

```
//-------------------------------------------------
using UnityEngine;
using System.Collections;
//-------------------------------------------------
public class ViewTester : MonoBehaviour
{
    //-------------------------------------------------
  void OnBecameVisible()
    {
        Debug.Log ("Became Visible");
    }
    /-------------------------------------------------
  void OnBecameInvisible()
    {
        Debug.Log ("Became Invisible");
    }
    //-------------------------------------------------
}
//-------------------------------------------------
```

There are several important caveats worth noting with the events `OnBecameVisible` and `OnBecameInvisible`. First, visibility here only means that an object has come within the camera frustum; thus, it can still be occluded by other, nearer objects, and so, it might not be truly visible at all. Second, the events pertain to all cameras and not to specific cameras. `OnBecameVisible` is called once to tell you that the object, while previously not visible, has now entered the frustum of at least one camera. Likewise, `OnBecameInvisible` is called once and tells you that the object, while previously visible, has now left the frustum of all cameras. Finally, and rather unhelpfully, these functions also include the visibility of the scene camera. This means that if you're testing your game with the **Scene** tab open and visible and the object is visible to you in the **Scene** tab, this will count as being visible. In short, the methods `OnBecameVisible` and `OnBecameInvisible` would be useful only if your behavior depends on the total visibility or invisibility in the scene, where visibility just corresponds to the frustum's presence. In other words, these events are a great place to toggle behaviors such as AI behaviors that depend on visibility, for example, NPC panic behaviors and other kinds of NPC-to-NPC interactions.

> More information on the functions `OnBecameVisible` and `OnBecameInvisible` can be found online in the Unity documentation at `http://docs.unity3d.com/ScriptReference/MonoBehaviour.OnBecameVisible.html` and `http://docs.unity3d.com/ScriptReference/MonoBehaviour.OnBecameInvisible.html`.

More on the object visibility

Another check that's important, besides testing when an object enters and leaves camera visibility, is to test whether an object is visible right now to a specific camera. Unlike `OnBecameVisible` and `OnBecameInvisible`, which were called on a one-off basis when an object enters or leaves the frustum, this kind of test is about the current state of an object that assumes no prior knowledge of it. To achieve this, the `OnWillRenderObject` event can be used. This event is called continuously on an object, once per frame for each camera to which it is visible as long as the object is visible to that camera. "Visible" here is taken to mean "within the camera frustum". Again, no occlusion testing is applied. Refer to the following code sample 5-3, and notice that inside this event, the `Camera.current` member can be used to retrieve a reference to the camera to which the object is currently visible, including the scene view camera:

```
void OnWillRenderObject()
{
    Debug.Log (Camera.current.name);
}
```

Frustum testing – renderers

There are many times when the Unity native camera events, as we saw earlier, are not sufficient for your visibility and frustum-testing requirements. Specifically, you might simply want to test whether just one specific camera can see a renderer, whether an invisible object would be seen if it were visible, whether a specified point in space is seen by the camera, or whether a camera would see a specific object if it were moved to a new location. All of these cases can be important visibility tests in different situations, and all of them require some degree of manual testing. To meet these camera visibility needs, we'll need to code more intensively. The functions in the following sections will be compiled together as static functions in a dedicated CamUtility class. Let's start by creating a function to test whether a specific renderer component is within the frustum of a specific Camera object, as shown in the following code sample 5-4:

```
01 using UnityEngine;
02 using System.Collections;
03 //-------------------------------------------------------------
04 public class CamUtility
05 {
06 //-------------------------------------------------------------
07 //Function to determine whether a renderer is within frustum of
   a specified camera
08 //Returns true if renderer is within frustum, else false
09 public static bool IsRendererInFrustum(Renderer Renderable,
   Camera Cam)

10 {
11         //Construct frustum planes from camera
12         //Each plane represents one wall of frustrum
13         Plane[] planes =
          GeometryUtility.CalculateFrustumPlanes(Cam);

14
15         //Test whether renderable is within frustum planes
16         return GeometryUtility.TestPlanesAABB(planes,
          Renderable.bounds);

17 }
18 //-------------------------------------------------------------
19 }
```

From lines 10–17, the `GeometryUtility` class is used to generate an array of plane objects that describe the camera frustum. Planes are to 3D space what lines are to 2D space; they mark out a flat, imaginary surface in 3D. The frustum planes are a collection of six planes that are rotated and aligned in 3D space to represent the complete trapezoidal camera frustum. This array is then used by the `TestPlanesAABB` function, **Axially Aligned Bounding Box (AABB)**, which determines whether the collision boundary of a mesh renderer exists inside the frustum as defined by the planes.

Frustum testing – points

Of course, you don't always want to test renderers for visibility. Instead, you might simply want to test for a point. This might be for two main reasons. First, you might want to know whether an object, such as a particle or a gun target location, is actually visible. Second, you might not only want to know whether a point is visible but also where in the screen space; this will be rendered by the camera. The following code sample 5-5 will do this. It will test whether a point is within the camera frustum, and if so, it would further return where the point would be rendered on screen in a normalized viewport space (between 1-0).

```
//----------------------------------------------------------
//Determines if point is within frustum of camera
//Returns true if point is within frustum, else false
//The out param ViewPortLoc defines the location

public static bool IsPointInFrustum(Vector3 Point, Camera Cam, out
Vector3 ViewPortLoc)
    {
        //Create new bounds with no size
        Bounds B = new Bounds(Point, Vector3.zero);

        //Construct frustum planes from camera
        //Each plane represents one wall of frustrum

        Plane[] planes =
        GeometryUtility.CalculateFrustumPlanes(Cam);

        //Test whether point is within frustum planes
        bool IsVisible = GeometryUtility.TestPlanesAABB(planes,
B);
```

```
        //Assign viewport location
        ViewPortLoc = Vector3.zero;

        //If visible then get viewport location of point
        if(IsVisible)
                ViewPortLoc = Cam.WorldToViewportPoint(Point);

        return IsVisible;
}
//------------------------------------------------------------
```

Frustum testing – occlusion

As mentioned earlier, visibility in its strictest sense is primarily a two-stage and not a one-stage process. All visibility testing so far has consisted only of checking for an object's presence within the frustum of a camera. Typically, this is enough, and it should always be preferred. However, sometimes, it's really not enough, because even among objects within the frustum, it's possible for one object to occlude another, as nearer objects can conceal objects further away, either fully or partially. This, in itself, is not always a problem though, because more often than not, the main interest in determining object visibility is simply to know whether the camera is near enough for a set of performance-intensive behaviors (such as AI behaviors) to be enabled. The aim is not truly visibility testing, but to know whether the camera is close enough. In these cases, it doesn't matter whether the objects are occluded; it only matters whether they are in the frustum. Yet, occasionally, occlusion matters, such as when displaying GUI elements or pop-up notifications as the player looks at specific objects. In these cases, occlusion is important, because GUI elements should not pop up for objects on the other side of a wall, for example. Sometimes, you can even get around these situations with an inventive use of colliders, triggers, and careful object placement, and sometimes, there's really no choice but to further filter objects in the frustum with occlusion testing. Now, occlusion testing among objects within the frustum is a deep subject that can, via some implementations, have a significant performance overhead. For this reason, one of the best methods is to use a simple `Physics.LineCast` method call to determine whether an imaginary line drawn between the camera and destination object is intersected by other colliders. This method usually works well, but its limitations should be recognized. First, it assumes that all visible objects have colliders; any exceptions to this rule will not be detected by the `LineCast` method. Second, as colliders only approximate the bounds of a mesh and do not wrap around the mesh vertex for vertex, it's possible for the `LineCast` method to fail when meshes have internal holes, as the surrounding collider will prevent `LineCast` from penetrating them. Finally, meshes with transparent materials that reveal objects behind them will always fail the `LineCast` method. Consider the following code sample 5-6:

```
//-----------------------------------------------------------
//Function to determine whether an object is visible
public static bool IsVisible(Renderer Renderable, Camera Cam)
{
    //If in frustrum then cast line
    if(CamUtility.IsRendererInFrustum(Renderable, Cam))
        return

//Is direct line between camera and object?
!Physics.Linecast(Renderable.transform.position,
Cam.transform.position);
        return false; //No line found or not in frustum
}
//-----------------------------------------------------------
```

Camera vision – front and back

In some games, such as RTS games or casual games, the camera horizon (or far clipping plane) does not have so great a significance, because the camera always sees everything that is in front of it. In these cases, when objects are outside the frustum, they are only outside in the x and y planes but not in the local z axis; that is, the hidden objects are only hidden because the camera is not directly looking at them. However, when the camera is appropriately orientated, objects can never be too far away in the distance to be seen beyond the far clipping plane. In situations like these, visibility tests can often be reduced to faster and simpler orientation tests. Thus, the question changes from, "Is the object within the frustum and not occluded?" to "Is the object in front of the camera or is it behind?" Here, the answer we need is different; the question is not one of visibility but of orientation, whether the camera and its subject are so oriented that the subject is in front of the camera or behind it. To test for this, the vector dot product can be used. The dot product accepts two vectors as input and reduces them to a single dimensional, numerical value as output. This value describes the angular relationship between the two input vectors. In the following code sample 5-7, the `CamFieldView` class can be attached to a camera, and it detects whether the camera can see a target object, that is, whether the target object is within a limited field of view in front of the camera:

```
using UnityEngine;
using System.Collections;
//-----------------------------------------------------
public class CamFieldView : MonoBehaviour
{
    //-----------------------------------------------------
    //Field of view (degrees) in which can see in front of us
    //Measure in degrees from forward vector (left or right)
```

```csharp
public float AngleView = 30.0f;

//Target object for seeing
public Transform Target = null;

//Local transform
private Transform ThisTransform = null;
//-------------------------------------------------
// Use this for initialization
void Awake ()
{
    //Get local transform
    ThisTransform = transform;
}
//-------------------------------------------------
// Update is called once per frame
void Update ()
{
    //Update view between camera and target
    Vector3 Forward = ThisTransform.forward.normalized;
    Vector3 ToObject = (Target.position -
    ThisTransform.position).normalized;

    //Get Dot Product
    float DotProduct = Vector3.Dot(Forward, ToObject);
    float Angle = DotProduct * 180f;

    //Check within field of view
    if(Angle >= 180f-AngleView)
    {
            Debug.Log ("Object can be seen");
    }
}
//-------------------------------------------------
}
//-------------------------------------------------
```

Orthographic cameras

Every newly created camera object in Unity is, by default, configured as a perspective camera, unless you change the default settings. This type of camera most closely corresponds to real-life cameras that have a position within the 3D space, a curved lens, and employ methods to convert captured images onto a flat, 2D surface, like a screen. The chief symptom of such a camera is foreshortening, the name given to the distortion applied to rendered objects. Specifically, rendered objects grow smaller as they recede into the distance, the shape and appearance of objects change as they move further from the center of vision, and all parallel lines converge at a vanishing point somewhere in the distance, whether on the horizon line itself or on a secondary line. In contrast to perspective cameras, however, there are orthographic cameras. These are useful for the creation of 2D and truly isometric games and not just for the semblance of isometric. With orthographic cameras, the lens is flattened out to a plane, and the result is a loss of foreshortening, that is, parallel lines remain parallel, objects don't shrink with distance, 2D remains 2D even when moved away from the center of the view, and so on. You can easily switch a camera from **Perspective** to **Orthographic** using the **Projection** type setting from the Object Inspector, as shown in the following screenshot:

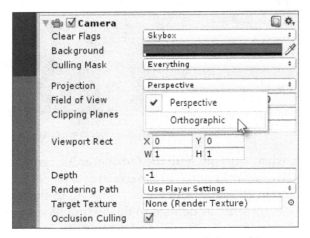

Changing a Perspective camera to an Orthographic one

After changing the **Perspective** type to **Orthographic**, the camera frustum will also change from a trapezoidal volume to a box. Everything within the box will be visible, and nearer objects will continue to obscure more distant ones, but all other senses of depth will be lost, as shown in the following screenshot. Hence, this camera is considered suitable for 2D games.

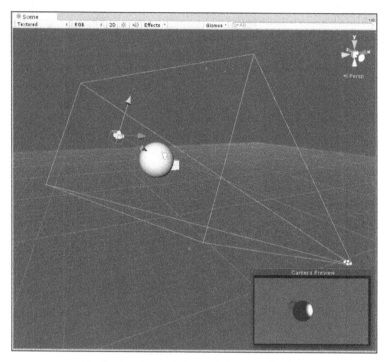

The frustum for an Orthographic camera is a box

The central problem when working with the **Orthographic** cameras is how to create a 1:1 relationship between world units (in the scene) and pixels (on screen). This problem arises because in 2D games and GUIs, it's useful to show graphics on screen at their default and correct sizes, as defined in the texture files. In most 3D games, by contrast, texture mapping, foreshortening, and perspective means textures are seen distorted, that is, projected onto the surface of 3D objects where they are viewed not directly as though in a photo-editing program, but in perspective. With 2D games and sprites, the situation is different. These graphics are typically viewed head on. For this reason, it's desirable to display them in their default sizes, pixel for pixel. This kind of display is called pixel perfection, because each pixel in the texture will be shown onscreen and in the game, unchanged. Achieving this in practice, however, requires a specific approach. In short, to map 1 world unit to 1 pixel, the **Size** field in the **Camera** tab should be set to half the vertical resolution of the game. Thus, if your game runs at 1024 x 768, the **Size** field should be 364, because 768 / 2 = 364, as shown here:

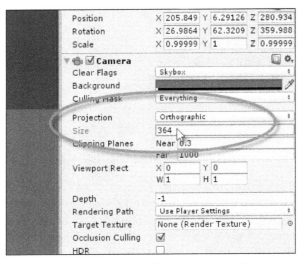

The Size field controls how world units map to pixels on screen

You can set the **Size** field directly in the editor, but this would only work if your game resolution is constant and never changes. If the user can resize the game window or change the game resolution, then you would need to update the camera size in script, as shown in the following code sample 5-8:

```
01 //---------------------------------------------------------
02 using UnityEngine;
03 using System.Collections;
04 //---------------------------------------------------------
05 [RequireComponent(typeof(Camera))]
06 //---------------------------------------------------------
07 public class OrthoCam : MonoBehaviour
08 {
09 //private reference to camera component
10 private Camera Cam = null;
11
12 //Reference to Pixels to World Units Scale
13 public float PixelsToWorldUnits = 200f;
14 //---------------------------------------------------------
15 // Use this for initialization
16 void Awake ()
17 {
18      //Get camera reference
19      Cam = GetComponent<Camera>();
20 }
21 //---------------------------------------------------------
22 // Update is called once per frame
```

```
23 void LateUpdate ()
24 {
25        //Update orthographic size
26        Cam.orthographicSize = Screen.height / 2f /
           PixelsToWorldUnits;

27 }
28 //-----------------------------------------------------------
29 }
30 //-----------------------------------------------------------
```

Notice that the member variable `PixelsToWorldUnits` has been added to line 13 to scale the orthographic size according to the **Pixels To Units** field of imported sprite textures, as shown in the following screenshot. This helps ensure that sprites will appear in their correct pixel sizes when shown on screen. This is so because all sprites are necessarily scaled by this value to map pixels in the texture to units in the world.

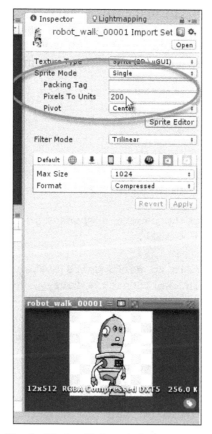

Setting the Pixels to Units scale for sprite textures

Camera rendering and postprocessing

The official Unity documentation concerning camera rendering and postprocessing is comparatively sparse. However, this should not be taken as an indication that there's little to be said on the subject. On the contrary, Unity cameras and objects offer extensive flexibility over how the scene is rendered. These topics fall under the umbrella term of postprocessing. Specifically, this refers to all the additional edits and amendments made to a camera's rendered output that is not included as part of the normal render. This includes blur effects, color adjustments, fish-eye effects, and so on. It should be said here that access to these features is included only in the professional version of Unity and not in the free version. For this reason, free users will not be able to follow along and complete this section. However, for professional version users, there is a wide range of camera-rendering features available, as shown in the following screenshot. This section considers them by creating a camera change system in which one camera will cross-fade smoothly into another. By cross-fade, I don't simply mean that one camera will cut to another, which (incidentally) can be achieved by changing a camera's depth field, as higher-order cameras are rendered above lower-order cameras. I rather mean that the rendered output of the first camera will gradually dissolve in opacity to reveal the output of the second camera. So, let's get started.

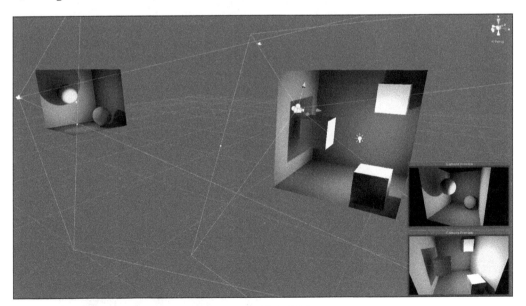

Creating a scene with multiple cameras

Start the project with a scene that contains two separate areas or regions, as shown in the preceding screenshot. The sample project is included in the book's companion files (code bundle) inside the Cameras folder of this chapter. Each region of the scene should be assigned a separate camera; this makes a total of two cameras in the scene, and each camera component should be disabled. This will prevent the cameras from rendering themselves automatically. Here, we'll be rendering the cameras manually; this will allow the render from each camera to be composited and faded on top of the other.

> For each camera, the AudioListener component was removed, because a Unity scene can have only one AudioListener active at any one time.

Next, create a third camera tagged as MainCamera at the scene's origin and set with a culling mask of nothing, making sure that the camera is active but can render nothing. This will represent the central main scene camera that composites together renders from all other cameras, as shown here:

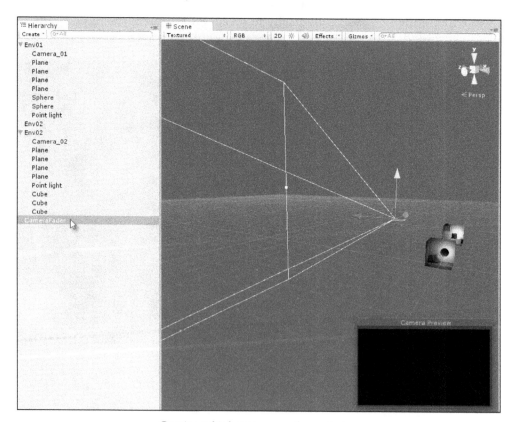

Creating a third main camera for rendering

Now, the scene should have three cameras: two separate and disabled cameras at different locations (cameras **X** and **Y**), and one main camera at the scene's origin (camera **Z**). On this basis, the following code sample 5-9 can be assigned to camera **Z**, and this allows fading between cameras **X** and **Y** when Space bar is pressed:

```
001 //Class to fade from camera 0 to 1, and back from 1 to 0
002 //This class assumes there are only two scene cameras
003 //---------------------------------------
004 using UnityEngine;
005 using System.Collections;
006 //---------------------------------------
007 public class CameraFader : MonoBehaviour
008 {
009         //---------------------------------------
010         //All cameras in the scene to be composited
011         public Camera[] Cameras;
012
013         //Color to multiply with render)
014         public Color[] CamCols = null;
015
016         //Fade in/out time in seconds
017         public float FadeTime = 2.0f;
018
019         //Material used as shader to final render
020         public Material Mat = null;
021         //---------------------------------------
022         // Use this for initialization
023         void Start ()
024         {
025              //Assign render textures to each camera
026              foreach(Camera C in Cameras)
027                   C.targetTexture = new
                      RenderTexture(Screen.width, Screen.height,
                      24); //Create texture

028         }
029         //---------------------------------------
030         //Called once per frame after the camera has
031         //finished rendering but before the render is shown
032         //Companion function: OnPreRender
033          void OnPostRender()
034         {
035              //Define screen rect
036              Rect ScreenRct = new
Rect(0,0,Screen.width,Screen.height);
```

```
037
038                //Source Rect
039                Rect SourceRect = new Rect(0,1,1,-1);
040
041                //Render each camera to their target texture
042                for(int i = 0; i<Cameras.Length; i++)
043                 {
044                    //Render camera
045                    Cameras[i].Render();
046
047                    //Draw textures to screen using camera
048                    GL.PushMatrix();
049                    GL.LoadPixelMatrix();
050                    Graphics.DrawTexture(ScreenRct,
                       Cameras[i].targetTexture, SourceRect,
                       0,0,0,0, CamCols[i]);
051                    GL.PopMatrix(); //Reset matrix
052                 }
053             }
054         //----------------------------------------
055         //This function is called after OnPostRender
056         //And when final pixels are to be shown on screen
057         //src = current render from camera
058         //dst = texture to be shown on screen
059         void OnRenderImage(RenderTexture src, RenderTexture dst)
060             {
061                //Now push final pixels to screen with Mat
062                Graphics.Blit(src, dst, Mat);
063             }
064         //----------------------------------------
065         //Lerp color over period TotalTime
066         //Fade alpha for topmost rendered camera CamCols[1]
067         public IEnumerator Fade(Color From, Color To, float
           TotalTime)

068         {
069             float ElapsedTime = 0f;
070
071             //Loop while total time is not met
072             while(ElapsedTime <= TotalTime)
073              {
074                 //Update color
075                 CamCols[1] = Color.Lerp(From, To,
                    ElapsedTime/TotalTime);
```

```
076
077                    //Wait until next frame
078                    yield return null;
079
080                //Update Time
081                ElapsedTime += Time.deltaTime;
082            }
083
084        //Apply final color
085        CamCols[1] = Color.Lerp(From, To, 1f);
086    }
087    //-------------------------------------
088    //Sample for testing camera functionality
089    //Press space bar to fade in and out between cameras
090    void Update()
091    {
092        //Fade camera in or out when space is pressed
093        if(Input.GetKeyDown(KeyCode.Space))
094        {
095            StopAllCoroutines();
096
097            //Should we fade out or in
098            if(CamCols[1].a <= 0f)
099                StartCoroutine(Fade(CamCols[1], new
                    Color(0.5f,0.5f,0.5f,1f), FadeTime));
                    //Fade in

100            else
101                StartCoroutine(Fade(CamCols[1], new
                    Color(0.5f,0.5f,0.5f,0f), FadeTime));
                    //Fade out

102        }
103    }
104    //-------------------------------------
105 }
```

The following are comments in code sample 5-9:

- **Lines 011-020**: The `CamerFader` class is responsible for cross fading between `Camera[0]` and `Camera[1]`. To achieve this, several variables are created. The `Cameras` array maintains a list of cameras: two cameras in this case. The `CamCols` array is linked to `Cameras`. It describes the color by which the render from the camera will be multiplied; this allows the alpha value to make the render transparent. The `FadeTime` variable defines the total time in seconds for a camera fade in one direction, either fade-out or fade-in. Finally, the `Mat` variable references any valid material that will be applied to the final render from the main camera, that is, the pixels of the completed render, including everything composited from all the other cameras.

- **Lines 023-038**: The `Start` method creates `RenderTexture` for each camera that assigns the texture to its `TargetTexture` member. In essence, this means each camera is assigned an internal texture to which its render is locally composited.

- **Lines 033-052**: The `OnPostRender` event is called automatically by Unity for any active camera objects in the scene, once for each frame and after the camera has completed its render as normal. It gives the object an opportunity to render additional cameras or elements on top of the normal rendered data. Here, the `Render` method of each camera in the `Cameras` array is called; this method manually renders the camera, not directly on screen but to its render texture. Once rendered to the texture, the `Graphics.DrawTexture` function draws `RenderTexture` for each camera onto the screen in the order of the array, one atop the other. Notice that each `DrawTexture` call multiplies the `CamCols` color to the texture; this also factors in the alpha component for transparency.

- **Lines 059-063**: Like `OnPostRender`, the `OnRenderImage` event is called automatically on active camera objects by Unity, once per frame. It's called after `OnPostRender` and just before the camera render is presented on screen. This event provides two arguments, namely, `src` and `dst`. The `src` argument is a reference to a render texture that contains the completed render from the camera, which was output from `OnPostRender`, and the `dst` argument reference defines the render texture that will be shown on screen when the `OnRenderImage` event completes. In short, this function gives us an opportunity to edit the pixels of the render either manually in code or via shader. Here, the `Graphics.Blit` function is called to copy the source to the destination render texture using the shader associated with the material reference `Mat`.

- **Lines 067-085**: `Fade` is a `CoRoutine` that transitions a `From` color to a `To` color over the time (`TotalTime`). This `CoRoutine` method is used to transition the alpha of a camera color between `0` and `1`, which refer to transparent and opaque, respectively.

The following screenshot shows the cross-fading camera effect:

Cross-fading cameras

Camera shake

Now, here's an effect we can achieve with the Unity free version: camera shake! For fighting, shooting, and action games generally, a camera shake effect can be important. It conveys impact, danger, action, dynamism, and excitement—a form of kinetic feedback. It can, in fact, be used to stand in for lots of other animations too that simulate a pervasive motion and emotion where there really isn't any to be found elsewhere in the scene. To this extent, camera shakes can save us lots of work by creating an overarching animation, as shown here:

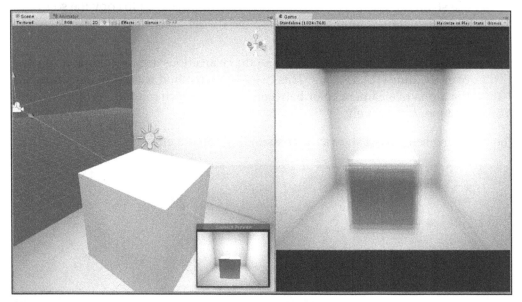

Camera shake effects

There are many ways to create camera shakes, but all of them involve fluctuation of the camera position between a minimum and maximum range using some kind of "randomness" function. Sometimes, the "randomness" is left raw, and sometimes, it's smoothened using the damping functionality to create a slower or more "flowing" shake. Refer to the following code sample 5-10 that can be attached to any camera to create a shake effect:

```
using UnityEngine;
using System.Collections;
//---------------------
public class CameraShake : MonoBehaviour
{
    private Transform ThisTransform = null;

    //Total time for shaking in seconds
    public float ShakeTime = 2.0f;
```

```
    //Shake amount - distance to offset in any direction
    public float ShakeAmount = 3.0f;

    //Speed of camera moving to shake points
    public float ShakeSpeed = 2.0f;

//---------------------
// Use this for initialization
void Start ()
{
    //Get transform component
    ThisTransform = GetComponent<Transform>();

    //Start shaking
    StartCoroutine(Shake());
}
//---------------------
//Shake camera
public IEnumerator Shake()
{
    //Store original camera position
    Vector3 OrigPosition = ThisTransform.localPosition;

     //Count elapsed time (in seconds)
     float ElapsedTime = 0.0f;

    //Repeat for total shake time
    while(ElapsedTime < ShakeTime)
    {
        //Pick random point on unit sphere
        Vector3 RandomPoint = OrigPosition +
Random.insideUnitSphere * ShakeAmount;

        //Update Position
        ThisTransform.localPosition =
Vector3.Lerp(ThisTransform.localPosition, RandomPoint,
Time.deltaTime * ShakeSpeed);

        //Break for next frame
        yield return null;

        //Update time
         ElapsedTime += Time.deltaTime;
    }
    //Restore camera position
    ThisTransform.localPosition = OrigPosition;
}
//---------------------
}
//---------------------
```

Cameras and animation

Camera fly-throughs are animations in which the camera is moved and rotated over time across specific positions to create a cinematic. Their importance is primarily to create cut-scenes, though not exclusively. It can be useful for the creation of stylized third-person cameras and other top-down views in which the camera motion must be mapped in a specific and deliberated way. One of the most common methods to create a camera motion like this is to predefine them either using Unity's animation editor or third-party tools such as Maya, Blender, and 3DS Max. However, there are times when more programmatic control is required over the camera to adjust its position manually, away from an average center, using smooth, curved motions, passing through a series of points or following a specific and predefined route. This section considers three approaches.

Follow cameras

Perhaps, one of the most common camera needs is a follow camera, that is, a camera that tracks a specified object in the scene and follows it. This camera maintains some distance between the object and the camera, as shown in the following screenshot. This is useful for third-person cameras, such as over-the-shoulder views and top-down views for RTS games.

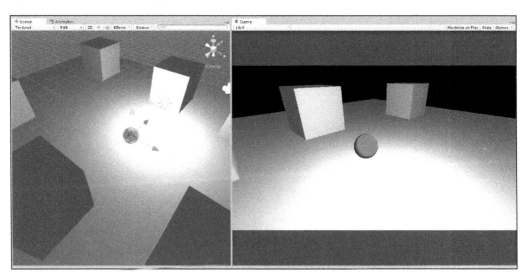

Making a camera smoothly follow an object

This project can be found in the book's companion files (code bundle) inside the `Camera_Smooth_Damp` folder of this chapter.

For such cameras, a simple follow behavior is usually not enough for your purposes. If it were, you could simply parent the camera to the object and leave it at that. However, typically, you'll want some degree of smoothing or damping to the camera motion, that is, a falling-off of speed that allows the camera to gradually slow down to a stop on reaching the target, as opposed to a sudden and immediate stop in which the camera is either travelling at full speed or not at all. To achieve this, the `Quaternion.Slerp` and `Vector3.SmoothDamp` functions can be used. Consider the following code sample 5-11 for a class that can be attached to any camera to smoothly follow an object:

```
using UnityEngine;
using System.Collections;
//-------------------------------------------------------------
public class CamFollow : MonoBehaviour
{
//-------------------------------------------------------------
    //Follow target
     public Transform Target = null;

    //Reference to local transform
    private Transform ThisTransform = null;

    //Linear distance to maintain from target (in world units)
    public float DistanceFromTarget = 10.0f;

    //Height of camera above target
    public float CamHeight = 1f;

    //Damping for rotation
    public float RotationDamp = 4f;

    //Damping for position
    public float PosDamp = 4f;
//-------------------------------------------------------------
    void Awake()
    {
        //Get transform for camera
        ThisTransform = GetComponent<Transform>();
    }
```

```
//----------------------------------------------------------------

// Update is called once per frame
void LateUpdate ()
{
    //Get output velocity
    Vector3 Velocity = Vector3.zero;

    //Calculate rotation interpolate
    ThisTransform.rotation =
Quaternion.Slerp(ThisTransform.rotation, Target.rotation,
RotationDamp * Time.deltaTime);

    //Get new position
    Vector3 Dest = ThisTransform.position =
Vector3.SmoothDamp(ThisTransform.position, Target.position, ref
Velocity, PosDamp * Time.deltaTime);

    //Move away from target
    ThisTransform.position = Dest - ThisTransform.forward *
DistanceFromTarget;

    //Set height
    ThisTransform.position = new
Vector3(ThisTransform.position.x, CamHeight,
ThisTransform.position.z);

    //Look at dest
    ThisTransform.LookAt(Dest);
}
//----------------------------------------------------------------
}
```

 More information on `Quaternion.Slerp` can be found online at
`http://docs.unity3d.com/ScriptReference/Quaternion.`
`Slerp.html`, and more information on `Vector3.SmoothDamp` can be
found online at `http://docs.unity3d.com/ScriptReference/`
`Vector3.SmoothDamp.html`.

Cameras and curves

For cut-scenes, menu backgrounds, or simpler camera fly-throughs, you might just need the camera to travel roughly in a straight line that allows some curvature and fluctuation in speed as the camera moves using a smooth-in and smooth-out motion. This means that the camera picks up speed at the beginning and slowly drops in speed towards the end of the path. To achieve this, you can use a prescripted animation via Unity's animation editor, or you can use animation curves, which offer a high degree of flexibility and control over object transformations across time, as shown here:

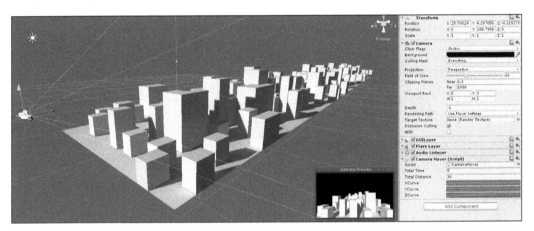

Moving cameras with animation curves

To create a camera control script that allows you to control object speed and motion over time, including curved motion and smoothing or damping of speed, the following code sample 5-12 can be used:

```
//----------------------------
using UnityEngine;
using System.Collections;
//----------------------------
public class CameraMover : MonoBehaviour
{
    //----------------------------
    //Total time for animation
    public float TotalTime = 5.0f;

    //Total Distance to move on each axis
    public float TotalDistance = 30.0f;
    //Curves for motion
```

```csharp
    public AnimationCurve XCurve;
    public AnimationCurve YCurve;
    public AnimationCurve ZCurve;

    //Transform for this object
    private Transform ThisTransform = null;
    //----------------------------
    void Start()
    {
        //Get transform component
        ThisTransform = GetComponent<Transform>();

        //Start animation
        StartCoroutine(PlayAnim());
    }
    //----------------------------
    public IEnumerator PlayAnim()
    {
        //Time that has passed since anim start
        float TimeElapsed = 0.0f;

         while(TimeElapsed < TotalTime)
         {
             //Get normalized time
             float NormalTime = TimeElapsed / TotalTime;

            //Sample graph for X Y and Z
            Vector3 NewPos = ThisTransform.right.normalized *
XCurve.Evaluate(NormalTime) * TotalDistance;

             NewPos += ThisTransform.up.normalized *
YCurve.Evaluate(NormalTime) * TotalDistance;

             NewPos += ThisTransform.forward.normalized *
ZCurve.Evaluate(NormalTime) * TotalDistance;

            //Update position
            ThisTransform.position = NewPos;

            //Wait until next frame
            yield return null;

            //Update time
            TimeElapsed += Time.deltaTime;
        }
    }
    //----------------------------

}
//----------------------------
```

A sample project using animation curves for camera movement can be found in the book's companion files (code bundle) inside the `Camera_Anim_Curves` folder of this chapter.

To use the `CameraMover` class, attach the script to a camera, and from the Object Inspector, click on each of the **X**, **Y**, and **Z** curve fields to plot the distance and speed of the camera over time. By clicking on a **Graph** swatch, you can edit the graph, thus adding points and defining a motion curve to apply for that axis. Notice that the **X**, **Y**, and **Z** motion is plotted to the object's local axes (forward, up, and right) and not to the world axes (x, y, and z). This allows the object motion to apply relatively that offers you root-level control of object motion while honoring the relevance of animation data, as shown here:

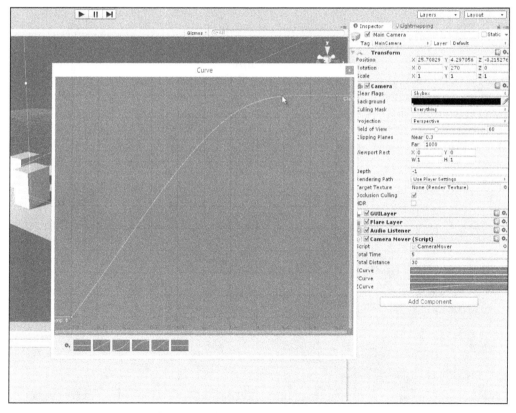

Plotting motion curves using animation curves

More information on animation curves can be found online in the Unity documentation at `http://docs.unity3d.com/Manual/AnimatorCurves.html`.

Camera paths – iTween

One very common feature request that, strangely, has not yet been implemented as a native Unity feature is programmable motion paths. This refers to the ability to have a `GameObject`, such as a camera, smoothly follow a path or spline using spherical interpolation, where the path is defined by a series of connected game objects. This feature already exists in the sense that camera motion can be defined through prescripted animations that are created using Unity's animation editor. However, there is a desire for more flexible and programmatic control over a motion path in which the path is defined by a set of waypoints that can be adjusted in code over time. This functionality is especially useful, for example, for space-shooter games where the trajectory of enemy ships clearly follows smooth, curved flight paths that sometimes change according to the position of the player's space ship, as shown in the following screenshot. There are many ways to achieve this in Unity, but a quick and easy solution is to use the freely available add-on, iTween by Bob Berkebile; this can be downloaded and imported directly from Unity's Asset Store. More information on iTween can be found at `http://itween.pixelplacement.com/index.php`.

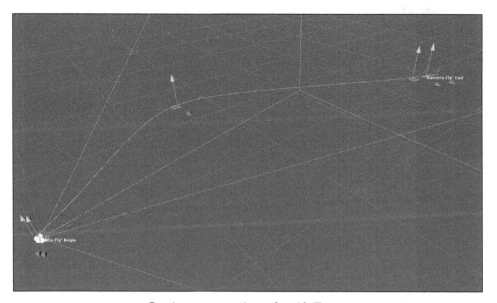

Creating camera motion paths with iTween

In addition to the default iTween package, you can also download the freely available extension for iTween, namely, the Visual iTween Path Editor, which is accessible from `http://pixelplacement.com/2010/12/03/visual-editor-for-itween-motion-paths/`.

After importing both iTween packages, the next step is to start using it to create an object animated along a path. To take the example of a camera fly-through, drag-and-drop the script `iTweenPath` onto a camera object. This script allows you to create an independent and named path that consists of multiple waypoints, as shown here:

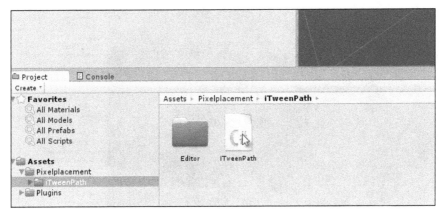

The iTweenPath script allows you to define a path of waypoints

To define multiple waypoints for a path, enter the total number of waypoints to create inside the **Node Count** field and then select each node gizmo in the **Scene** viewport that transforms each into place. Notice the curved path drawn between the points that outline the path for the camera to take:

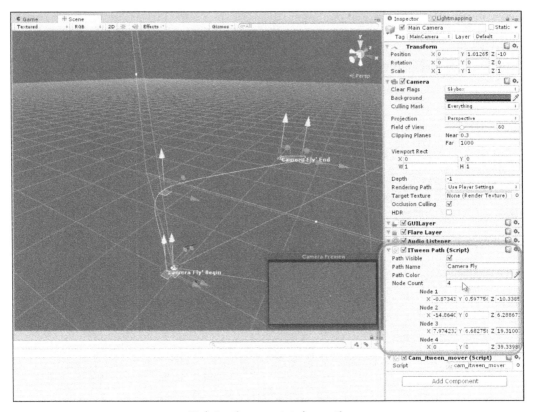

Defining the waypoints for a path

Then, to make the camera follow the path at runtime, add the following code sample 5-13 script to the camera :

```
using UnityEngine;
using System.Collections;

public class cam_itween_mover : MonoBehaviour
{
    // Use this for initialization
    void Start ()
    {
```

```
        iTween.MoveTo(gameObject, iTween.Hash("path",
iTweenPath.GetPath("Camera Fly") , "time", 4f, "easetype",
iTween.EaseType.easeInOutSine));
    }
}
```

More information on iTween and its usage can be found online at
`http://itween.pixelplacement.com/gettingstarted.php`.

Summary

This chapter concentrated on many common tasks expected or needed of cameras. Cameras are essential in Unity and in any game engine, because they represent the perspective from which the scene is rendered to the screen. Most of the camera functionality is commonly taken for granted in Unity, and as a result, much of the flexibility and control that cameras offer us is lost and not discussed. Specifically, here, we first considered gizmo rendering, that is, how to permanently render the camera gizmo in the scene viewport even when the camera is deselected. Second, we saw how to determine which objects are visible to the camera and which are not. This included several kinds of important tests such as frustum presence and occlusion testing. Third, we saw how to create and configure orthographic cameras that render 2D elements without perspective distortion. Fourth, we saw how to edit and enhance a camera render through render textures. This involved overriding a series of camera-critical events and blending renders from other cameras to create a camera cross-fade effect. Fifth, we saw how to create more advanced camera motions, such as camera shake. Finally, you learned about camera paths, that is, the ability for a camera to follow a specified path, whether this path was defined by a series of game object waypoints or was simply an object to follow. Next up, we'll explore the Mono Framework further.

6
Working with Mono

Unity supports two main scripting languages, namely, C# and JavaScript. Developers should select one of these two from the outset and apply it consistently throughout their project; this writes all scripts in the selected language. Failure to do so (by mixing script files in different languages) typically causes unnecessary headache and confusion. However, once you've settled on a language, such as C#, it usually won't offer everything you need it to do to create games. C#, on its own, can neither load and parse XML files to support save-game data, nor can it create window objects and GUI widgets to perform advanced search and query behaviors on complex data sets and collections. To achieve these additional behaviors and lots more, we must turn to external libraries. Some libraries can be purchased directly from the Unity's Asset Store, and these are typically used for a specific and dedicated purpose. However, Unity ships with the Mono Framework, which is a free, cross-platform, and open source implementation of the Microsoft .NET Framework (a programming library), and it offers most classes available in this library. The .NET Framework features classes to handle strings, file input-output, search and sort data, keep track of dynamic lists, parse XML, and more. This means that through Mono an extensive toolkit is open to you to effectively and efficiently manage data in your application. This chapter explores some of the many ways in which Mono can be deployed in a Unity application by considering lists, stacks, **Language Integrated Query (Linq)**, regular expressions, enumerators, and so on.

The following screenshot shows the Mono Framework interface:

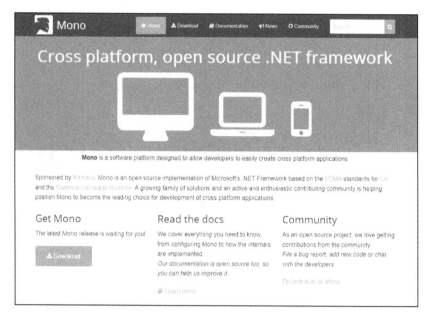

The Mono Framework ships with the Unity engine

Lists and collections

Perhaps, the most common task when programming games is to store lists of data. The nature of this data varies tremendously: high scores, player stats, enemy stats, inventory items, weapons, power-ups, level lists, and more. Wherever possible, choose static arrays to hold data due to their speed and efficiency. Static arrays were considered in detail in *Chapter 1, Unity C# Refresher*. In short, static arrays are created ahead of time, and their maximum capacity is fixed from the outset. Items can be added and removed from them at runtime, but their total size can never change. If their maximum capacity is not utilized, then space would be wasted. Static arrays, as their name implies, are an excellent choice for storing lists of data that remain constant, such as all levels in the game, all weapons that can possibly be collected, all power-ups that can possibly be collected, and so on.

However, you'll often need dynamic arrays, which can grow and shrink in capacity to exactly accommodate the data you need as it changes, such as when enemies are spawned and destroyed, inventory items come and go, weapons are collected and discarded, and so on. The Mono Framework offers many classes to maintain lists of data. The three main classes are List, Stack, and Dictionary. Each of these is useful for a specific purpose.

The List class

If you need an unordered, sequential list of items of any single data type, that is, a list that grows and shrinks to match the size of the stored data, then the `List` class is ideal. `List` is especially good to add and remove items and sequentially iterating through all stored items. In addition, the `List` objects are editable from the Unity Object Inspector. The following code sample 6-1 uses a sample C# file `Using_List.cs`:

```
01 using UnityEngine;
02 using System.Collections;
03 using System.Collections.Generic;
04 //---------------------------------------
05 //Sample enemy class for holding enemy data
06 [System.Serializable]
07 public class Enemy
08 {
09 public int Health = 100;
10 public int Damage = 10;
11 public int Defense = 5;
12 public int Mana = 20;
13 public int ID = 0;
14 }
15 //---------------------------------------
16 public class Using_List : MonoBehaviour
17 {
18 //---------------------------------------
19 //List of active enemies in the scene
20 public List<Enemy> Enemies = new List<Enemy>();
21 //---------------------------------------
22 // Use this for initialization
23 void Start ()
24 {
25         //Add 5 enemies to the list
26         for(int i=0; i<5; i++)
27             Enemies.Add (new Enemy());
                //Add method inserts item to end of the list
28
29         //Remove 1 enemy from start of list (index 0)
30         Enemies.RemoveRange(0,1);
31
32         //Iterate through list
33         foreach (Enemy E in Enemies)
34         {
35             //Print enemy ID
```

```
36                Debug.Log (E.ID);
37        }
38 }
39 }
40 //------------------------------------------
```

More details on using `List` can be found in the book's companion files (code bundle) at `Chapter06\Collections`. You can also see the `List` class reference documentation in the MSDN at `http://msdn.microsoft.com/en-us/library/6sh2ey19%28v=vs.110%29.aspx`.

The following are the comments for code sample 6-1:

- **Line 03**: To use the `List` class, you must include the `System.Collections.Generic` namespace.

- **Line 06**: If your list data type is declared as a `System.Serializable` class, then the list would be shown in the Object Inspector.

- **Line 20**: You can declare and initialize a new list instance in just one statement inside the class members' declaration.

- **Line 27**: New objects are immediately added to the end of the list using the `Add` method.

- **Line 30**: Items can be removed using several methods. `RemoveRange` lets you delete several consecutive items from the list. Other removal methods include `Remove`, `RemoveAll`, and `RemoveAt`.

- **Line 33**: You can cycle through all items in a list using a `foreach` loop.

- **Lines 27-33**: Generally, don't add or remove items to or from a list while looping through it.

The following screenshot shows the `List` class in the Object Inspector:

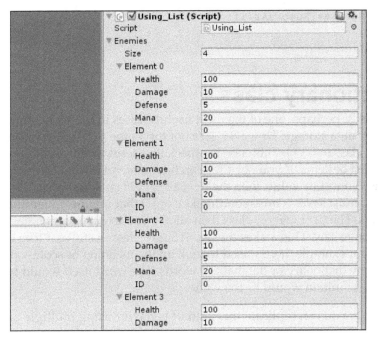

Viewing the List class in the Object Inspector

The `List` class supports several methods to remove items either individually or collectively, and these are intended to be used outside list iterations (loops). However, there are times when it's convenient, or seems simplest, to remove items while iterating through a loop, such as when you need to remove each item after processing it. A classic case is when you need to delete all reference type objects in the scene, such as enemies, while also removing their entry in the array to avoid null references. Item removal in a loop, however, can cause problems, because it's easy for an iterator to lose track of where it is and where it should go within the array as the total item count changes during the loop. To loop and remove in one process, you should traverse the array backwards from the end to the start, as opposed to forwards, as shown in the following code sample 6-2:

```
//Remove all items from a loop
void RemoveAllItems()
{
    //Traverse list backwards
    for(int i = Enemies.Count-1; i>=0; i--)
    {
        //Call function on enemy before removal
        Enemies[i].MyFunc();
```

```
        //Remove this enemy from list
        Enemies.RemoveAt(i);
    }
}
```

The Dictionary class

The `List` class is, perhaps, one of the most useful classes in the Mono Framework for in-memory data storage. However, let's not forget the `Dictionary` class (similar to the `std::map` class in C++). This class is especially useful when you need more than just a simple list of items. If you need to search for and get instant access to specific elements based on a key value, then the `Dictionary` class is essential. For each item in the list, you must save a corresponding key or ID that uniquely identifies the item from all others. The `Dictionary` class then allows you to get instant access to this item, based solely on its key. This makes the `Dictionary` class useful as a true dictionary for word games, for example, if you need to look up the meaning or score-value of specific words in a large dictionary or database of words. The word itself would be the key, and the word definition would be the value.

Now, of course, you can replicate this kind of behavior using multiple `List` objects instead of the `Dictionary` class. However, the `Dictionary` class is extremely fast in terms of performance, almost lightning fast. You can store vast quantities of data inside the dictionary at very little performance cost. This makes them highly valuable for a quick data lookup from key values, as shown in the following code sample 6-3;

```
01 using UnityEngine;
02 using System.Collections;
03 using System.Collections.Generic;
04
05 public class Using_Dictionary : MonoBehaviour
06 {
07 //Database of words. <Word, Score> key-value pair
08 public Dictionary<string, int> WordDatabase = new
   Dictionary<string, int>();

09
10 // Use this for initialization
11 void Start ()
12 {
13         //Create some words
14         string[] Words = new string[5];
15         Words[0]="hello";
16         Words[1]="today";
```

```
17          Words[2]="car";
18          Words[3]="vehicle";
19          Words[4]="computers";
20
21          //add to dictionary with scores
22          foreach(string Word in Words)
23              WordDatabase.Add(Word, Word.Length);
24
25          //Pick word from list using key value
26          //Uses array syntax!
27          Debug.Log ("Score is: " +
            WordDatabase["computers"].ToString());

28 }
29 }
```

The following are the comments for code sample 6-3:

- **Line 03**: As with the `List` class, you must include the `System.Collections.Generic` namespace

- **Line 08**: Here, the dictionary is declared and created in one line; unlike the `List` class, `Dictionary` does not appear in the Unity Object Inspector

- **Lines 13-23**: The `Dictionary` class is populated using the `Add` method

- **Line 27**: Elements in the `Dictionary` class are accessed much like arrays, except by specifying each element using its key data instead of an array index

More details on using `Dictionary` can be found in *Chapter 4, Event-driven Programming*, when considering event-driven programming with an `EventManager`.

The Stack class

If you're making a card game where players should pick the top card from a deck, if you need an undo history, if you're coding customized path finding, or if you're creating a complex spell-casting system or even a Tower of a Hanoi puzzle game (`http://en.wikipedia.org/wiki/Tower_of_Hanoi`), the chances are high that you'll need a stack somewhere along the line. A stack is a special kind of list based on the **Last in, first out (LIFO)** model. The concept is about stacking. You can push items into the list, and these stack up one atop the other in a vertical tower, with the most recently pushed item always at the top. Then, you can pop items from the top of the stack (remove them from the array) one by one. The order in which you pop items is always the inverse of the order in which they were pushed.

This is why `Stack` is especially useful for the undo or rewind functionality. Refer to the following code sample 6-4 for an example on how to use `Stack`:

```
using UnityEngine;
using System.Collections;
using System.Collections.Generic;
//---------------------------------------------
[System.Serializable]
public class PlayingCard
{
    public string Name;
    public int Attack;
    public int Defense;
}
//---------------------------------------------
public class Using_Stack : MonoBehaviour
{
    //---------------------------------------------
    //Stack of cards
    public Stack<PlayingCard> CardStack = new Stack<PlayingCard>();
    //---------------------------------------------
    // Use this for initialization
    void Start ()
    {
        //Create card array
        PlayingCard[] Cards = new PlayingCard[5];

        //Create cards with sample data
        for(int i=0; i<5; i++)
        {
            Cards[i] = new PlayingCard();
            Cards[i].Name = "Card_0" + i.ToString();
            Cards[i].Attack = Cards[i].Defense = i * 3;

            //Push card onto stack
            CardStack.Push(Cards[i]);
        }

        //Remove cards from stack
while(CardStack.Count > 0)
        {
            PlayingCard PickedCard = CardStack.Pop();

            //Print name of selected card
```

```
            Debug.Log (PickedCard.Name);
        }
    }
    //-------------------------------------------
}
//-------------------------------------------
```

IEnumerable and IEnumerator

When you're working with collections of data, whether `List`, `Dictionary`, `Stack`, or others, you'll typically want to iterate (or traverse) all items in the list or at least some items, based on a specific criteria. In some cases, you'll want to loop through all items in sequence or some items. Most often, you'll want to traverse the items forwards in sequence, but as we've seen, there are times when reverse traversing is also suitable. You can loop through items using a standard for loop. However, this raises some annoyances that the interfaces of `IEnumerable` and `IEnumerator` can help us solve. Let's see what the annoyances are. Consider the `for` loop in the following code sample 6-5:

```
//Create a total variable
int Total = 0;

//Loop through List object, from left to right
for(int i=0; i<MyList.Count; i++)
{
    //Pick number from list
    int MyNumber = MyList[i];

    //Increment total
    Total += MyNumber;
}
```

There are three main annoyances while using a `for` loop. Let's start with the first two. The first is that the syntax is not especially inviting for a loop that just cycles from left to right, from beginning to end, and we must always use an integer iterator variable (`i`) to access each array element as the loop proceeds. The second is that the iterator itself is not truly "bounds safe". It can, in fact, be incremented or decremented either above or below the array limits and cause an out-of-bounds error.

These issues can, to some extent, be fixed using the neater `foreach` loop, which is bounds safe and uses a simpler syntax, as shown in following code sample 6-6:

```
//Create a total variable
int Total = 0;

//Loop through List object, from left to right
foreach(int Number in MyList)
{
    //Increment total
    Total += Number;
}
```

The `foreach` loop is simpler and is to be preferred for readability, but there's more going on here than first meets the eye. The `foreach` loop works only for classes that implement the `IEnumerable` interface. Objects that implement `IEnumerable` must return a valid instance to an `IEnumerator` interface. So, for an object to work in a `foreach` loop, it must depend on two other interfaces. The question that then arises is why is there all this internal complexity for simple looping or traversal behavior. The answer is, not only do the `IEnumerable` and `IEnumerator` solve the first two problems of simpler syntax and bounds-safe iteration by way of the `foreach` loop, but they also solve a third problem. Specifically, they allow us to loop through or iterate groups of objects that are not even truly array types; that is, they let us iterate through many different types of objects, whether or not they're in an array, as though they were in an array. This can be very powerful. Let's see this in action in a practical example.

Iterating through enemies with IEnumerator

Take, for example, an RPG game that features a medieval world inhabited by many different and evil wizard characters (coded in class `Wizard`). For the sake of example, these wizards will spawn into the level at random places and random intervals, potentially causing untold trouble for the gamer, casting spells, and performing evil deeds. The result of such random spawning is that, by default, we cannot know in advance how many wizards there will be in the scene at any one time, nor can we know where they've been spawned, because it's random. However, there are still legitimate reasons why we'd need to find all the wizards; perhaps, all the wizards must be disabled, hidden, paused, or killed, or, perhaps, we need a head count to prevent overspawning. So, regardless of the wizard spawning and its randomness, there are still good justifications for being able to access all the wizards in the level on demand.

We've seen already, in *Chapter 2, Debugging,* one way in which we can retrieve a traversable list of all wizards, as shown in the following code sample 6-7:

```
//Get all wizards
Wizard[] WizardsInScene = Object.FindObjectsOfType<Wizard>();

//Cycle through wizards
foreach (Wizard W in WizardsInScene)
{
    //Access each wizard through W
}
```

The problem with the `FindObjectsOfType` function is that it's slow and performance prohibitive when used frequently. Even the Unity documentation at `http://docs.unity3d.com/ScriptReference/Object.FindObjectsOfType.html` recommends against its repeated use.

 A sample Unity project using the `IEnumerator` and `IEnumerable` interfaces can be found in the book's companion files (code bundle) at `Chapter06\Enumerators`.

So, instead, we can achieve similar behavior using `IEnumerable` and `IEnumerator`, and this avoids significant performance penalties. Using these two interfaces, we'll be able to efficiently iterate through all the wizards in the scene, using a `foreach` loop, as though they were in an array, as shown in the following code sample 6-8:

```
01 using UnityEngine;
02 using System.Collections;
03 using System.Collections.Generic;
04 //-----------------------------------------------------
05 //Class derives from IEnumerator
06 //Handles bounds safe iteration of all wizards in scene
07 public class WizardEnumerator : IEnumerator
08 {
09 //Current wizard object pointed to by enumerator
10 private Wizard CurrentObj = null;
11 //-----------------------------------------------------
12 //Overrides movenext
13 public bool MoveNext()
14 {
15       //Get next wizard
16       CurrentObj = (CurrentObj==null) ? Wizard.FirstCreated :
          CurrentObj.NextWizard;

17
```

```
18        //Return the next wizard
19        return (CurrentObj != null);
20 }
21 //----------------------------------------------------
22 //Resets the iterator back to the first wizard
23 public void Reset()
24 {
25        CurrentObj = null;
26 }
27 //----------------------------------------------------
28 //C# Property to get current wizard
29 public object Current
30 {
31        get{return CurrentObj;}
32 }
33 //----------------------------------------------------
34 }
35 //----------------------------------------------------
36 //Sample class defining a wizard object
37 //Derives from IEnumerable, allowing looping with foreach
38 [System.Serializable]
39 public class Wizard : MonoBehaviour, IEnumerable
40 {
41 //----------------------------------------------------
42 //Reference to last created wizard
43 public static Wizard LastCreated = null;
44
45 //Reference to first created wizard
46 public static Wizard FirstCreated = null;
47
48 //Reference to next wizard in the list
49 public Wizard NextWizard = null;
50
51 //Reference to previous wizard in the list
52 public Wizard PrevWizard = null;
53
54 //Name of this wizard
55 public string WizardName = "";
56 //----------------------------------------------------
57 //Constructor
58 void Awake()
59 {
60        //Should we update first created
61        if(FirstCreated==null)
```

```
62              FirstCreated = this;
63
64        //Should we update last created
65        if(Wizard.LastCreated != null)
66        {
67                Wizard.LastCreated.NextWizard = this;
68                PrevWizard = Wizard.LastCreated;
69        }
70
71         Wizard.LastCreated = this;
72 }
73 //----------------------------------------------------
74 //Called on object destruction
75 void OnDestroy()
76 {
77        //Repair links if object in chain is destroyed
78        if(PrevWizard!=null)
79                PrevWizard.NextWizard = NextWizard;
80
81        if(NextWizard!=null)
82                NextWizard.PrevWizard = PrevWizard;
83 }
84 //----------------------------------------------------
85 //Get this class as enumerator
86 public IEnumerator GetEnumerator()
87 {
88         return new WizardEnumerator();
89 }
90 //----------------------------------------------------
91 }
92 //-------------------------------------------------------------
---
```

The following are the comments for code sample 6-8:

- **Lines 07 and 39**: Two classes are created here: the first is `WizardEnumerator`, which implements `IEnumerator`, and the second is `Wizard`, which implements `IEnumerable`. The `WizardEnumerator` class is instantiated simply to iterate over a collection of wizards that keeps track of the current wizard in the iteration process. To loop through or iterate over all wizards in the scene, it relies on member variables for the `Wizard` class, as we'll see in the upcoming sections.

- **Lines 13, 23, and 29**: The WizardEnumerator class implements the methods and properties of IEnumerator, specifically, MoveNext (which iterates over to the next wizard in the cycle), Reset (which resets the iterator back to the first wizard), and Current (which returns the active wizard in the cycle).

- **Line 39**: The Wizard class encapsulates a wizard character in the scene and inherits from two classes: MonoBehaviour and IEnumerable. This means that all the features of both classes come together in this derived class. It internally maintains several variables that allow the enumerator to loop through all the wizard instances in the scene at any time. First, Wizard holds the FirstCreated and LastCreated static members (which are global to all the wizard instances). These variables are set when objects are created (see the Awake function in line 58). FirstCreated always refers to the instance of a wizard that was created first, and LastCreated always to the most recently created instance.

- **Lines 48 and 52**: The Wizard class also maintains the instance variables, NextWizard and PrevWizard. This implements a doubly-linked list; that is, each instance of the wizard points to the previously and subsequently created instance, which allows a chain-like connection between all wizards. The first wizard will have PrevWizard or null, and the last wizard will have NextWizard or null. These variables make it possible for the iterator to cycle through all wizard instances even when none of them are in an array.

- **Line 86**: The GetEnumerator method returns an instance to an Enumerator object. This is required by the IEnumerable interface and allows a foreach loop across all wizards.

Together, the Wizard and WizardEnumerator classes offer fast, direct, and efficient Wizard object cycling, even though no array of wizards need to truly exist. To see this in practice, in a scene of wizards, the following code sample 6-9 can enumerate all wizards:

```
void Update()
{
    //Press space to list all wizards in scene
    if(Input.GetKeyDown(KeyCode.Space))
    {
        //Get first wizard through static member
        Wizard WizardCollection= Wizard.FirstCreated;

        //If there is at least one wizard, then loop them all
        if(Wizard.FirstCreated != null)
        {
            //Loop through all wizards in foreach
            foreach(Wizard W in WizardCollection)
```

```
                    Debug.Log (W.WizardName);


            }
        }
    }
```

You can also enumerate through all wizards outside a `foreach` loop by accessing the `Enumerator` object directly, as shown in the following code sample 6-10:

```
void Update()
{
    //Press space to list all wizards in scene
    if(Input.GetKeyDown(KeyCode.Space))
    {
            //Get Enumerator
            IEnumerator WE = Wizard.FirstCreated.GetEnumerator();

            while(WE.MoveNext())
            {
                    Debug.Log(((Wizard)WE.Current).WizardName);
            }
    }
}
```

Strings and regular expressions

Working with text data is critical and for many reasons. If you need to display subtitles, show in-game text, and implement localization functionality (supporting multiple languages), then you would be working with text, specifically with Text Assets. In Unity, Text Assets refer to any text files included in the Unity project, and each asset is treated as one long string even when multiple lines are involved (each line is separated by a \n escape character). Once your code is presented with a string like this, however, there're typically many ways in which you'll want to process it. Let's see some common but important string operations.

Null, empty strings, and white space

When processing strings, you can't always guarantee validity; sometimes, strings are badly formed and don't make sense. For this reason, you'll frequently need to validate them before processing. A common way to validate them initially is to see whether a string is null, and then (if not null) check the string's length, because if the length is 0, then the string is empty and, therefore, invalid, even though it's not null.

Again, you'll probably also want to eliminate the possibility that a string consists entirely of spaces, because a string that is not `null` and features only white space characters will not, in fact, be of `0` length, even though it usually means there's nothing to process. You can validate a string for each of these states individually, but the string class in .NET offers a compound or all-in-one convenience check for you, specifically the method `IsNullOrWhiteSpace`. However, this method was introduced in .NET 4.5, and Mono does not support this version. This means a manual implementation is required for equivalent behavior, as shown in the following code sample 6-11:

```csharp
using UnityEngine;
using System.Collections;
//-------------------------------------------------------------
//Class extension to add Null or White Space functionality
public static class StringExtensions {
    public static bool IsNullOrWhitespace(this string s){
        return s == null || s.Trim().Length == 0;
    }
}
//-------------------------------------------------------------
public class StringOps : MonoBehaviour
{
    //Validate string
    public bool IsValid(string MyString)
    {
        //Check for null or white space
        if(MyString.IsNullOrWhitespace()) return false;

        //Now validate further
        return true;
    }
}
//-------------------------------------------------------------
```

String comparison

You'll frequently need to compare two separate strings, typically, for equality to determine whether two strings are identical. You can do this using the `==` operator such as `string1 == string2`, but for best performance, use the `theString.Equals` method. This method has several versions, all of varying computational expense. In general, you should prefer any version that contains an argument of type `StringComparison`. When the comparison type is explicitly stated, the operation will perform best, as shown in the following code sample 6-12:

```
//Compare strings
public bool IsSame(string Str1, string Str2)
{
        //Ignore case
        return string.Equals(Str1, Str2,
System.StringComparison.CurrentCultureIgnoreCase);
}
```

 More information on the `String.Compare` method can be found online in MSDN at `http://msdn.microsoft.com/en-us/library/system.string.compare%28v=vs.110%29.aspx`.

Another method to quickly and regularly compare the same two strings for equality is to use string hashes, that is, to convert each string into a unique integer and then to compare the integers instead, as shown in the following code sample 6-13:

```
//Compare strings as hash
public bool StringHashCompare(string Str1, string Str2)
{
        int Hash1 = Animator.StringToHash(Str1);
        int Hash2 = Animator.StringToHash(Str2);

        return Hash1 == Hash2;
}
```

 You can also use the `String.GetHashCode` function from the Mono library to retrieve a string's hash code. For more information, visit `http://msdn.microsoft.com/en-us/library/system.string.gethashcode%28v=vs.110%29.aspx`.

Sometimes, however, you don't want to compare for equality. Your intention might be to determine which string takes more priority alphabetically, that is, whether one string would appear before the other if they were both listed alphabetically in a dictionary. You can achieve this using the `String.Compare` function. However, again, be sure to use a version that features a `StringComparison` type in the arguments, as shown in the following code sample 6-14. With this version, `-1` would be returned if `Str1` comes before `Str2`, `1` would be returned if `Str2` comes before `Str1`, and `0` would be returned if the two strings are equal:

```
//Sort comparison
public int StringOrder (string Str1, string Str2)
{
        //Ignores case
        return string.Compare(Str1, Str2,
System.StringComparison.CurrentCultureIgnoreCase);
}
```

Although `String.Compare` returns 0 to indicate that two strings are equal, never use this function for equality testing. For equality testing, use `String.Equals` or hashes, as both perform much faster than `String.Compare`.

String formatting

If you're creating GUI elements, such as high-score HUDs, player names, cash counters, or resources indicators, you'll not only need to show literal text but also numerical values inside the strings, for example, by combing the word `Score:` with a string representation of the actual score, which will change over time depending on player performance. One way to achieve this is the `String.Format` method, as shown in the following code sample 6-15:

```
//Construct string from three numbers
public void BuildString(int Num1, int Num2, float Num3)
{
    string Output = string.Format("Number 1 is: {0}, Number 2 is:
{1}, Number 3 is: {2}", Num1, Num2, Num3);

    Debug.Log (Output.ToString("n2"));
}
```

String looping

So far, we've seen `IEnumerable` and `IEnumerator`. Thankfully, these interfaces apply to strings and can be used to loop or cycle through every letter in a string. This can be achieved using either the `IEnumerator` interface itself or via a `foreach` loop. Let's see both ways, as shown in the following code sample 6-16 and 6-17:

```
//Sample 6-16
//Loops through string in foreach
    public void LoopLettersForEach(string Str)
    {
        //For each letter
        foreach(char C in Str)
        {
            //Print letter to console
            Debug.Log (C);
```

```
        }
    }

//Sample 6-17
    //Loop through string as iterator
    public void LoopLettersEnumerator(string Str)
    {
        //Get Enumerator
        IEnumerator StrEnum = Str.GetEnumerator();

        //Move to nextletter
        while(StrEnum.MoveNext())
        {
            Debug.Log ((char)StrEnum.Current);
        }
    }
```

Creating strings

To make your code read better, work in a cleaner way, and generally, be more consistent with .NET and the way it's intended to be used. It's a good practice to avoid initializing string variables as: `string MyString = ""`;. Instead, try the following code for string declaration and assignment using `String.empty`:

```
string MyString = string.Empty;
```

Searching strings

If you're dealing with multiple lines of text read from a file, such as a Text Asset, you might need to find the first occurrence of a smaller string inside the larger one, for example, finding a smaller and separate word within the larger string. You can achieve this using the `String.IndexOf` method. If a match is found, the function would return a positive integer that indicates the position in the larger string of the first character of the found word as a measured offset from the first letter. If no match is found, the function returns -1, as shown in the following code sample 6-18:

```
    //Searches string for a specified word and returns found index
of first occurrence
    public int SearchString(string LargerStr, string SearchStr)
    {
        //Ignore case
        return LargerStr.IndexOf(SearchStr,
System.StringComparison.CurrentCultureIgnoreCase);
    }
```

Regular expressions

Occasionally, you might need to perform more complex searches on very large strings, such as finding all words in a string beginning with a specific letter, all words starting with a and ending in t, and so on. In these cases, you would want the results available in an array if there are any. You can achieve this effectively using regular expressions (Regex). Regular expressions let you define a string value using a conventional and specialized syntax, specifying a search pattern. For example, the string [dw]ay means "find all words that end with ay and that also begin with either d or w. Thus, find all occurrences of either day or way". The regular expression can then be applied to a larger string to perform a search using the Regex class. The .NET framework provides access to regular expression searches through the RegularExpressions namespace, as shown in the following code sample 6-19:

```
01 //----------------------------------------------------------
02 using UnityEngine;
03 using System.Collections;
04 //Must include Regular Expression Namespace
05 using System.Text.RegularExpressions;
06 //----------------------------------------------------------
07 public class RGX : MonoBehaviour
08 {
09 //Regular Expression Search Pattern
10 string search = "[dw]ay";
11
12 //Larger string to search
13 string txt = "hello, today is a good day to do things my way";
14
15 // Use this for initialization
16 void Start ()
17 {
18         //Perform search and get first result in m
19         Match m = Regex.Match(txt, search);
20
21         //While m refers to a search result, loop
22         while(m.Success)
23         {
24              //Print result to console
25              Debug.Log (m.Value);
26
27              //Get next result, if any
28              m = m.NextMatch();
29         }
```

```
30 }
31 }
32 //---------------------------------------------------------
```

The following are the comments for code sample 6-19:

- **Line 05**: The RegularExpressions namespace must be included in all source files using regular expression searches.

- **Lines 09 and 13**: The string Search defines the regular expression itself. The string txt defines the larger string to be searched by the regular expression. The string Search searches for all occurrences of the words, day and way.

- **Line 19**: The method Regex.Match is called to apply a regular expression search on the string txt. The results are stored in the local variable m. This variable can be iterated to scan for all results.

- **Line 25**: The results in m will include three matches (not two) based on the string txt. These will include *day* as found in to*day* as well as *day* and *way* by themselves.

 More information on regular expressions can be found online at http://en.wikipedia.org/wiki/Regular_expression.

Infinite arguments

Though not technically a part of .NET or Mono, our exploration of both these libraries has touched several times on functions that accept seemingly an endless chain of arguments, such as the String.Format function. With String.Format, it's possible to plug in as many object arguments as you need for inclusion into a formatted string. In this section, I want to take a small (and very quick) diversion to show that you can code your own functions that accept and process limitless arguments; they're simple to create. Refer to the following code sample 6-20 for a function that can sum a potentially limitless array of integers:

```
01 public int Sum(params int[] Numbers)
02 {
03 int Answer = 0;
04
05 for(int i=0; i<Numbers.Length; i++)
06         Answer += Numbers[i];
07
08 return Answer;
09 }
```

The following are the comments for code sample 6-20:

- **Line 01**: To accept a potentially infinite number of arguments, use the `params` keyword and declare the argument as an array type

- **Line 05**: The `params` argument can be accessed like a regular array

Language Integrated Query

Obviously, games work with lots of data. They work with not just strings but also with objects, databases, tables, documents, and plenty more, too many to list here. However, despite the extensiveness and variety of data, there's always a common need to filter it, viewing smaller subsets of it as is relevant to our needs at the time. For example, given a complete array (or enumerated list) of all wizard objects in the scene, we might want to restrict the results even further, viewing only wizards whose health is less than 50 percent and whose defense points are less than 5. The purpose is, perhaps, to initiate a mass flee behavior on the wizards to find a nearby potion and restore their health before resuming an attack on the player. Let's now consider the implementation of this scenario and how a technology, Linq, can help us.

A complete Linq sample project can be found in the book's companion files (code bundle) at `Chapter06\Linq\`.

First, a very basic and sample definition of a wizard enemy class can be given, as shown in the following code sample 6-21. This class includes both the `Health` and `Defense` member variables that are critical to our behavior logic:

```
//-------------------------------------------
using UnityEngine;
using System.Collections;
//-------------------------------------------
public class Enemy : MonoBehaviour
{
    public int Health = 100;
    public int Mana = 20;
  public int Attack = 5;
    public int Defense = 10;
}
//-------------------------------------------
```

Now, given a collection of all enemy objects in the scene, we could filter the data into a smaller array according to our criteria with the code, as shown in the following code sample 6-22.

This code effectively loops through all members, runs them through a conditional `if` statement, and then, finally adds the enemy to a results array if it passes the condition. The condition, in this case, is whether an enemy's health is less than 50 percent and their defense is less than 5:

```
//Get list of enemies matching search criteria
public void FindEnemiesOldWay()
{
    //Get all enemies in scene
    Enemy[] Enemies = Object.FindObjectsOfType<Enemy>();

    //Filtered Enemies
    List<Enemy> FilteredData = new List<Enemy>();

    //Loop through enemies and check
    foreach(Enemy E in Enemies)
    {
        if(E.Health <= 50 && E.Defense < 5)
        {
            //Found appropriate enemy
            FilteredData.Add (E);
        }
    }

    //Now we can process filtered data
    //All items in FilteredData match search criteria
    foreach(Enemy E in FilteredData)
    {
        //Process Enemy E
        Debug.Log (E.name);
    }
}
```

This code works insofar as it restricts a larger data set into a smaller one on the basis of a specific criterion. However, Linq lets us achieve the same results with less code and often greater performance. Linq is a high-level and specialized language to run queries on data sets, including arrays and objects, as well as on databases and XML documents. The queries are translated automatically by Linq, under the hood, into an appropriate language for the data set used (for example, SQL for databases). The aim is to extract the results we need into a regular array.

The following code sample 6-23 demonstrates an alternative approach to the preceding code sample 6-22 using Linq:

```
01 using UnityEngine;
02 using System.Collections;
03 using System.Collections.Generic;
04 using System.Linq;
05 //------------------------------------------------
06 public void FindEnemiesLinqWay()
07 {
08 //Get all enemies in scene
09 Enemy[] Enemies = Object.FindObjectsOfType<Enemy>();
10
11 //Perform search
12 Enemy[] FilteredData = (from EnemyChar in Enemies
13         where EnemyChar.Health <= 50 && EnemyChar.Defense < 5
14         select EnemyChar).ToArray();
15
16 //Now we can process filtered data
17 //All items in FilteredData match search criteria
18 foreach(Enemy E in FilteredData)
19 {
20         //Process Enemy E
21         Debug.Log (E.name);
22 }
23 }
24 //------------------------------------------------
```

The following are the comments for code sample 6-23:

- **Lines 03-04**: To use Linq, you must include the `System.Collections.Linq` namespace, and to use `List` objects, you must include the `System.Collections.Generic` namespace.

- **Lines 12-14**: The main body of Linq code occurs here. It consists of three main parts. First, we indicated the items to pick from the source data, specifically, enemy objects from the data set `Enemies`. Second, we defined the criteria to search for, specifically where `EnemyChar.Health <= 50 && EnemyChar.Defense < 5`. Then, when the criterion is met, we selected that object to add to the results; we selected `EnemyChar`. Finally, we converted the results to an array with the `ToArray` function.

More information on Linq can be found online in MSDN at
`http://msdn.microsoft.com/en-gb/library/bb397926.aspx`.

Linq and regular expressions

Linq, of course, need not work in isolation. It can, for example, be combined with regular expressions to extract specific string patterns from a larger string that converts the matched results into a traversable array. This can be especially useful in processing comma-separated value files (CSV files), for example, where data is formatted inside a text file, each entry being separated by a comma character. Both Linq and regular expressions can be used to read each value into a unique array element very quickly and easily. For example, consider an RTS game where human names must be generated for new units. The names themselves are stored in a CSV format and are divided into two groups: male and female. On generating a character, it can be either male or female, and an appropriate name must be assigned to them from the CSV data, as shown in the following code sample 6-24:

```
01 //Generate female name
02 //Regular Expression Search Pattern
03 //Find all names prefixed with 'female:' but do not include the
   prefix in the results
04 string search = @"(?<=\bfemale:)\w+\b";
05
06 //CSV Data - names of characters
07 string CSVData =
   "male:john,male:tom,male:bob,female:betty,female:jessica,male:dirk
   ";

08
09 //Retrieve all prefixed with 'female'. Don't include prefix
10 string[] FemaleNames = (from Match m in Regex.Matches(CSVData,
   search)

11          select m.Groups[0].Value).ToArray();
12
13 //Print all female names in results
14 foreach(string S in FemaleNames)
15 Debug.Log (S);
16
17 //Now pick a random female name from collection
18 string RandomFemaleName = FemaleNames[Random.Range(0,
   FemaleNames.Length)];
```

The following are the comments for code sample 6-24:

- **Line 04**: The member variable `Search` defines a regular expression search pattern. The `Search` variable, in this case, is for all words prefixed with `female:`. More than this, however, the prefix itself should not be included in the resultant strings.

- **Line 07**: The member variable `CSVData` defines a complete CSV string with both male and female names that are structured in the expected format. This string essentially represents the database or data source.

- **Lines 10-11**: Here, Linq is used in conjunction with a regular expression search to retrieve all female names from the CSV, minus the prefixes. This list is then converted into a string array `FemaleNames`.

Strings and the @ symbol

Notice from line 04 of the code sample 6-24 that the regular expression string is prefixed with the symbol @. This is a C# convention that allows you to write a string literal in a source file; this string literal can contain escape sequences (such as \) without breaking or invalidating the string itself.

Working with Text Data Assets

Throughout all examples so far, we've considered text directly stored in string objects, but you can also work with text files in Unity. Specifically, you can load in text from external sources. Here, I will demonstrate how.

Text Assets – static loading

The first method is to drag-and-drop a text file into a Unity project that imports the text asset. The file is imported as a **TextAssets** type, as shown here:

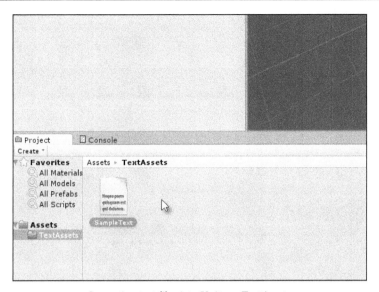

Importing text files into Unity as TextAssets

You can access the file and its text data from any script file by exposing a TextAsset public member, as shown in the following code sample 6-25:

```
//-------------------------------------------------
using UnityEngine;
using System.Collections;
//-------------------------------------------------
public class TextFileAccess : MonoBehaviour
{
    //Reference a text file
    public TextAsset TextData = null;

    // Use this for initialization
    void Start ()
    {
        //Display text in file
```

```
            Debug.Log (TextData.text);
    }
}
//------------------------------------------------------
```

This code means you just need to drag-and-drop the `TextAsset` file onto the **Text Data** slot in the Object Inspector, as shown here:

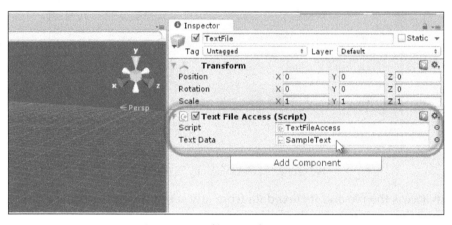

Accessing text file assets from script

Text Assets – loading from the local files

Another method to load in text data is externally from the project, that is, from files on the local hard drive. Text Data loaded in this way is read into the project dynamically from script, not necessarily at scene startup, but whenever you execute the necessary code. This means that for longer text files that involve heavy processing, lag becomes a serious consideration. In general, therefore, it is best to prefer statically loaded Text Assets to dynamic forms. For any dynamic assets, I recommend that you load and process them at scene startup to avoid in-game lagging, as shown in the following code sample 6-26:

```
using UnityEngine;
using System.Collections;
using System.IO;

//Function to load text data from external file
public static string LoadTextFromFile(string Filename)
{
    //If file does not exist on system, then return empty string
    if(!File.Exists(Filename)) return string.Empty;
```

```
    //File exists, now load text from file
    return File.ReadAllText(Filename);
}
```

The code sample 6-26 loads a complete text file into one string object. You might, however, prefer to process a text file line by line instead, especially if the file is a configuration file where values are specified in separate lines. For this, see the following code sample 6-27:

```
//Function to load text data, line by line, into a string array
public static string[] LoadTextAsLines(string Filename)
{
    //If file does not exist on system, then return empty array
    if(!File.Exists(Filename)) return null;

    //Get lines
    return File.ReadAllLines(Filename);
}
```

Text Assets – loading from the INI files

Among the many text file types, you can load a common format is the INI file. It's, perhaps, not as common with Unity games, because many developers use the `PlayerPreferences` class instead to store application settings. Even so, the INI files offer the advantage of storing application configuration data in only one place and in the same format across many different platforms. For this reason, there are strong reasons to use INI files. Refer to the code sample 6-28 for an example INI that uses a key-value pairing format:

```
ApplicationName=MyTestApp
Date=1st Nov 2014
Author=Alan Thorn
Engine=Unity
Build=Production
```

An ideal data structure to load INI files is the dictionary that mirrors a key-value pair structure. For this reason, it'd be great to load an INI file into a dictionary.

However, neither Unity nor Mono offers native support for this, which means we have to code the functionality ourselves, as shown in the following code sample 6-29:

```
using UnityEngine;
using System.Collections;
using System.Collections.Generic;
using System.IO;
using System.Text;


//Function to read basic ini file to dictionary
public static Dictionary<string, string> ReadINIFile(string
Filename)
{
    //If file does not exist on system, then return null
    if(!File.Exists(Filename)) return null;

    //Create new dictionary
    Dictionary<string, string> INIFile = new Dictionary<string,
string>();

    //Create new stream reader
    using (StreamReader SR = new StreamReader(Filename))
    {
        //String for current line
        string Line;

        //Keep reading valid lines
        while(!string.IsNullOrEmpty(Line = SR.ReadLine()))
        {
            //Trim line of leading and trailing white space
            Line.Trim();

            //Split the line at key=value
            string[] Parts = Line.Split(new char[] {'='});

            //Now add to dictionary
            INIFile.Add(Parts[0].Trim(), Parts[1].Trim());
        }
    }

    //Return dictionary
    return INIFile;
}
```

A dictionary returned from this function will match the structure of the INI file. Therefore, values can be accessed in the form string `Value = MyDictionary["Key"];`. You can also enumerate through all key and value members of a dictionary inside a `foreach`, as shown in the following code sample 6-30:

```
//Build a dictionary from an INI file
Dictionary<string,string> DB = ReadINIFile(@"c:\myfile.ini");

//List all entries in dictionary
foreach(KeyValuePair<string, string> Entry in DB)
{
    //Loop through each key and value pair
    Debug.Log("Key: " + Entry.Key + " Value: " + Entry.Value);
}
```

Text Assets – loading from the CSV files

Earlier in this chapter, we saw how to process a CSV file that features character names, both male and female. Let's now see some source code to load CSV from a file on disk into an array of strings, with each string separated by a comma, as shown in the following code sample 6-31:

```
//Function to load a string array from a CSV file
public static string[] LoadFromCSV(string Filename)
{
    //If file does not exist on system, then return null
    if(!File.Exists(Filename)) return null;

    //Get all text
    string AllText = File.ReadAllText(Filename);

    //Return string array
    return AllText.Split(new char[] {','});
}
```

Text Assets – loading from the Web

If you're making multiplayer games and need to access player or game data across the Web, if you need to verify passwords with hashes online, or if you need to access a web page to process its elements, then you will need the WWW class to retrieve text data online, as shown in the following code sample 6-32:

```
//Gets text from the web in a string
public IEnumerator GetTextFromURL(string URL)
{
    //Create new WWW object
    WWW TXTSource = new WWW(URL);

    //Wait for data to load
    yield return TXTSource;

    //Now get text data
    string ReturnedText = TXTSource.text;
}
```

More information on the WWW class can be found in the online Unity documentation at http://docs.unity3d.com/ScriptReference/WWW.html.

Summary

This chapter considered a wide range of applications for the Mono Framework in practical contexts. It took a three-part structure. First, we explored common data structures used in C#, including List, Dictionary, and Stack. From there, we moved on to investigate their common usages in storing and searching data and in organizing and processing strings. We also explored regular expressions for searching strings for patterns of data and the Linq language for filtering not only strings but all the collection-type objects available in Mono. Then, finally, we examined various methods to import text data, both internally to the project and from local files, as well as text data streamed across the Web. The next chapter moves into the world of artificial intelligence; it considers path-finding, finite state machines, line of sight, decision making, ray casting, and more.

7
Artificial Intelligence

This chapter takes a highly practical and specialized focus. Here, we'll cover the development of a single Unity project from start to finish in creating a maze scene that features enemy characters with **Artificial Intelligence (AI)**; these characters have the ability to search for and chase us, attack us, and also flee from us while looking for health-restore potions. The following screenshot shows the maze scene in Unity:

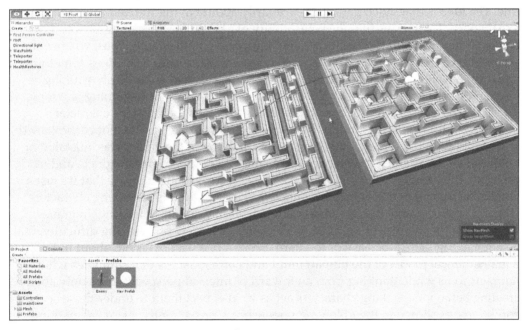

The maze scene

[The AI project for this book can be found in the book's companion files (code bundle) in the `ai` folder of this chapter.]

In creating this project, we'll apply nearly all the concepts and ideas seen so far in an isolated and pure form, looking at how they come together in the project, alongside a unique range of AI concepts, such as **Finite State Machines** (**FSMs**), navigation meshes, line of sight, and more. To follow this chapter and get the most from it, I recommend that you create a new and blank Unity project and take each step from start to finish. The final, completed project arrived at by the end of this chapter can be found in the book's companion files (code bundle) in the `ai` folder of this chapter.

Artificial Intelligence in games

The concept of intelligence can be understood in many senses: psychological, scientific, philosophical, spiritual, sociological, and others. Many of them are profound. However, in video games, it's primarily about appearances, namely, the appearance of intelligence. Perhaps, this is why the word "artificial" enters the title. The idea is that video games are primarily about having fun and interesting experiences. This means that the believability of a game for the gamer rests on how engaged they are with the events actually happening in the game. Thus, whenever a **non-player character** (**NPC**), such as an enemy wizard in an RPG, does something "silly" (like walking through solid walls for no good reason or aimlessly walking back and forth as though stuck), then the gamer perceives that something is wrong. They regard the characters as not acting intelligently just because the character's behavior, in those specific circumstances, is not appropriate and cannot be explained reasonably with reference to anything else happening in the game. The "mistake" or "silliness" of the character's behavior forces the player to recognize a glitch, and in doing so, the gamer is removed from the experience, becoming aware that it's just a game. The upshot of this is that for games, AI largely consists of making characters respond appropriately to their situation whenever the gamer is looking. In games where AI is for enemies or opponents, this consists largely of tweaking difficulty, that is, not making the AI too easy or too hard. Seen in this way, AI is not about building a mathematical model of the human mind and consciousness that simulates what happens to us while thinking from an inward or internal perspective. It's only about creating behaviors, making characters act as we'd expect them to under those specific conditions, as shown in the following screenshot. Consequently, there's something "hollow" about AI for games, but this philosophical observation need not concern us here any further.

The enemy AI character to be created using the Unity constructor mesh

In this chapter, we'll create a first-person sample game set inside a maze environment. Here, the player can attack enemies, and enemies can attack the player. The enemy mesh itself is based on the animated constructor character that ships with Unity and features the walk, run, and jump animations. The constructor character (not class constructors) will search the environment, look for the player, and when they are found, chase and attack them. The constructor can also be attacked, and when attacked, they will flee and search for power-ups if their health runs low. So, let's get started!

Starting the project

To start, create a blank, new Unity project with a new scene. For this sample, I've imported several Unity asset packages via the file menu command by selecting the **Import Package** option from **Asset**. The packages are **Character Controller**, **Skyboxes**, and **Particles**, as shown in the following screenshot. **Character Controllers** features the constructor mesh and animations, as well as a first-person controller prefab.

The **Skyboxes** package adds some eye candy for a sky that the camera will see, and the **Particles** package will be used to create a teleporter device, as we'll see.

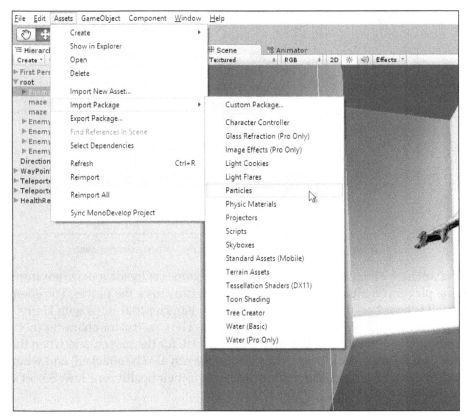

Importing assets into the project

Also, add a first-person controller and the maze mesh to the scene (the mesh is included in the book's companion files in the `assets` folder of this chapter) and create some lighting and light mapping to make things look good initially. The mesh was created in a 3D modeling program, in this case, Blender (http://www.blender.org/).None of these assets are, however, critical to AI per se, but they create a presentable gray-box scenario with which you can work. Lightmapping details are outside the scope of this book, but Lightmapping features can be accessed by selecting **Lightmapping** in the **Window** option from the application menu, as shown in the following screenshot.

More details on Lightmapping can be found in the online Unity documentation at
`http://docs.unity3d.com/Manual/Lightmapping.html`.

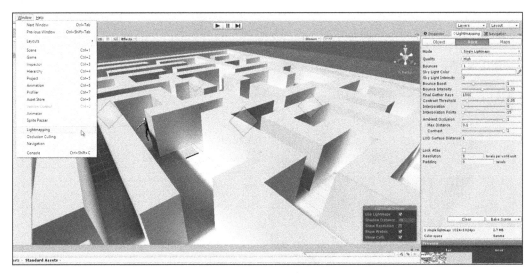

Creating the initial scene

Baking a navigation mesh

The enemy to be created needs to walk intelligently around the level to find and
chase the player as well as to find health-restore power-ups. The AI cannot simply
walk in a straight line between any two points, as there might be intervening
obstacles such as walls and other characters. The AI should instead navigate
around these objects when they're encountered. To achieve this in the long term, a
navigation mesh should be used. This is an invisible mesh asset that Unity generates
automatically to approximate all walkable, horizontal surfaces in the level, that
is, surfaces classified as a floor. The navigation mesh itself contains no AI. It does
not make anything walk. The navigation mesh is rather a mathematical model that
contains all the necessary data that allows AI units to successfully calculate and
travel a path that avoids obstacles as and when required. To generate a navigation
mesh for the level, select the **Navigation** option from the **Window** tab of the
application menu. This displays the **Navigation Mesh** tab, which can be docked
into the Object Inspector.

For the basics on navigation mesh baking, see the online Unity
documentation at `http://docs.unity3d.com/Manual/Navmeshes.html`.

When baking a navigation mesh, there are some additional details to keep in mind, as shown in the following screenshot:

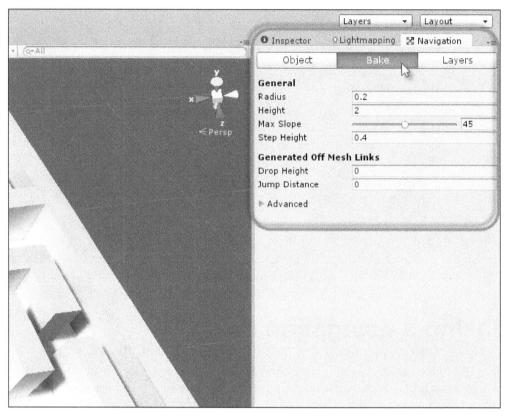

Preparing to bake a navigation mesh

First, the **Radius** setting will likely require adjusting from its default. In short, this setting defines an imaginary circle around the feet of your characters; this circle indicates their approximate size as walking agents. If the radius is too large, the navigation mesh appears broken or fractured, and if it is too small, the mesh takes a long time to generate, and additionally, your agents will penetrate through walls while walking. A certain degree of trial and error and refinement lets you reach a value that works best for your project. For this sample, a value of 0.2 works best. If the radius is too high, your navigation mesh will fracture in narrow areas, which is not good because agents cannot travel across gaps, as shown in the following screenshot:

Navigation mesh fracture in narrow areas

Second, a navigation mesh (once generated) might appear raised above or offset upwards, away from the true mesh floor. If this happens, you could reduce the **Height Inaccuracy** % setting to 1 from the **Advanced** group, as shown in the following screenshot. This prevents your agents from appearing to hover in midair. Remember that after adjusting any settings, you need to rebake the navigation mesh to apply the changes.

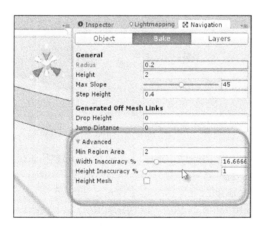

Reducing Height Inaccuracy % moves the generated navigation mesh closer to the true floor

From the figures, you can see that the maze scene features two separate maze areas (left and right) with no connecting mesh between them that allows the creation of a path. For this sample, the intelligent agents should be able to move freely between each section using a teleporter to transport them from one area to another, if required.

To achieve a connection like this between a break in the navigation mesh that allows the AI to compute valid paths across surfaces, we could use off-mesh links. Add a new mesh to the level that should act as a teleporter pad or platform when stepped upon. For this example, I used a standard box mesh with a particle system for enhanced effect, but this is not essential. Then, attach an off-mesh link component to the mesh object, as shown here:

Creating a teleporter pad using off-mesh links

Repeat the procedure for the destination teleporter pad. For each teleporter, assign the object's transform to the **Start** field of the off-mesh link component. This indicates the selected teleporter as the start point. Then, for the **End** field, assign the destination transform. This establishes a connection between the two teleporters that creates a path between them. When the connection is established, a connection arrow should be drawn in-between the scene viewport when the **Navigation** panel is open and active in the editor, as shown in the following screenshot. You can also generate off-mesh links automatically. For more information, visit `https://www.youtube.com/watch?v=w3-sSozYph4`.

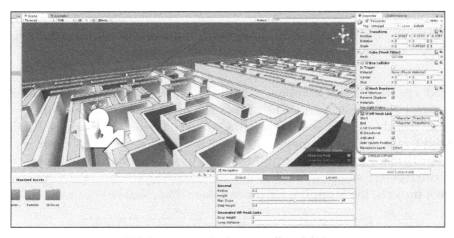

Defining a connection between off-mesh links

 The starting project for this chapter, ready for AI coding, can be found in the book's companion files (code bundle) in the `Start` folder of this chapter.

Starting an NPC agent

Now, let's create an AI agent for the level, something that can interact with the player. First, the agent needs a physical mesh representation in the scene. For this, I used the `Constructor` mesh, which is part of the Unity **Character Controllers** package imported earlier. Drag-and-drop this from the **Project** panel into the scene and then remove any animator component that might be created, as shown in the following screenshot. The animations will be important, but a custom-made animator controller will be created later.

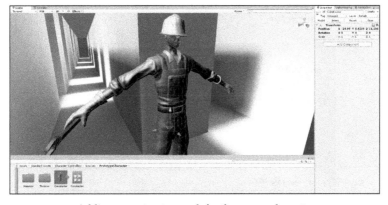

Adding a constructor mesh for the enemy character

Remember that we're not using the third-person controller prefab; it's just the constructor mesh alone.

Next, add a `NavMeshAgent` component to the object by navigating to **Component | Navigation | Nav Mesh Agent**. This allows the object to work with the navigation mesh, and it is able to find and travel paths when instructed. Set both the **Radius** and **Height** values of the component to match the dimensions of the mesh. Set the **Stopping Distance** to 2; this controls how close to a destination that the player should reach before stopping, as shown in the following screenshot. Of course, for your own projects, the **Stopping Distance** value will probably need to be edited.

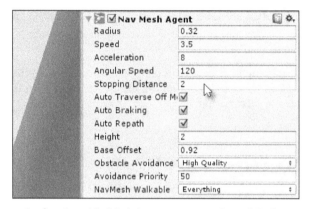

Configuring a NavMeshAgent component for pathfinding

Now, add a `Rigidbody` component and enable the **Is Kinematic** checkbox, as shown in the following screenshot. This allows the object to enter trigger volumes and be a part of the physics system by both causing and receiving physics events. However, with **Is Kinematic** checked, Unity will not override the object's transformation (position, rotation, and scale). This allows the `NavMeshAgent` exclusively to control the movement of the character.

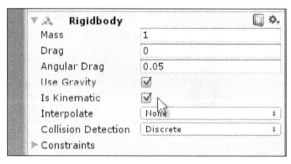

Configuring a Rigidbody component for physics

Now, add a `BoxCollider` component to the object and enable the **Is Trigger** checkbox to convert it into a trigger volume, that is, a volume that allows physical objects to pass through as opposed to blocking them. This will be used by the AI to approximate an agent's field of view or viewing area. It will follow the agent, and only other objects entering its field are classified as worthy of further consideration. To size the volume to the agent's field of view, use the **X**, **Y**, and **Z** size fields, as shown here:

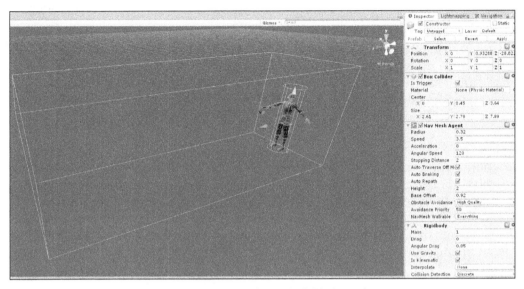

Using a BoxCollider component to configure the field of view for an enemy agent

Finally, create a new C# script file, `AI_Enemy.cs`, in the project to define the enemy intelligence. This script will encapsulate the complete AI for the enemy character and will be developed over the course of this chapter. Once the file is initially created, attach it to the enemy object in the scene. We're now ready to jump into the AI coding and graph building! We'll start by creating FSMs and their attendant states that specify how the enemy should behave.

Finite State Machines in Mecanim

From this point onwards, we'll concentrate mainly on coding AI for the enemy character both in C# and in terms of visual coding for a Mecanim graph. Mecanim refers to the Unity's Animation System (`http://docs.unity3d.com/Manual/MecanimAnimationSystem.html`). In the upcoming sections, we'll piece together a complete class that looks at and discusses specific sections of code, and the full class source code will be pieced together as we go along. It can be viewed in the completed project in the `AI_Enemy.cs` file.

To start, let's examine FSMs conceptually. When thinking about the enemy character, we can observe in them a specific set of behaviors. The enemy begins the scene by standing idle and then proceeds to wander around on patrol. During their patrol, they might see the player character. If they do so, they'll chase the player until the player comes into attack range. When the player enters attack range, they'll attack the player. Now, the only exception to these rules is if the enemy sustains serious health damage that brings them close to death. On reaching critical levels like this, the enemy will, instead of acting aggressively, flee and search for a health-restore potion until their health level is returned to normal.

In summarizing the enemy behavior sets like this, we've identified a number of discrete and critical states for enemy intelligence. These are idle, patrol, chase, attack, and flee. The enemy can be in one and only one of these states at any one time, and each state determines how the enemy will behave. To implement this logic, we can use an FSM design. This refers not to a specific class or object type (such as `MonoBehaviour` or `ScriptableObject`) but rather to a design pattern, a way of coding. An FSM begins with a finite set of states (idle, patrol, chase, and so on, as mentioned earlier) and then manages how the states are connected to one another logically. This determines when and how one state changes to another. The enemy for our situation here will depend, in fact, on two-state machines under the hood: one in C# code and the other in a Mecanim animator graph. The latter controls only the animation that should play for the enemy mesh during each state. Let's build the Mecanim graph first.

Right-click on the **Project** panel and create a new **Animator Controller** asset. Open the asset inside the **Animator** window that is accessible by selecting the **Animator** option in **Window** from the application main menu, as shown here:

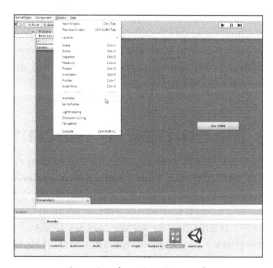

Accessing the animation graph

The Mecanim animator graph defines all the possible animation states for the mesh, and these should correspond to the enemy states already outlined, namely, idle, patrol, chase, attack, and flee. To configure the animations for these states, select the **Constructor** mesh asset in the **Project** panel and make all animations loopable by enabling the **Loop Time** and **Loop Pose** checkboxes in the Object Inspector, as shown in the following screenshot. This prevents the character animations from stopping after playing only once:

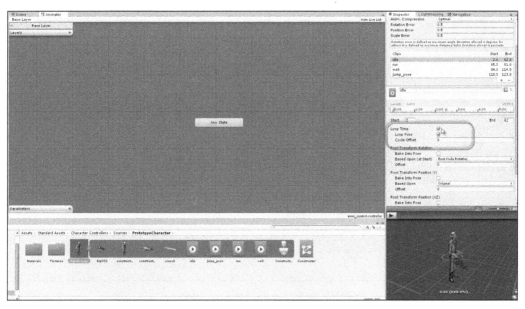

Preparation of animation assets for a Mecanim FSM

Now, let's add animation states to the graph, one animation per state. For the **Idle** state, the idle animation should play. For the **Patrol** state, the walk animation should play as the character should be walking around. For the **Chase** and **Flee** states, the run animation should play, and for the **Attack** state, the jump animation should play. The **Constructor** model lacks a dedicated animation for attacks, so (for this sample) the jump animation will suffice as an attack animation.

Go ahead and add these to the graph by dragging-and-dropping each animation from the **Project** panel into the Graph Editor, and name each state as appropriate, as shown here:

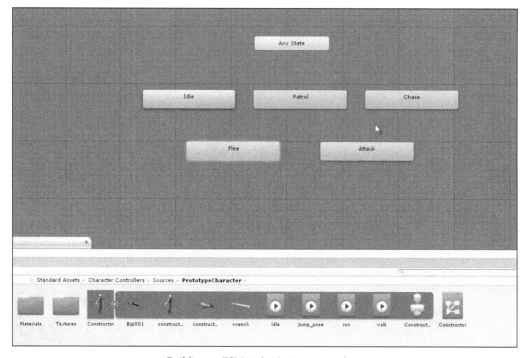

Building an FSM in the Animator window

In addition to the standard animation states added so far, let's add an additional empty state too. This will be the initial and default state of the enemy; this state plays no animation and represents, effectively, a stateless state until we explicitly put the enemy into a specific state at level startup. To create an empty and default state, right-click on the empty space inside the Graph Editor and choose the **Empty** option in **Create State** from the context menu (rename it appropriately to Start or Init), and then make it the default state by right-clicking on the state and choosing **Set As Default**, as shown here:

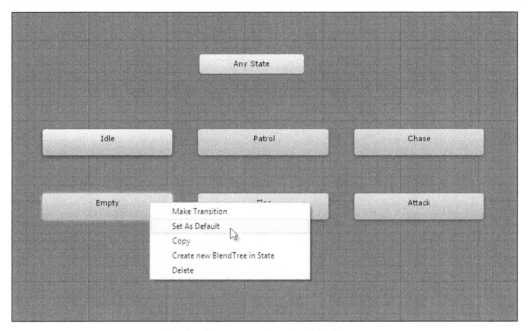

Setting the empty node as the default state

The graph now features one animation per state for the character, but the states are not connected; each state is isolated. Specifically, there's no logic that governs the conditions by which one state moves to another. To fix this, create five new triggers using the **Parameters** box in the bottom-left corner of the Mecanim window. A trigger variable is a special Boolean type that Unity will automatically reset to `false`; every time it's made `true`, it allows behaviors to be initiated once, such as state changes. The triggers, as we'll see, can be accessed in C# code.

For now, create five triggers: **Idle**, **Patrol**, **Chase**, **Attack**, and **SeekHealth**, as shown here:

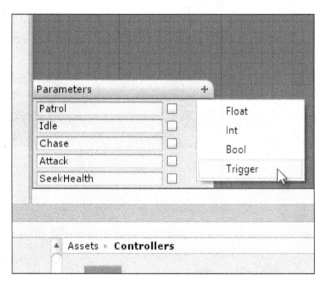

Creating a Trigger variable for each animation state

With both the states and triggers created, the connection between the states in the graph can now be defined more precisely. Specifically, the **Idle** state should change to the **Patrol** state when the trigger **Patrol** is activated, the **Patrol** to the **Chase** state when trigger **Chase** is activated, the **Chase** state to the **Attack** state when trigger **Attack** is activated, and so on. In addition, there's a two-way linkage between most states: **Patrol** can transition to **Chase** (such as when the enemy sees the player) and **Chase** can transition back to **Patrol** (when the enemy loses sight of the player).
To create connections between states, right-click on a state, select **Make Transition** from the context menu, and then click on the destination state to which a connection should be made.

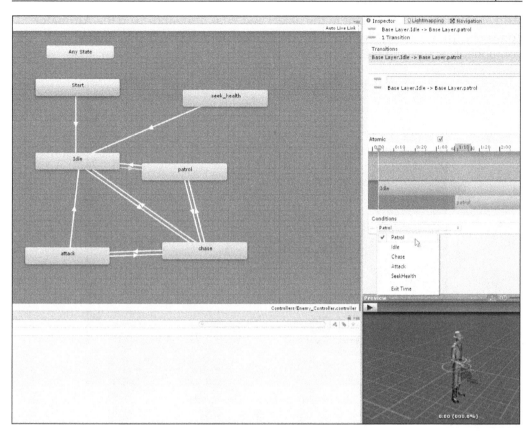

Setting the condition for a state transition

The graph now defines a complete animation state machine (FSM) for an enemy object. Attaching this to the enemy object in the scene is simple.

Add an **Animator** component to the object and then drag-and-drop the **Animator** controller from the **Project** panel into the **Controller** field on the **Animator** component, as shown here:

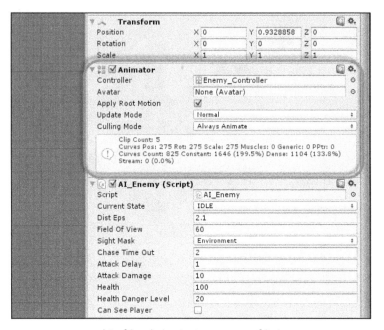

Attaching Animator to an enemy object

Finite State Machines in C# – getting started

Now that the FSM for animation is completed, we should turn our attention to an FSM in C# that governs the behavior of the enemy as well as initiates our triggers in the Mecanim graph to play the appropriate animations (walk and run) at the right time. To begin the implementation, add the following public enumeration to the top of the AI_Enemy.cs script file, as shown in the following code sample 7-1. This enumeration defines all the possible states in the FSM for the enemy, and each state is assigned its unique string hash code; that is, the IDLE state is assigned the value of 2081823275, which is the hash code for the string IDLE, and so on. This will be important later to work with Mecanim and specifically to initiate triggers. You can retrieve the hash code for a string using the StringToHash function of the Animator class, as shown here:

```
//Define possible states for enemy
public enum AI_ENEMY_STATE {IDLE = 2081823275,
                            PATROL=207038023,
                            CHASE= 1463555229,
                            ATTACK=1080829965,
                            SEEKHEALTH=-833380208};
```

 More information can be found online at http://docs.unity3d.com/ ScriptReference/Animator.StringToHash.html.

On the basis of the enumeration AI_ENEMY_STATE, the AI_Enemy class will maintain a public variable CurrentState, which expresses the active state of the enemy object right now. This variable will change over time as the states change, as shown in the following code:

```
//Current state of enemy
public AI_ENEMY_STATE CurrentState = AI_ENEMY_STATE.IDLE;
```

Like most objects, the class AI_Enemy features an Awake function to retrieve cached component references to other components, including the NavMeshAgent and the local Transform, as well as to other objects in the scene, such as the Player object. These references will be used elsewhere in the script, as shown in the following code sample 7-2:

```
//Get Animator
ThisAnimator = GetComponent<Animator>();

//Get Navigation Mesh Agent
ThisAgent = GetComponent<NavMeshAgent>();

//Get Transform Component
ThisTransform = transform;

//Get Player Transform
PlayerTransform =
GameObject.FindGameObjectWithTag("Player").transform;

//Get Collider
ThisCollider = GetComponent<BoxCollider>();
```

This code uses cached variables: ThisAnimator, ThisTransform, ThisAgent, and ThisCollider. This lets us retrieve immediate and direct references to attached components at level startup, which saves us from having to call C# property functions (get and set) every time we need access to an object. Thus, This.Transform carries a greater performance overhead than the optimized, cached variable, ThisTransform.

Each state in the FSM will be coded as a separate Coroutine, one Coroutine per state. The Coroutine will loop infinitely and exclusively as long as the state is active, defining all behaviors for the enemy in that state. The primary job of the state machine is to select and initiate the appropriate state under the correct conditions. Let's start by creating the Idle state—the default or normal state for the enemy.

Creating the Idle state

The enemy object begins in the Idle state (a "doing nothing" state), which is primarily transitional. In this state, the enemies stand where they are, playing the idle animation. The state is entered once at scene startup, but we'll also return to it when exiting some other states, as an intermediary step before moving onto a new state. Effectively, in this state, the enemy should always play the idle animation just once and then leave the state when the animation is completed. The enemy can further move to the Patrol state automatically, where they begin searching the scene for the player. This involves a two-step process. First, we'll need to start playing the idle animation as the Idle state begins. Second, we'll need to be notified when the idle animation has completed, to initiate a change to the Patrol state. Refer to the following code sample 7-3 for the Idle state:

```
01 //-----------------------------------------------
02 //This coroutine runs when object is in idle state
03 public IEnumerator State_Idle()
04 {
05     //Set current state
06     CurrentState = AI_ENEMY_STATE.IDLE;
07
08     //Activate idle state with Mecanim
09     ThisAnimator.SetTrigger((int) AI_ENEMY_STATE.IDLE);
10
11     //Stop nav mesh agent movement
12      ThisAgent.Stop();
13
14     //Loop forever while in idle state
15     while(CurrentState == AI_ENEMY_STATE.IDLE)
```

```
16          {
17                  //Check if we can see player
18                  if(CanSeePlayer)
19                  {
20                          // can see player?, chase to attack
21                          StartCoroutine(State_Chase());
22                          yield break;
23                  }
24
25                  //Wait for next frame
26                  yield return null;
27          }
28 }
29 //-------------------------------------------------------
```

The following are the comments for code sample 7-3:

- **Line 03**: `State_Idle` is coded as a Coroutine. For more information on Coroutines, see the online Unity documentation at `http://docs.unity3d.com/Manual/Coroutines.html`. In short, a Coroutine works like an asynchronous function (as a code block that runs in the background, parallel to other functions). For this reason, the infinite loop in line 15 will not cause a crash because a Coroutine runs like a separate thread. Coroutines always return type `IEnumerator` and always feature a yield statement somewhere within their body.

- **Line 09**: The animator `SetTrigger` function is called in this line; it passes the hash code for the string `Idle` as an argument to set the `Idle` trigger in the Mecanim graph, initiating a playback of the idle animation. This links the C# FSM to the Mecanim FSM. Notice that in line 12, the `Stop` function is called for the `NavMeshAgent` component to stop any movement that the object might have been performing. This is because while the idle animation is playing, the enemy should not be moving.

- **Line 15**: Here, the `State_Idle` function enters an infinite loop; that is, it'll loop frame by frame as long as the enemy is in an `Idle` state. While the `Idle` state is active, everything within the loop executes every frame that allows the object to update and change its behavior over time.

- **Line 18**: One exit condition for the `Idle` state, other than waiting for the idle animation to complete, is if the player is seen in the interim. Player visibility is determined by the Boolean variable `CanSeePlayer` (the details of line of sight are considered later). If `CanSeePlayer` is `true`, the `Chase` state is activated using the `StartCoroutine` function, and the `Idle` state is terminated with a call to yield break.

The `Idle` state, as implemented so far, loops infinitely and never changes to another state unless the player is seen. However, the `Idle` state should only be temporary; the idle animation should play once and then notify us of its completion. To achieve this playback notification, we can use Animation Events. To configure this, select the **Constructor** character mesh in the **Project** panel and open the **Animation** tab to examine the idle animation in the Object Inspector. From here, open the **Events** tab, as shown in the following screenshot:

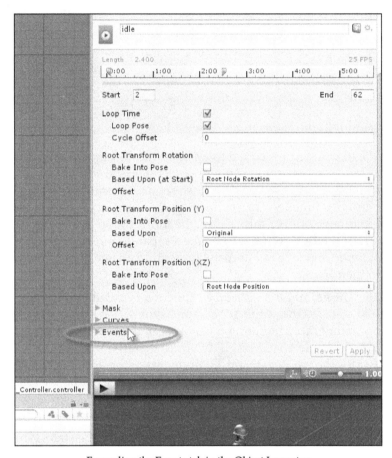

Expanding the Events tab in the Object Inspector

Then, double-click on the animation timeline at time **1** (at the end) to insert a function call at that time. This sends a message to the enemy object when the animation completes, as shown in the following screenshot. For this purpose, I've coded a method `OnIdleAnimCompleted` inside the `AI_Enemy` class:

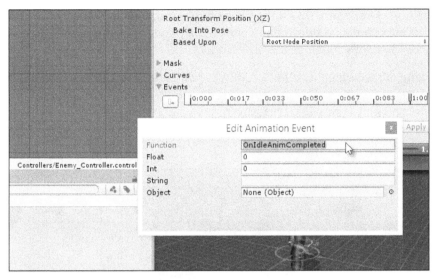

Calling a function at animation end

The function `OnIdleAnimCompleted` is called automatically by Unity when the idle animation completes. The following code sample 7-4 shows how this method is implemented:

```
//Event called when Idle animation is completed
public void OnIdleAnimCompleted()
{
    //Stop active Idle state
    StopAllCoroutines();
    StartCoroutine(State_Patrol());
}
```

Creating the Patrol state

In the `Patrol` state, the enemy should wander the environment and look for the player. This state can be entered from the `Idle` state, after the idle animation is completed, and also from the `Chase` state, if the enemy loses sight of the player during a chase. Patrol involves a looping logic. Specifically, the enemy should pick a random destination somewhere on the navigation mesh and then travel to that destination. When the destination is reached, the process should repeat and so on. The only condition that causes the enemy to leave this state is a sighting of the player, which demands a `Chase` state.

Though simple to explain, this state relies on two more complex issues: first, a random location must be selected and second, a player visibility check should be performed. First, let's consider the random location selection.

In the **Scene** tab, I created a collection of waypoints (empty game objects) that are tagged **Waypoint** and do nothing but mark locations on the NavMesh floor. Together, these represent all the possible locations to which an enemy could travel during a patrol. The enemy, therefore, needs to randomly select one of these destinations, as shown here:

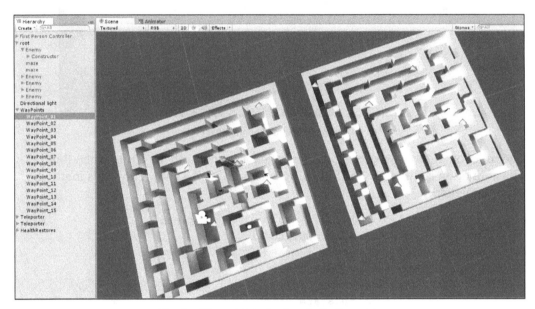

Creating Waypoint destinations in the Scene tab

To implement the destination selection for a Patrol state, the Awake function of AI_Enemy will first retrieve a list of all waypoints in the scene to be used later. We can do this using Linq, as shown in the following code sample 7-5. This example code retrieves a static array of all transforms for waypoints in the scene, in a private variable named Waypoints:

```
01 //Find all gameobjects with waypoint
02 GameObject[] Waypoints =
   GameObject.FindGameObjectsWithTag("Waypoint");
03
04 //Select all transform components from waypoints using Linq
05 WayPoints = (from GameObject GO in Waypoints
06                  select GO.transform).ToArray();
```

Having retrieved a list of all waypoints, the Patrol state can be coded, as shown in the following code sample 7-6, which regularly selects waypoints as move new targets:

```
01 //----------------------------------------------------
02 //This coroutine runs when object is in patrol state
03 public IEnumerator State_Patrol()
04 {
05 //Set current state
06 CurrentState = AI_ENEMY_STATE.PATROL;
07
08 //Set Patrol State
09 ThisAnimator.SetTrigger((int) AI_ENEMY_STATE.PATROL);
10
11 //Pick a random waypoint
12 Transform RandomDest = WayPoints[Random.Range(0,
   WayPoints.Length)];
13
14 //Go to destination
15 ThisAgent.SetDestination(RandomDest.position);
16
17 //Loop forever while in patrol state
18 while(CurrentState == AI_ENEMY_STATE.PATROL)
19 {
20         //Check if we can see player
21         if(CanSeePlayer)
22         {
23             //If we can see player, then chase to attack
24             StartCoroutine(State_Chase());
25             yield break;
26         }
27
28         //Check if we have reached destination
29         if(Vector3.Distance(ThisTransform.position,
           RandomDest.position) <= DistEps)

30         {
31             //Reached destination. Changed state back to Idle
32             StartCoroutine(State_Idle());
33             yield break;
34         }
35
36         //Wait for next frame
37         yield return null;
38 }
39 }
40 //----------------------------------------------------
```

The following are the comments for code sample 7-6:

- **Line 12**: Here, the Random.Range function selects a random destination from the Waypoints array. This is passed as a destination argument to the SetDestination function of the NavMeshAgent component that sends the enemy to the destination.

- **Line 28**: The function Vector3.Distance is used to determine whether the agent has reached the destination. This does not check for equality between the enemy position and destination position, because floating-point inaccuracy means we cannot guarantee that the two will ever be the same. Instead, it checks whether the enemy has come within a specified distance of the destination (DistEps), classifying that as having arrived.

- **Line 32**: If the destination is reached, the enemy would return to Idle. After waiting for one cycle of the idle animation, the enemy would again enter into the Patrol state.

- **Line 21**: Again, the Patrol state depends on whether the player is visible to the enemy. If so, they enter the Chase state.

The Boolean variable CanSeePlayer indicates, for any frame, whether the player is currently visible to the enemy. This variable is updated on each frame. The process for this begins inside the Update function, as shown in the following code sample 7-7:

```
01 void Update()
02 {
03 //Assume we cannot see player
04 CanSeePlayer = false;
05
06 //If player not inside bounds then exit
07 if(!ThisCollider.bounds.Contains(PlayerTransform.position)) return;

08
09 //Player is inside bounds, update line of sight
10 CanSeePlayer = HaveLineSightToPlayer(PlayerTransform);
11 }
```

The key question for the Update function is whether the player is inside the box collider attached to the enemy; this box collider represents the enemy's view or range. If the player is inside that box, the player could possibly be visible to the enemy. In this case, further checks are required to be sure. This is where the HaveLineSightToPlayer function is essential. This function returns a Boolean (true/false) value that indicates whether the player is visible to the enemy, as shown in the following code sample 7-8:

```
//Function to return whether player can be seen right now
private bool HaveLineSightToPlayer(Transform Player)
{
//Get angle between enemy sight and player
float Angle = Mathf.Abs(Vector3.Angle(ThisTransform.forward,
(Player.position-ThisTransform.position).normalized));


    //If angle is greater than field of view, we cannot see player
    if(Angle > FieldOfView) return false;

    //Check with raycast- make sure player is not on other side of
wall
    if(Physics.Linecast(ThisTransform.position, Player.position,
SightMask)) return false;

    //We can see player
    return true;
}
```

As we saw in the earlier chapters, visibility is determined by a two-stage process. First, the angle between the enemy look at vector and the normalized vector, which points from the enemy to the player, decides the visibility. If the angle is less than the enemy's field-of-view angle, then the player would be in front of the enemy and they would be seen, provided no obstacles, such as walls, lie between the enemy and the player. The second test, performed by `Physics.Linecast`, determines whether an unbroken line can be drawn between the enemy and the player. If it can, then no obstacle would exist between them and the player would be seen.

Creating the Chase state

If the player is seen by the enemy and is not within attacking distance, the enemy would run to attack the player. This state, in which the enemy runs towards the player with hostile intent, is the Chase state. There are two main exit conditions for this state. If the enemy reaches attacking distance, they should change from the Chase state to the Attack state. In contrast, if the player disappears from sight, the enemy should continue to chase as best as they can for a while and then give up the chase if, after an interval, the player still cannot be sighted. Refer to the following code sample 7-9:

```
01 //This coroutine runs when object is in chase state
02 public IEnumerator State_Chase()
03 {
04 //Set current state
```

```
05 CurrentState = AI_ENEMY_STATE.CHASE;
06
07 //Set Chase State
08 ThisAnimator.SetTrigger((int) AI_ENEMY_STATE.CHASE);
09
10 //Loop forever while in chase state
11 while(CurrentState == AI_ENEMY_STATE.CHASE)
12 {
13        //Set destination to player
14         ThisAgent.SetDestination(PlayerTransform.position);
15
16      //If we lose sight of player, keep chasing
17      if(!CanSeePlayer)
18      {
19             //Begin time out
20             float ElapsedTime = 0f;
21
22             //Continue to chase
23             while(true)
24             {
25                  //Increment time
26                  ElapsedTime += Time.deltaTime;
27
28                  //Set destination to player
29 ThisAgent.SetDestination( PlayerTransform.position);
30
31                  //Wait for next frame
32                  yield return null;
33
34                  //Has timeout expired?
35                  if(ElapsedTime >= ChaseTimeOut)
36                  {
37                       //If cannot see player, change to idle
38                       if(!CanSeePlayer)
39                       {
40                            //Change to idle
41                            StartCoroutine(State_Idle());
42                            yield break;
43                       }
44                       else
45                            break; //can see player again
46                  }
47             }
48      }
```

```
49
50          //If we have reached player then attack
51 if(Vector3.Distance(ThisTransform.position,
   PlayerTransform.position) <= DistEps)

52          {
53                  //We have reached distance, now attack
54                  StartCoroutine(State_Attack());
55                  yield break;
56          }
57
58          //Wait until next
59          yield return null;
60 }
61 }
```

The following are the comments for code sample 7-9:

- **Lines 17-48**: During this phase, the State loop determines that the player visibility has been lost. When this happens, the enemy will continue to chase the player for a period of ChaseTimeOut. After this time elapses, the enemy checks for player visibility again. If the player is sighted at that time, the chase resumes as it did earlier. Otherwise, the enemy changes to the Idle state, ready to begin a new patrol in search of the player again.

- **Lines 51-59**: Here, the Chase state checks whether the enemy has come within the attack range (DistEps). If so, the FSM would enter State_Attack.

Creating the Attack state

In the Attack state, the enemy continually attacks the player as long as they're visible. After an attack, the enemy must recover before launching a new attack. The only exit condition for this state is losing sight of the player. When this happens, the enemy returns to the Chase state and, from there, they either go back to the attack state or into Idle, depending on whether the player has been found, as shown in the following code sample 7-10:

```
//This coroutine runs when object is in attack state
 public IEnumerator State_Attack()
 {
    //Set current state
    CurrentState = AI_ENEMY_STATE.ATTACK;

    //Set Chase State
    ThisAnimator.SetTrigger((int) AI_ENEMY_STATE.ATTACK);
```

```
    //Stop nav mesh agent movement
    ThisAgent.Stop();

    //Set up timer for attack interval
    float ElapsedTime = 0f;

    //Loop forever while in attack state
    while(CurrentState == AI_ENEMY_STATE.ATTACK)
    {
        //Update timer
        ElapsedTime += Time.deltaTime;

        //Check if player has passed beyond the attack distance
if(!CanSeePlayer || Vector3.Distance(ThisTransform.position,
PlayerTransform.position) > DistEps)
            {
                //Change to chase
                StartCoroutine(State_Chase());
                yield break;
            }

            //Check attack delay
            if(ElapsedTime >= AttackDelay)
            {
                 //Reset counter
                 ElapsedTime = 0f;

                //Launch attack
                PlayerTransform.SendMessage("ChangeHealth",
-AttackDamage, SendMessageOptions.DontRequireReceiver);
            }

            //Wait until next frame
            yield return null;
    }
 }
```

Creating the Seek-Health (or flee) state

The `Seek-Health` state occurs when the enemy runs low on health and can restore it by collecting a medikit. This state is unlike most others, in that, it can be reached or entered from any state. The entering of this state doesn't depend on its relationship to others, but only on the player's health. Specifically, this state should be entered when the enemy's health is reduced beyond a minimum floor. As a result of this configuration, be sure to hook up the `Seek-Health` animation state in the Mecanim graph to the **Any State** node that allows the run animation to be triggered in any state, as shown here:

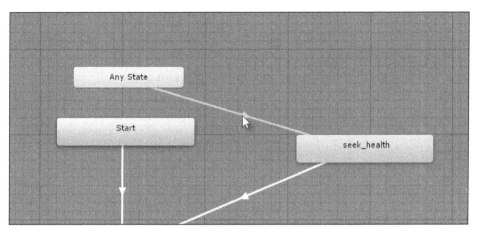

The Seek-Health state can be accessed from Any State

Each enemy maintains a `Health` variable; this variable is adjusted either up or down, depending on whether the enemy finds a medikit or is attacked. The change occurs inside the method `ChangeHealth`, and this is where we can determine whether a `SeekHealth` state must be initiated. The `ChangeHealth` function is public; it allows `SendMessage` and `BroadcastMessage` to trigger it as an event, if required, as shown in the following code sample 7-11:

```
//Event called health changed
 public void ChangeHealth(float Amount)
 {
    //Reduce health
    Health += Amount;

    //Should we die?
    if(Health <= 0)
```

```
        {
            StopAllCoroutines();
            Destroy(gameObject);
            return;
        }

        //Check health danger level
        if(Health > HealthDangerLevel) return;

        //Health is less than or equal to danger level, now seek
    health restores, if available
        StopAllCoroutines();
        StartCoroutine(State_SeekHealth());
    }
```

The `State_SeekHealth` method can be coded, as shown in the following code sample 7-12:

```
01 //This coroutine runs when object is in seek health state
02 public IEnumerator State_SeekHealth()
03 {
04 //Set current state
05 CurrentState = AI_ENEMY_STATE.SEEKHEALTH;
06
07 //Set Chase State
08 ThisAnimator.SetTrigger((int) AI_ENEMY_STATE.SEEKHEALTH);
09
10 //This is the nearest health restore
11 HealthRestore HR = null;
12
13 //Loop forever while in seek health state
14 while(CurrentState == AI_ENEMY_STATE.SEEKHEALTH)
15 {
16        //If health restore is not valid, then get nearest
17        if(HR == null) HR = GetNearestHealthRestore(ThisTransform);
18
19        //There is an active health restore, so move there
20        ThisAgent.SetDestination(HR.transform.position);
21
22        //If HR is null, then no more health restore, go to idle
23        if(HR == null || Health > HealthDangerLevel)
24        {
25               //Change to idle
26               StartCoroutine(State_Idle());
27               yield break;
```

```
28        }
29
30        //Wait until next frame
31        yield return null;
32 }
33 }
```

The following are the comments for code sample 7-12:

- **Line 17**: The `Health-Seek` state begins by finding the nearest medikit in the scene and uses it for the agent destination. This is, in a sense, cheating, because (of course) without remote viewing powers, the enemy should not be able to know where the nearest medikit is. However, remember that what matters is not what the enemy really knows but how it appears to the gamer. If the gamer doesn't know about this logic and cannot learn about it from appearances, then it would be of no significance. Also note that it's possible for the player or another enemy to collect the medikit before the enemy arrives at the destination. For this reason, on each frame, the enemy must determine whether the destination medikit is still valid, and if not, they must pick the next, nearest one.

- **Line 23**: If there is no medikit available or the health has been restored to safe limits, the enemy would return to the `Idle` state.

The `SeekHealth` state demands that we find and retrieve a reference to the nearest medikit in the scene. This is achieved using a `GetNearestHealthRestore` method, as shown in the following code sample 7-13:

```
01 //Function to get nearest health restore to Target in scene
02 private HealthRestore GetNearestHealthRestore(Transform Target)
03 {
04 //Get all health restores
05 HealthRestore[] Restores =
Object.FindObjectsOfType<HealthRestore>();

06
07 //Nearest
08 float DistanceToNearest = Mathf.Infinity;
09
10 //Selected Health Restore
11 HealthRestore Nearest = null;
12
13 //Loop through all health restores
14 foreach(HealthRestore HR in Restores)
15 {
16         //Get distance to this health restore
```

```
17 float CurrentDistance = Vector3.Distance(Target.position,
   HR.transform.position);

18
19      //Found nearer health restore, so update
20      if(CurrentDistance <= DistanceToNearest)
21      {
22          Nearest = HR;
23          DistanceToNearest = CurrentDistance;
24      }
25 }
26
27 //Return nearest or null
28 return Nearest;
29 }
```

Summary

The complete AI project created in this chapter can be found in the book's companion files (code bundle) in the `ai` folder of this chapter. I recommend that you open it and then test it out. Using the first-person controller, the player can navigate the level, avoid enemies, and also attack when enemies are in range using the Space bar, as shown here:

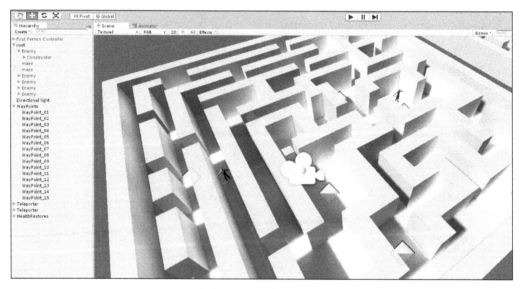

Testing the AI_Enemy class

There are, nonetheless, many ways in which the project can be improved further, for example, by adding multiple enemy types as well as varied strategies for each type, from taking cover to playing dead, and so on. However, nonetheless, we've come a long way and have developed Artificial Intelligence that relies on both a C# FSM as well as on a Mecanim FSM for animation playback.

In the next chapter, we'll leap out of the world of AI and into the world of editor customization to make game development smoother!

8
Customizing the Unity Editor

The Unity Editor is a powerful, general purpose game development tool. Nevertheless, there are times during development when you probably wished the editor offered a specific feature that it doesn't have or behaved in a particular way, simply because it would be more convenient for you and your specific game. Maybe you'd like the path editing features, batch renaming functionality, or mesh creation tools, among others. In such cases, you can search the Asset Store for add-ons that meet your needs. But even then, you may still not find what you need. Consequently, the focus then turns to how the editor can be adapted or customized to achieve your purpose. Thankfully, there are many ways Unity can be changed as a tool, and this chapter focuses on particular case studies. First, it explores how to create a **Batch Rename** tool for renaming multiple selected objects in one operation. Second, it covers how to create a color range field in the Object Inspector to blend between two colors using a slider. Third, it explores how to expose public C# properties in the Object Inspector for both setting and getting values. Lastly, it covers how to use C# attributes to create a localization toolkit that allows you to automatically change all in-game strings to a chosen language (English, French, and so on) at the touch of a button.

Batch renaming

When creating scenes with multiple enemies, power-ups, props, or other object instances, you'll typically use the duplicate feature to clone objects (*Ctrl* + *D*). This leads to many objects sharing the same name. Now, while there's nothing technically wrong in name duplication per se, it's both inconvenient and untidy. It results in a hierarchy panel of many identically named objects, and it's practically impossible to distinguish between specific objects by their name alone. Furthermore, object searches in script using the `GameObject.Find` function cannot be relied on to retrieve the specific object that you need, since it could return any one of the identically named objects. The solution, then, is to name each object uniquely and appropriately. But doing this can be tedious, especially if you're working with many objects. Thus, there's a need for a Batch Rename tool.

This would, in theory, allow you to select multiple objects in the hierarchy panel and then to rename them automatically according to a numbered convention. The only technical problem with this is that Unity doesn't natively support such a feature. But we can code it ourselves, as shown in the following screenshot:

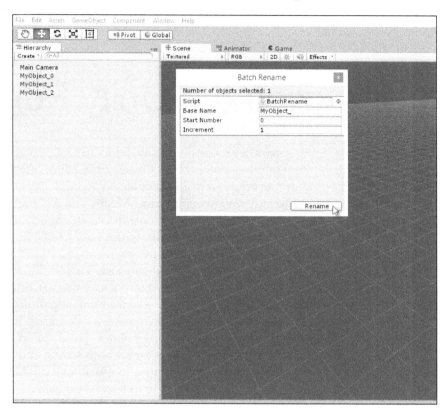

Creating a Batch Rename editor add-on

To begin customizing the Unity Editor, first create a folder named `Editor` inside the project. This is important. `Editor` is a special folder recognized by Unity as a place to house all the editor customizing scripts. Thus, if you plan on changing the Unity Editor, be sure all customizing scripts are inside the `Editor` folder. It doesn't matter whether your project features multiple folders named `Editor`; the only thing that matters is that there's at least one `Editor` folder and an editor script inside it, as shown here:

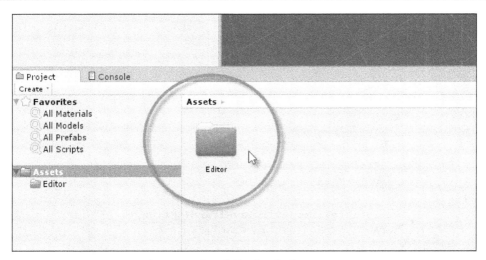

Create an Editor folder for all editor scripts

Next, we'll create a Batch Rename utility from the `ScriptableWizard` class. This class is an ancestor from which we derive new classes. All derived classes will work much like a pop-up utility dialog that can be launched from the Unity main menu. Their purpose is to present a set of options from which the user can choose before pressing a confirmation button that performs a one-time process. In other words, classes derived from `ScriptableWizard` are ideal for performing automated, one-time operations on single or multiple objects.

 More information on the `ScriptableWizard` class can be found in the online Unity documentation at `http://docs.unity3d.com/ ScriptReference/ScriptableWizard.html`.

The following code sample 8-1 lists the complete source code for a Batch Rename utility:

```
01 //------------------------------------
02 using UnityEngine;
03 using UnityEditor;
04 using System.Collections;
05 //------------------------------------
06 public class BatchRename : ScriptableWizard
07 {
```

```
08 //Base name
09 public string BaseName = "MyObject_";
10
11 //Start Count
12 public int StartNumber = 0;
13
14 //Increment
15 public int Increment = 1;
16
17 [MenuItem("Edit/Batch Rename...")]
18     static void CreateWizard()
19     {
20         ScriptableWizard.DisplayWizard("Batch
           Rename",typeof(BatchRename),"Rename");
21     }
22 //----------------------------------
23 //Called when the window first appears
24 void OnEnable()
25 {
26     UpdateSelectionHelper();
27 }
28 //----------------------------------
29 //Function called when selection changes in scene
30 void OnSelectionChange()
31 {
32     UpdateSelectionHelper();
33 }
34 //----------------------------------
35 //Update selection counter
36 void UpdateSelectionHelper()
37 {
38     helpString = "";
39
40     if (Selection.objects != null)
41 helpString = "Number of objects selected: " +
   Selection.objects.Length;
42 }
43 //----------------------------------
44 //Rename
45 void OnWizardCreate()
```

```
46 {
47          //If selection empty, then exit
48          if (Selection.objects == null)
49                  return;
50
51          //Current Increment
52          int PostFix = StartNumber;
53
54          //Cycle and rename
55          foreach(Object O in Selection.objects)
56          {
57                  O.name = BaseName + PostFix;
58                  PostFix += Increment;
59          }
60 }
61 //------------------------------------
62 }
63 //------------------------------------
```

The following are the comments for code sample 8-1:

- **Line 03**: The editor extensions should include the `UnityEditor` namespace that allows you to access editor classes and objects.

- **Line 06**: The `BatchRename` class derives not from `MonoBehaviour`, as with most script files, but from `ScriptableWizard`. Classes deriving from here will be treated by Unity like independent utilities that may be launched from the application menu.

- **Lines 17-21**: The `MenuItem` attribute is prefixed to the `CreateWizard` function. This creates a menu entry in the application menu listed under **Edit/Batch Rename** and invokes the `CreateWizard` function when clicked on to display the **Batch Rename** window.

- **Lines 8-16**: After `CreateWizard` is invoked, the `BatchRename` window shows. From here, all public class members (including **Base Name**, **Start Number**, and **Increment**) will automatically feature in the window as editable fields for the user.

- **Lines 45-60**: The OnWizardCreate function is invoked as an event when the user presses the **Rename** button from the **Batch Rename** window. The button is called **Rename** in this case because of line 20. The OnWizardCreate function iterates through all selected objects in the scene, if any, and renames them in sequence according to the **Base Name**, **Start Number**, and **Increment** fields, as shown here:

The Batch Rename tool

To use the Batch Rename tool, just select a group of objects in the scene and then click on the **Batch Rename** option in **Edit** from the application menu. The **Base Name** field defines a string that needs to be prefixed to all object names, and the **Increment** field defines the amount by which an integer counter should increase that is prefixed to the base name. The **Start Number** value is the point from which all incrementing begins, as shown in the following screenshot:

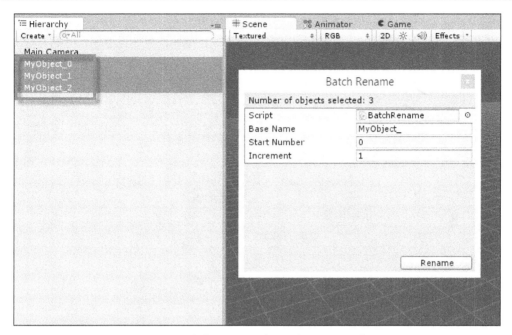

Renamed objects using the Batch Rename tool

C# attributes and reflection

From this point forward in the chapter, all editor extensions will rely heavily on the concepts of attributes and reflection. These concepts are not specific to Unity but refer to more general ideas in computer science, programming, and to their application in languages such as C# as well as in the .NET framework. Before proceeding to the next editor extension, let's consider attributes and the related concept of reflection using the example of the Range attribute, which is native to Unity. Consider the following line of code:

```
public float MyNumber = 0;
```

This public variable will be displayed in the Object Inspector with an edit field that allows the user to type in any valid floating point number thereby setting the value of MyNumber, as shown in the following screenshot:

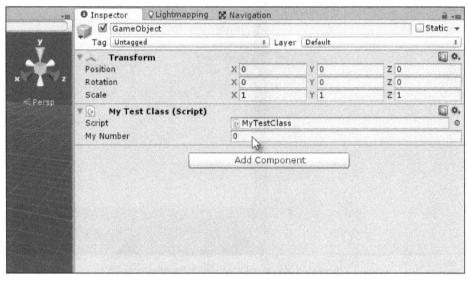

Entering in floating point values from the Object Inspector

This code works fine and is suitable in many cases, but there are times when it's preferable to validate the numerical entry to within a range, clipping the numbers between a minimum and maximum. You can do this in the code using the Mathf.Clamp function but you can also validate the entry using an attribute. You can attach a Range attribute to the floating point variable (MyNumber) to display a slider instead of an edit box, as shown in the following code:

```
[Range(0f,1f)]
public float MyNumber = 0;
```

> More information on attributes can be found in the online Unity documentation at http://unity3d.com/learn/tutorials/ modules/intermediate/scripting/attributes.

When this code is compiled, the MyNumber variable displays differently in the Object Inspector, honoring the numerical range between 0 and 1, as shown in the following screenshot. Notice that all numbers provided to the Range attribute as arguments must be explicit values known at compile time and not expressions, which depend on variables that can vary at runtime. All attribute values must be known at compile time.

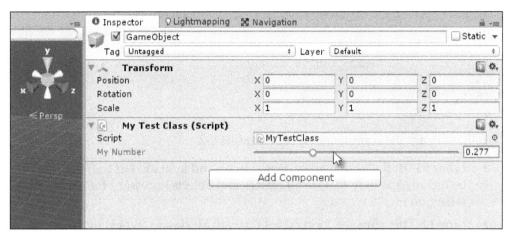

Using attributes to customize inspector display

So how do attributes work? In short, attributes are a form of metadata; they work like tags. Programmers can attach an attribute to a class, variable, or a method to associate data with it, which is known to the compiler. The attribute itself is entirely descriptive because it does nothing; it's simply data. The importance of attributes arises because all the code based on .NET (or Mono) has the ability to step outside itself and become self-conscious, that is, the ability to look at all the classes and data types and instances contained inside the program. For each object in the program, its metadata (attributes) can be queried and examined. This ability of a program to "look at itself from the outside" is known as reflection as it's like looking in a mirror. Of course, the program does not see itself in reverse or in distorted terms but rather as it truly is, including all its metadata. To give a quick example of reflection, try out the following code sample 8-2. This code will cycle through all the custom-made classes in your Unity application across all source files. Notice it doesn't just list all the instances of classes in the scene but all classes themselves (that is, the blueprints, metaphorically speaking):

```
01 using UnityEngine;
02 using System.Collections;
03 using System.Reflection;
04 using System;
05
06 public class MyTestScript : MonoBehaviour
07 {
08 // Use this for initialization
09 void Start ()
10 {
11        //List all classes in assembly
```

```
12 foreach(Type t in Assembly.GetExecutingAssembly().GetTypes())

13              {
14                      Debug.Log (t.Name);
15              }
16 }
17 }
```

The following are the comments for code sample 8-2:

- **Lines 03-04**: Both the namespaces System and System.Reflection should be included as they feature all classes and objects necessary for performing reflection in .NET.

- **Line 12**: This foreach loop cycles through all classes (types) in the active assembly (that is, the compiled code, including all your custom made script files).

You can take the concept of reflection even further. For example, having listed all types from code sample 8-2, you can even list the methods, properties, and variables (Fields) for a type. Refer to the following code sample 8-3 that, given a specific type as an argument, will list all its public member variables:

```
//Function to list all public variables for class t
public void ListAllPublicVariables(Type t)
{
    //Loop through all public variables
    foreach(FieldInfo FI in t.GetFields(BindingFlags.Public |
BindingFlags.Instance)
    {
        //Print name of variable
        Debug.Log (FI.Name);
    }
}
```

 More information on bitwise operations, as used in this code sample, can be found online at http://www.blackwasp.co.uk/ CSharpLogicalBitwiseOps.aspx.

Most crucially, however, you can list the attributes assigned to a type too. This lets you query a type for its metadata and examine its properties at runtime as shown in the following code sample 8-4:

```
01 public void ListAllAttributes(Type t)
02 {
03 foreach(Attribute attr in t.GetCustomAttributes(true))
04 {
05         //List the type of attribute found
06         Debug.Log (attr.GetType());
07 }
08 }
```

The code sample 8-4 demonstrates that all attribute data can be retrieved for a given data type in the code at runtime. This means data types and variables may have metadata associated with them, which can be retrieved and used to further influence how the objects should be handled. This is powerful for editor plugins because by creating our own custom-defined attributes that can be attached to data types and member variables, we can integrate our code with the Unity Editor without making its logical or runtime structure invalid. That is, we can tag variables in code with attributes to customize how they appear in the Unity Editor without invalidating or affecting it in terms of its logic or structure at runtime. Next, we'll see how to create custom attributes to customize the editor.

Color blending

The Range attribute explored previously may be attached to integer and floating-point variables, by way of their declarations, to limit the accepted values for them between a minimum and maximum in the Unity Editor. In the Unity Editor, a slider control is substituted for an editable field that controls the accepted values for the variable. This does not, of course, affect the values assigned to the same variables in the code. In the code, at runtime, the Range attribute has no effect itself. Rather, the Range attribute simply controls how numerical public variables are presented in the Object Inspector, and how they are entered there via user input. Behind the scenes, an Editor class is querying object Attribute data through reflection to control how the data type is rendered in the Object Inspector.

The Range attribute works well for numbers. But it'd be great to deploy similar behavior for other data types besides just numbers. For example, it's common to fade between different colors, such as fading from black to transparency to create fade-in and fade-out effects for scene transitions. This is known as Color Lerping (linear interpolation). That is, an intermediary color is generated between two extremes using a normalized float (between 0 and 1).

An appropriate `Inspector` property for this data type would be a slider control as with the `Range` attribute, which controls the interpolated color between 0 and 1, as shown here:

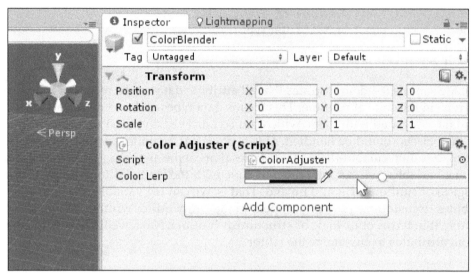

Lerping between two colors

In essence then, we need to customize the editor such that whenever an object is selected in the scene, which has a public member of a custom type we specify, we'll want to customize how the member is rendered inside the Object Inspector. This lets us present custom controls and inputs in the Object Inspector, which validates data entry for that member as opposed to simply accepting its defaults. To begin this process, let's create a custom class and define all data for a total color blend. A color blend requires four variables, namely the `SourceColor` and `DestColor` marking the limits of the blend. Next, the `BlendFactor` is a normalized float between 0 and 1 (start and end) which determines which intermediary color should be generated through Lerping. And then, finally, the output color itself (`BlendedColor`). The complete class definition for this process is included in the following code sample 8-5:

```
[System.Serializable]
public class ColorBlend : System.Object
{
    public Color SourceColor = Color.white;
    public Color DestColor = Color.white;
    public Color BlendedColor = Color.white;
    public float BlendFactor = 0f;
}
```

As the `ColorBlend` class uses the `[System.Serializable]` attribute, Unity will automatically render the class and its members inside the Object Inspector when it's added as a public member of a class. By default, all public members of `ColorBlend` will be rendered, and the `BlendFactor` field will be rendered as an editable field inside which numbers can be directly entered, including numbers outside 0 and 1, as shown here:

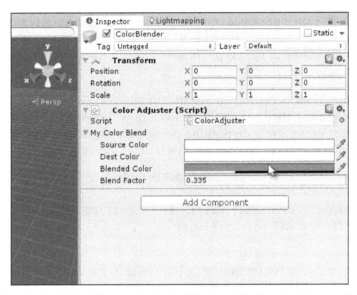

Exposing the Color Adjuster class by its defaults and by changing its properties

Let's now start customizing how Unity should render this class inside the Object Inspector. Begin by creating a new attribute class called `ColorRangeAttribute`, as shown in the following code sample 8-6:

```
01 public class ColorRangeAttribute : PropertyAttribute
02 {
03 //-------------------------------------------------------------
04 public Color Min;
05 public Color Max;
06 //-------------------------------------------------------------
07 public ColorRangeAttribute(float r1, float g1, float b1, float a1,
08                            float r2, float g2, float b2, float a2)
09 {
10       this.Min = new Color(r1, g1, b1, a1);
11       this.Max = new Color(r2, g2, b2, a2);
12 }
13 //-------------------------------------------------------------
14 }
```

The following are the comments for code sample 8-6:

- **Line 01**: The `ColorRangeAttribute` class defines a metadata structure that we can tag to other data types. Notice that it derives from `PropertyAttribute`. This signifies, above everything else, that `ColorRangeAttribute` is an attribute and metadata structure but not a regular class. It's not supposed to be instantiated as a standard class is.

- **Line 07**: The attribute has a constructor function that accepts eight floating-point values defining the RGBA channels for the source and destination colors of the Lerp. These will be used soon when attaching the attribute to a variable.

Now, we'll write a class declaring an instance of `ColorBlend` with the `ColorRangeAttribute` attribute attached. Even now, however, the addition of `ColorRangeAttribute` will do nothing per se because no `Editor` class has yet been written to handle it. We can see this in the following code:

```
public class ColorAdjuster : MonoBehaviour
{
    [ColorRangeAttribute(1f,0f,0f,0f,   0f,1f,0f,1f)]
    public ColorBlend MyColorBlend;
}
```

Creating an `Editor` class for rendering `ColorBlend` in the Object Inspector with a slider control involves handling the `ColorRangeAttribute` class. Specifically, Unity offers us the extension `PropertyDrawer` base class from which we can derive new classes to override the Object Inspector rendering for any specific attribute we add to our variables. In short, the `PropertyDrawer` class lets us customize inspector drawing for any and all variables tagged with a common attribute. Therefore, inside the `Editor` folder of your project, create a new `ColorRangeDrawer` class, as shown in the following code sample 8-7:

```
01 using UnityEngine;
02 using UnityEditor; //Be sure to include UnityEditor for all
   extension classes
03 using System.Collections;
04 //---------------------------------------------------------------
05 //CustomPropertyDrawer attribute for overriding drawing of all
   ColorRangeAttribute members

06 [CustomPropertyDrawer(typeof(ColorRangeAttribute))]
```

```
07 public class ColorRangeDrawer : PropertyDrawer
08 {
09 //-------------------------------------------------------------
10 //Event called by Unity Editor for updating GUI drawing of controls

11 public override void OnGUI (Rect position, SerializedProperty
   property, GUIContent label)

12 {
13        //Get color range attribute meta data
14 ColorRangeAttribute range  = attribute as ColorRangeAttribute;
15
16        //Add label to inspector
17 position = EditorGUI.PrefixLabel (position, new GUIContent
   ("Color Lerp"));
18
19        //Define sizes for color rect and slider controls
20 Rect ColorSamplerRect = new Rect(position.x, position.y, 100,
   position.height);

21 Rect SliderRect = new Rect(position.x+105, position.y, 200,
   position.height);
22
23       //Show color rect control
24 EditorGUI.ColorField(ColorSamplerRect,
   property.FindPropertyRelative("BlendedColor").colorValue);
25
26       //Show slider control
27 property.FindPropertyRelative("BlendFactor").floatValue =
   EditorGUI.Slider(SliderRect,
   property.FindPropertyRelative("BlendFactor").floatValue, 0f, 1f);
28
29       //Update blended color based on slider
30 property.FindPropertyRelative("BlendedColor").colorValue =
   Color.Lerp(range.Min, range.Max,
   property.FindPropertyRelative("BlendFactor").floatValue);
31 }
32 //-------------------------------------------------------------
33 }
34 //-------------------------------------------------------------
```

The following are the comments for code sample 8-7:

- **Line 01**: The `CustomPropertyDrawer` attribute is used here to associate the `PropertyDrawer` class with the `ColorRangeAttribute` attribute. The Unity Editor uses this metadata internally to determine which types require custom rendering in the Object Inspector. In this case, all members with `ColorRangeAttribute` will be drawn manually by the `OnGUI` function of the `PropertyDrawer` class.

- **Line 11**: The `OnGUI` function is overridden from the base class to define how all fields with `ColorRangeAttribute` should be rendered in the Object Inspector. `EditorGUI` is a native Unity Editor utility class for drawing GUI elements, such as buttons, textboxes, and sliders. For more information on `EditorGUI`, see the online documentation at `http://docs.unity3d.com/ScriptReference/EditorGUI.html`.

- **Line 14**: The `OnGUI` function is called once, perhaps many times per second, for each unique member to render manually in the Object Inspector. The attribute data for `ColorRangeAttribute` is retrieved here with typecasting, and this gives us access directly to all its members for the current object being rendered. To access the member variables of the object itself (for read/write access), as opposed to its attribute, the `SerializedProperty` argument should be used, such as the `FindPropertyRelative` method. For more information, see the online Unity documentation at `http://docs.unity3d.com/ScriptReference/SerializedProperty.html`.

- **Line 24**: From here onwards, the `FindPropertyRelative` function is called to retrieve public member variables, such as the `SourceColor`, `DestColor`, and `BlendedColor` in the selected object. This is where the values are actually set by moving the slider component.

 More information on the `PropertyDrawer` class can be found in the online Unity documentation at `http://docs.unity3d.com/Manual/editor-PropertyDrawers.html`.

The code sample 8-7 overrides the Object Inspector drawing for any `ColorBlend` instances when tagged with the `ColorRangeAttribute` attribute. This offers an accessible and easy-to-use way of creating blended colors. Remember, you can make your source and destination colors public, in order to be accessible from the **Inspector** tab, as shown here:

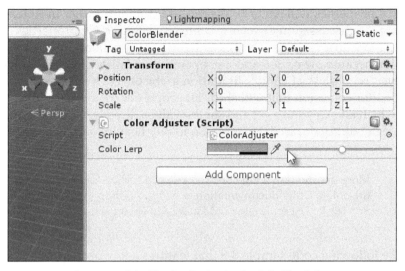

Creating a ColorBlender display for the ColorBlend class

Property exposing

By default, the Object Inspector displays all public member variables of a class unless it's in **Debug** mode or a private member is explicitly marked with the `SerializeField` attribute and in these cases private member variables will be shown too:

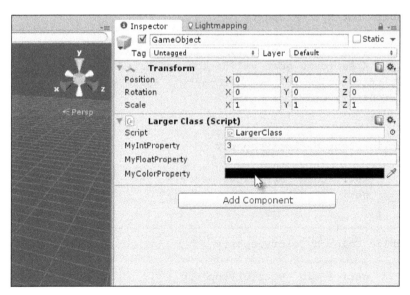

Property accessing from the Object Inspector

However, C# properties will never be displayed by default, either in **Release** or **Debug** mode. As discussed in *Chapter 1, Unity C# Refresher*, C# properties act like accessor functions to a variable. They essentially permit validation on each `get` and `set` operation because every `get` and `set` operation entails an internal function call. However, regardless of Unity's limitation in the Object Inspector, it's possible to write an editor extension that will show all properties for a class in the Object Inspector, which allows you to get and set the values directly. This section considers how in more detail. Again, we'll have reason to rely heavily on reflection.

> More information on the `SerializeField` class can be found in the online Unity documentation at `http://docs.unity3d.com/ScriptReference/SerializeField.html`.

Consider the following code sample 8-8 that features a few properties:

```csharp
//-----------------------------------------------
using UnityEngine;
using System.Collections;
//-----------------------------------------------
[System.Serializable]
public class ClassWithProperties : System.Object
{
    //Class with some properties
    //-------------------------------------------
    public int MyIntProperty
    {
        get{return _myIntProperty;}
        //Performs some validation on values
    set{if(value <= 10)_myIntProperty = value;else
_myIntProperty=0;}
    }
    //-------------------------------------------
    public float MyFloatProperty
    {
        get{return _myFloatProperty;}
        set{_myFloatProperty = value;}
    }
    //-------------------------------------------
    public Color MyColorProperty
    {
        get{return _myColorProperty;}
        set{_myColorProperty = value;}
```

```
        }
        //------------------------------------------------
        //Private members
        private int _myIntProperty;
        private float _myFloatProperty;
        private Color _myColorProperty;
        //------------------------------------------------
}
//------------------------------------------------
```

This class will be used internally by a different class as a public member, as shown in the following code sample 8-9:

```
using UnityEngine;
using System.Collections;

public class LargerClass : MonoBehaviour
{
    public ClassWithProperties MyPropClass;
}
```

By default, the public `MyPropClass` member (although tagged as `System. Serializable`) will not show its members in the Object Inspector. This is because C# properties are not natively supported:

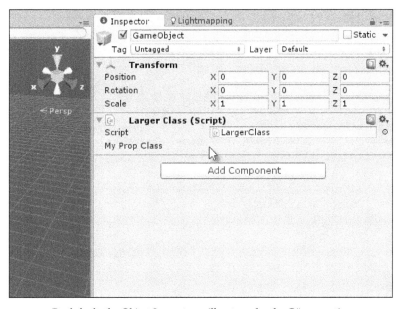

By default, the Object Inspector will not render the C# properties

To solve this issue, we can return to the `PropertyDrawer` class; this time associating the class with a specific class rather than an attribute, as shown in the following code sample 8-10:

```
01 //Custom Editor class to expose global properties of a class
02 //------------------------------------------------
03 using UnityEngine;
04 using UnityEditor;
05 using System.Collections;
06 using System.Reflection;
07 //------------------------------------------------
08 [CustomPropertyDrawer(typeof(ClassWithProperties))]
09 public class PropertyLister : PropertyDrawer
10 {
11 //Height of inspector panel
12 float InspectorHeight = 0;
13
14 //Height of single row in pixels
15 float RowHeight = 15;
16
17 //Spacing between rows
18 float RowSpacing = 5;
19
20 // Draw the property inside the given rect
21 public override void OnGUI(Rect position, SerializedProperty
   property, GUIContent label)
22 {
23          EditorGUI.BeginProperty(position, label, property);
24
25          //Get referenced object
26          object o = property.serializedObject.targetObject;
27 ClassWithProperties CP =
   o.GetType().GetField(property.name).GetValue(o) as
   ClassWithProperties;
28
29          int indent = EditorGUI.indentLevel;
30          EditorGUI.indentLevel = 0;
31
32          //Layout
33 Rect LayoutRect = new Rect(position.x, position.y,
   position.width, RowHeight);
34
35          //Find all properties for object
```

```
36 foreach(var prop in
   typeof(ClassWithProperties).GetProperties(BindingFlags.Public |
   BindingFlags.Instance))
37       {
38               //If integer property
39               if(prop.PropertyType.Equals(typeof(int)))
40               {
41 prop.SetValue(CP, EditorGUI.IntField(LayoutRect, prop.Name,
   (int)prop.GetValue(CP,null)), null);

42 LayoutRect = new Rect(LayoutRect.x, LayoutRect.y +
   RowHeight+RowSpacing, LayoutRect.width, RowHeight);
43               }
44
45               //If float property
46               if(prop.PropertyType.Equals(typeof(float)))
47               {
48 prop.SetValue(CP, EditorGUI.FloatField(LayoutRect, prop.Name,
   (float)prop.GetValue(CP,null)), null);

49 LayoutRect = new Rect(LayoutRect.x, LayoutRect.y +
   RowHeight+RowSpacing, LayoutRect.width, RowHeight);
50               }
51
52               //If color property
53                if(prop.PropertyType.Equals(typeof(Color)))
54               {
55 prop.SetValue(CP, EditorGUI.ColorField(LayoutRect, prop.Name,
   (Color)prop.GetValue(CP,null)), null);

56 LayoutRect = new Rect(LayoutRect.x, LayoutRect.y +
   RowHeight+RowSpacing, LayoutRect.width, RowHeight);
57               }
58          }
59
60       //Update inspector height
61       InspectorHeight = LayoutRect.y-position.y;
62
63       EditorGUI.indentLevel = indent;
64       EditorGUI.EndProperty();
65 }
```

```
66 //------------------------------------------------
67 //This function returns how high (in pixels) the field should be
68 //This is to make controls not overlap
69 public override float GetPropertyHeight (SerializedProperty
   property, GUIContent label)
70 {
71         return InspectorHeight;
72 }
73 //------------------------------------------------
74 }
75 //------------------------------------------------
```

The following are the comments for code sample 8-10:

- **Line 08**: Notice that the CustomPropertyDrawer attribute is now associated with a regular class as opposed to an attribute. In this case, the rendering of a specific class is being customized for the Object Inspector as opposed to various properties of different types, which can share a common attribute.

- **Lines 12-18**: Some public members are declared, primarily to calculate the height (in pixels) of a single row in the Object Inspector. By default, the Object Inspector allocates one row (or line) for our custom rendering and all drawing is supposed to fit within that space. If the total height of our rendering exceeds the height of one line, all additional controls and data will overlap and mix with controls and widgets beneath. To address this problem, the GetPropertyHeight (at line 69) function can be used to return a pixel height allocated for our custom drawing.

- **Lines 26-27**: These lines are especially important. They use reflection to retrieve a type-correct object reference to the ClassWithProperties instance currently being drawn for this call to OnGUI. Specifically, a reference to targetObject is retrieved (the object selected), and then an instance to ClassWithProperties is retrieved from that. The result is that this code gives us direct and immediate access to the ClassWithProperties object.

- **Lines 37-58**: Each public property on the object is cycled in sequence, and for valid or supported data types, an inspector property is drawn that allows both read/write access to the property, provided the property itself supports both methods.

The following screenshot shows the C# properties:

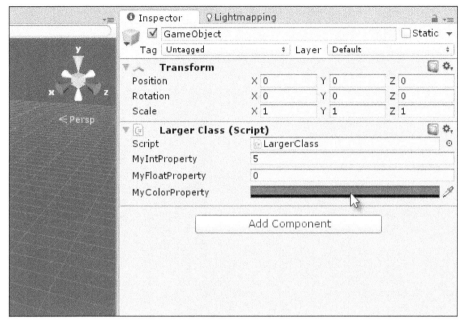

Accessing C# properties

Localization

Perhaps one of the most underappreciated and underdocumented aspect of game development is localization. This refers to the broad range of technical, economic, and logistical measures a developer takes to support multiple natural languages in their game, such as English, French, German, Spanish, Esperanto, and so on. The technical aim is not so much to support this or that specific language, but rather to establish an infrastructure that could support any arbitrary language chosen at any time, now or later. The entire scope and role of localization in development is beyond the scope of this book, but here we'll examine one way in which the Unity Editor can be customized to facilitate a quick and easy localization workflow. For example, consider the following sample XML file, in which game text for the buttons in a main menu system is defined in both English and a "spoof language" called Yoda:

```
<?xml version="1.0"?>
<text>
    <language id="english">
        <text_entry id="text_01"><![CDATA[new
game]]></text_entry>
        <text_entry id="text_02"><![CDATA[load
game]]></text_entry>
        <text_entry id="text_03"><![CDATA[save
game]]></text_entry>
        <text_entry id="text_04"><![CDATA[exit
game]]></text_entry>
    </language>
    <language id="yoda">
        <text_entry id="text_01"><![CDATA[new game, you
start]]></text_entry>
        <text_entry id="text_02"><![CDATA[load game, you
will]]></text_entry>
        <text_entry id="text_03"><![CDATA[game save, you
have]]></text_entry>
        <text_entry id="text_04"><![CDATA[leave now, you
must]]></text_entry>
    </language>
</text>
```

 Notice, the CDATA element encloses all custom text nodes to allow the use of any characters and symbols. More information on CDATA can be found online at http://www.w3schools.com/xml/xml_cdata.asp.

The XML defined earlier creates four text elements, one for each button on a sample user interface menu. Each text element is assigned a unique ID: text_01, text_02, text_03, and text_04. These IDs uniquely identify each item of text in the game and will match across all specified languages. The purpose here is to import the text file into Unity that allows the developer to switch between languages at the touch of a button, and have all relevant text elements in the game change automatically to accommodate the language switch. Let's see how this works.

First import the localized text into a Resources folder in a Unity project. Create a folder named Resources and then import the localized text file into it, as shown in the following screenshot. In code, this means any object or class can load or open the text file using a Resources.Load call, as we'll see soon.

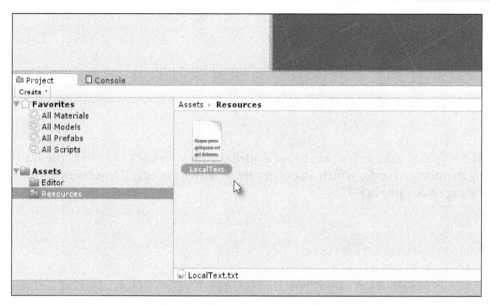

Importing localized text into a project

 More information on resources can be found online at the Unity documentation at `http://docs.unity3d.com/ScriptReference/Resources.html`.

The imported text file simply contains all text data to be included in the game, where each element is associated with its ID. Thus, each string value is married to an ID, and the ID is consistent across language schemes that allow a seamless transition between languages. The ID is the one common denominator that makes an automated localization possible. To implement the localization system in code, we'll first create an attribute that should be applied to all localized strings. The attribute defines only the ID to be attached to a specific string variable, as shown in the following code sample 8-11:

```
using UnityEngine;
using System.Collections;

//Attribute to attach to string objects
public class LocalizationTextAttribute : System.Attribute
{
    //ID to assign
```

```
        public string LocalizationID = string.Empty;

        //Constructor
        public LocalizationTextAttribute(string ID)
        {
                LocalizationID = ID;
        }
}
```

With the `LocalizationTextAttribute` attribute now created, we can apply it to string members in code, which associates them with a specific ID, as shown in the following code sample 8-12:

```
//------------------------------------------------
using UnityEngine;
using System.Collections;
//------------------------------------------------
public class SampleGameMenu : MonoBehaviour
{
    [LocalizationTextAttribute("text_01")]
    public string NewGameText = string.Empty;

    [LocalizationTextAttribute("text_02")]
    public string LoadGameText = string.Empty;

    [LocalizationTextAttribute("text_03")]
    public string SaveGameText = string.Empty;

    [LocalizationTextAttribute("text_04")]
    public string ExitGameText = string.Empty;
}
//------------------------------------------------
```

The `SampleGameMenu` class appears as a regular class in the Object Inspector, as shown in the following screenshot. Later, through our `Editor` class, we'll develop the ability to automatically change all string members to the selected language.

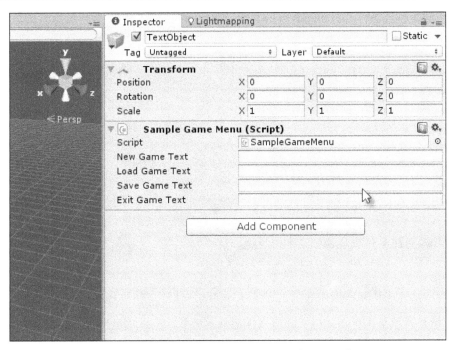

A SampleGameMenu class features all texture required for a sample menu screen

Now, we'll code an `Editor` class to switch between languages. This class will add menu entries on the application menu, which when clicked will change the active language, as shown in the following code sample 8-13. This sample draws on a range of related concepts we've seen already, including new ones. Specifically, it uses the `Reflection`, `Linq`, and `Editor` classes as well as the Mono Framework XML handling classes:

```
01 //-------------------------------------------
02 using UnityEngine;
03 using UnityEditor;
04 using System.Collections;
05 using System.Xml;
06 using System.Linq;
07 using System.Reflection;
08 //-------------------------------------------
```

```
09 public class LanguageSelector
10 {
11 [MenuItem ("Localization/English")]
12 public static void SelectEnglish()
13 {
14         LanguageSelector.SelectLanguage("english");
15 }
16
17 [MenuItem ("Localization/French")]
18 public static void SelectFrench()
19 {
20         LanguageSelector.SelectLanguage("french");
21 }
22
23 [MenuItem ("Localization/Yoda")]
24 public static void SelectYoda()
25 {
26         LanguageSelector.SelectLanguage("yoda");
27 }
28
29 public static void SelectLanguage(string LanguageName)
30 {
31         //Access XML Text File in Project
32 TextAsset textAsset = Resources.Load("LocalText") as TextAsset;
33
34         //Load text into XML Reader object
35         XmlDocument xmlDoc = new XmlDocument();
36         xmlDoc.LoadXml(textAsset.text);
37
38         //Get language nodes
39 XmlNode[] LanguageNodes = (from XmlNode Node in
   xmlDoc.GetElementsByTagName("language")

40 where
   Node.Attributes["id"].Value.ToString().Equals(LanguageName.ToLower
()
)
41         select Node).ToArray();
42
43         //If no matching node found, then exit
44         if(LanguageNodes.Length <= 0)
```

```
45              return;
46
47       //Get first node
48       XmlNode LanguageNode = LanguageNodes[0];
49
50       //Get text object
51 SampleGameMenu GM = Object.FindObjectOfType<SampleGameMenu>()
as SampleGameMenu;
52
53       //Loop through child xml nodes
54       foreach (XmlNode Child in LanguageNode.ChildNodes)
55          {
56              //Get text Id for this node
57              string TextID = Child.Attributes["id"].Value;
58               string LocalText = Child.InnerText;
59
60              //Loop through all fields
61 foreach(var field in GM.GetType().GetFields(BindingFlags.Instance
   | BindingFlags.Public | BindingFlags.NonPublic |
   BindingFlags.FlattenHierarchy))
62                 {
63                      //If field is a string then is relevant
64                      if(field.FieldType == typeof(System.String))
65                      {
66                          //Get custom attributes for field
67 System.Attribute[] attrs = field.GetCustomAttributes(true) as
   System.Attribute[];
68
69                      foreach (System.Attribute attr in attrs)
70                      {
71      if(attr is LocalizationTextAttribute)
72                                  {
73                                      //We've found text
74 LocalizationTextAttribute LocalAttr = attr as
   LocalizationTextAttribute;
75
76              if(LocalAttr.LocalizationID.Equals( TextID ))
```

```
77                                    {
78                                    //id matches, now set value
79                                    field.SetValue(GM, LocalText);
80                                    }
81                            }
82                    }
83                    }
84            }
85            }
86 }
87 }
88 //--------------------------------------------
```

The following are the comments for code sample 8-13:

- **Lines 02-07**: Remember to include wide range of namespaces as shown here. Our code will rely on them all to some degree.

- **Lines 11-23**: For this sample application, the three languages: **English, French**, and **Yoda** are selectable from the application menu. For your own projects, your language list may be different. But crucially, based on the localization system given here, integration of additional languages, even at a much later time, is easy.

- **Line 32**: The `Resources.Load` function is called here to open the XML text file from the `Resources` folder in the project that extracts its text contents into one single concatenated string variable.

- **Lines 35-36**: The XML string is loaded into an `XmlDocument` object, which is a Mono class encapsulating a complete XML file, either on disk or in memory. The class also validates the document on loading, which means an exception will be generated here if the file contains syntax errors.

- **Line 53**: Once a language is selected from the XML file, all child nodes of the language (each node a unique string) are cycled to find a matching ID.

- **Line 61**: For each string entry, all public string members for the text class are searched for an appropriate `LocalizationTextAttribute` and when found, the string ID is compared to check for a match. When a match is found, the string variable is assigned the corresponding localized string.

To use the localization framework given here, first add a `SampleGameMenu` object to the scene as shown here:

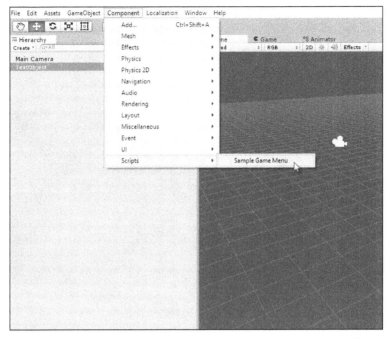

Adding a Sample Game Menu object to the scene with localized text members

Then, choose a language from the application main menu by selecting **English** or **Yoda** from the **Localization** tab, as shown here:

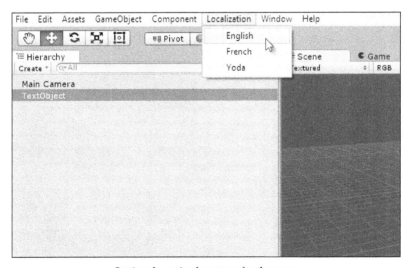

Setting the active language for the game

Once the active language is specified, all strings with the
LocalizationTextAttribute attribute will be updated, as shown in the
following screenshot:

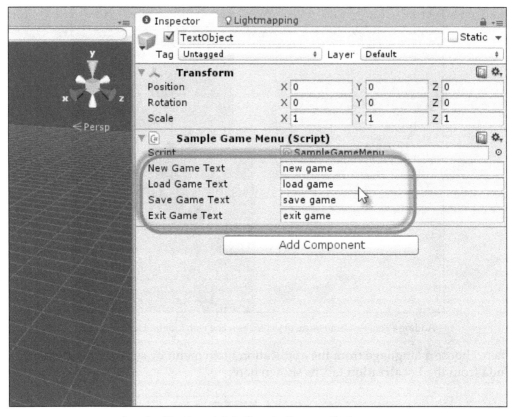

Localized text is updated after selecting an active language

Summary

This chapter explored in depth the relationship between reflection, as a concept, and its practical use for creating `Editor` classes that extended the editor behavior beyond its defaults to accommodate custom intentions. The ability to do this is not always essential to building Unity games themselves but it can make your work easier. Furthermore, it can lead to making money via the Asset Store, should you wish to develop custom add-ons that can help other developers. Here, you saw how to create a Batch Rename tool with the `ScriptableWizard` class and then a color blending property for the Object Inspector. Next, we made extensive use of reflection to expose all public C# properties in the Object Inspector that allowed us direct access to the set and get property values as if we'd accessed them at runtime. Further, we moved on to see how a localization framework could be implemented from XML files via the `Editor` classes that allow string variables to be automatically changed to match a selected language. For more information, you can visit `http://catlikecoding.com/unity/tutorials/editor/custom-data/` and `http://catlikecoding.com/unity/tutorials/editor/custom-list/`. In the next chapter, we'll move our conceptual and technical baggage to explore the world of 2D from more unconventional angles.

9
Working with Textures, Models, and 2D

Most game engines today orient their feature set towards the creation of 3D games rather than 2D in a general sense. This often, ironically, makes 3D tasks and workflows simpler than 2D ones, at least to pick up and get started with initially. In this chapter, we'll explore a variety of 2D issues with some provisos. Since the release of Unity 4.3, a wide range of 2D features have been added to the editor: initially, a native sprite system and then, a new GUI system. While these are both useful in their respective ways, the main focus of this chapter will not be on these features specifically. The first reason is that a lot of tutorials already explain them in considerable detail, but the second and most important reason is that even with the added 2D features, there are still more fundamental questions that arise about working in 2D, in a looser sense. These include questions such as how to manipulate geometry such as the vertices and edges of 2D planes, how to adjust and animate texture coordinates, how to edit textures and also how to texture paint onto textures in real time using a brush-like system to create decals and blood splats, and so on. These questions are more 2D than 3D insofar as they pertain to geometry and textures in the 2D plane, but their relevance is to both 2D and 3D games generally. Their importance is highly significant today, though their coverage is somewhat under-represented in the tutorials available, so I have covered them here. Consequently, I'll restrict this chapter mostly to the unconventional side of 2D.

Skybox

The Skybox might seem a strange place to begin an analysis of 2D, but it demonstrates an important feature set for cameras, specifically layering. The Skybox is essentially a cube-based background that's attached to a camera to show clouds, skies, and other distant details that should always act as the backdrop to a scene, but it never represents anything that the player can move close to. It is always distant, as shown here:

Skybox assets display a sky background for cameras

The main problem with the default Skyboxes native to Unity is that they remain static and motionless by default. Most developers, however, want their skies and clouds to gently rotate, even when the camera is standing motionless, to portray the procession of a day or of time passing. Now, let's create an improved Skybox prefab using the Unity Skybox assets, two layered cameras, and a C# script file.

> The final project for a rotating Skybox can be found in the book's companion files.

For the sample project created here, let's import the **Character Controllers** package for a first-person controller asset, the **Terrain Assets** package for terrain textures that we can paint onto a sample terrain, and the **Skyboxes** package for the Skybox textures, as shown in the following screenshot.

All these will be useful in building a sample project with a rotating Skybox.

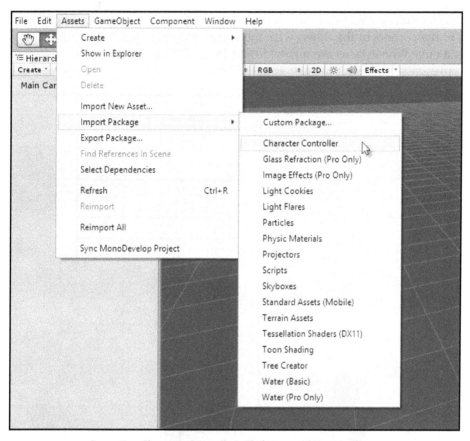

Importing Character Controllers, Skyboxes, and Terrain Assets

Next, let's begin by creating the rotating Skybox prefab to make a reusable object. This object consists of three main parts or subobjects: a first-person controller that allows player movement and renders most scene objects, a second camera (the Skybox camera) that is rendered below the first-person camera and shows only the Skybox, and a cube object with inverted normals that surrounds the Skybox camera and shows each Skybox texture on each face.

To start, create a new empty object at the scene origin (named `SkyBoxCamera`) and add a first-person controller object as a child. Then, create six **Quad** objects from the main menu (by navigating to **GameObject | 3D Object | Quad**), aligning each object to the corners of the other, with the vertex snapping to form an inverted cube, that is, a cube whose faces are turned inwards, as shown in the following screenshot. This represents the mesh for the manual Skybox.

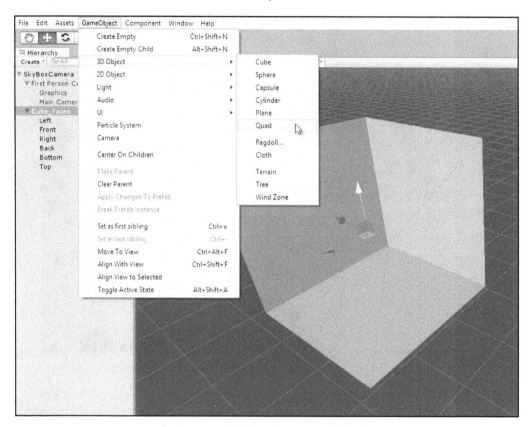

Create a manual Skybox from six Quad objects

 Scale the Quads if required and make sure that they contain and enclose the first-person controller, which should be at the center of the Skybox.

Assign the Skybox faces to a new layer, SkyBoxLayer, select the first-person controller camera, and then change the **Culling Mask** field to exclude the SkyBoxLayer layer. The first-person camera should render only foreground objects and not background ones. To achieve this, change the **Clear Flags** field to **Depth only** in the Object Inspector, as shown in the following screenshot. This renders the camera background to transparent, which allows lower-order cameras to show through, if any.

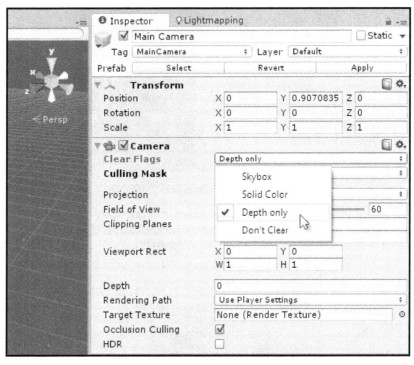

Making the camera background transparent

Now, create a new and additional Camera object as a direct child object of the first-person camera and match its position, rotation, and scale. This allows the camera to inherit all the transformations from the first-person camera. The purpose of the secondary camera is to render only the Skybox object as a layer beneath the first-person camera while matching the first-person position and rotation.

To this end, change the **Depth** value of the new camera to any value less than the depth of the first-person camera; such as -1. Remove any audio listener components where required.

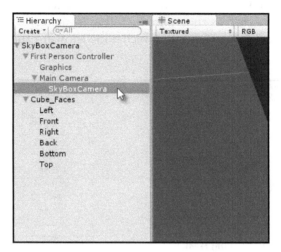

Creating a second camera for Skybox rendering

Assign a unique Skybox texture to each cube face and take care to align them seamlessly by rotating or adjusting the Quad alignment as needed. Then, change the material **Shader** type for the Skybox textures to **Unlit/Texture**, making the Skybox immune to scene lighting. The Skybox mesh should start taking shape, as shown here:

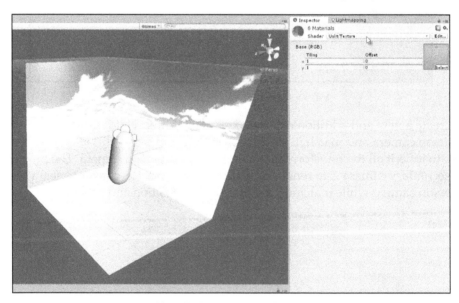

Adding Skybox textures to the Quads

Finally, apply the following code sample 9-1 to the Skybox parent object to create its rotation behavior and to align it continuously to the camera position. This ensures that the Skybox is always centered on the camera wherever it travels in the scene:

```
01 //-------------------------------------------------
02 using UnityEngine;
03 using System.Collections;
04 //-------------------------------------------------
05 public class SkyBox : MonoBehaviour
06 {
07 //-------------------------------------------------
08 //Camera to follow
09 public Camera FollowCam = null;
10
11 //Rotate Speed (Degrees per second)
12 public float RotateSpeed = 10.0f;
13
14 //Transform
15 private Transform ThisTransform = null;
16 //-------------------------------------------------
17 // Use this for initialization
18 void Awake () {
19         ThisTransform = transform;
20 }
21 //-------------------------------------------------
22 // Update is called once per frame
23 void Update () {
24         //Update position
25         ThisTransform.position = FollowCam.transform.position;
26
27         //Update rotation
28 ThisTransform.Rotate(new Vector3(0,RotateSpeed *
   Time.deltaTime,0));
29 }
30 //-------------------------------------------------
31 }
32 //-------------------------------------------------
```

From this, you now have a completed and enhanced Skybox, one that surrounds the camera and rotates to produce greater realism and life in your scenes. You can even go further by adding multiple stacked skyboxes within each other, each with transparency, to create additional effects such as fog, mist, and so on:

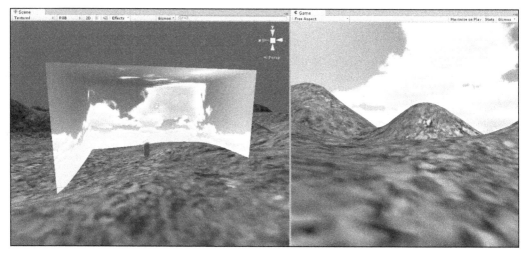

Completing a manual Skybox prefab

Procedural meshes

Although Unity now offers a Quad primitive from the application menu, which you can access by navigating to **GameObject | 3D Object | Quad**, it's still useful to know how to create geometry manually, such as Quads. There are several reasons for this. First, you'll frequently need to edit vertices in the script to move, animate, or distort meshes for various effects to create, for example, a jelly-like surface in a platform game that bends and wobbles whenever characters step on it. Second, you'll need to edit the UV coordinates of a mesh, perhaps, to create animated or scrolling-texture effects, as shown here:

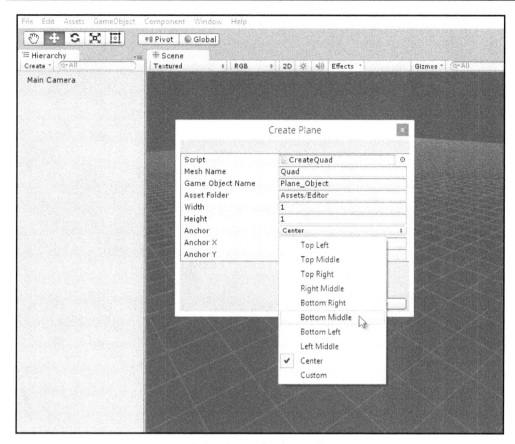

Generating meshes from script

Consider the following code sample 9-2, which should be included inside the `Editor` folder of a project. It creates an editor add-on that generates a Quad in script with full customization over the location of the mesh pivot point. As we'll see in the code comments, this sample features many useful tips:

```
001 //EDITOR CLASS TO CREATE QUAD MESH WITH SPECIFIED ANCHOR
002 //-----------------------------------------------
003 using UnityEngine;
004 using UnityEditor;
005 using System.IO;
006 //-----------------------------------------------
007 //Run from unity editor
```

```
008 public class CreateQuad : ScriptableWizard
009 {
010       //Anchor point for created quad
011       public enum AnchorPoint
012     {
013         TopLeft,
014         TopMiddle,
015         TopRight,
016         RightMiddle,
017         BottomRight,
018         BottomMiddle,
019         BottomLeft,
020         LeftMiddle,
021         Center,
022             Custom
023     }
024
025     //Name of Quad Asset
026     public string MeshName = "Quad";
027
028     //Game Object Name
029     public string GameObjectName = "Plane_Object";
030
031     //Name of asset folder
032     public string AssetFolder = "Assets";
033
034     //Width of quad in world units (pixels)
035     public float Width = 1.0f;
036
037     //Height of quad in world units (pixels)
038     public float Height = 1.0f;
039
040     //Position of Anchor
041     public AnchorPoint Anchor = AnchorPoint.Center;
042
043     //Horz Position of Anchor on Plane
044     public float AnchorX = 0.5f;
045
046    //Vert Position of Anchor on Plane
047     public float AnchorY = 0.5f;
048     //-------------------------------------------------
049     [MenuItem("GameObject/Create Other/Custom Plane")]
050     static void CreateWizard()
051     {
```

```
052             ScriptableWizard.DisplayWizard("Create
                Plane",typeof(CreateQuad));
053         }
054
055     //-----------------------------------------------
056     //Function called when window is created
057     void OnEnable()
058     {
059             //Call selection change
060             OnSelectionChange();
061      }
062     //-----------------------------------------------
063     //Called 10 times per second
064     void OnInspectorUpdate()
065     {
066             switch(Anchor)
067             {
068                     //Anchor is set to top-left
069                     case AnchorPoint.TopLeft:
070                             AnchorX = 0.0f * Width;
071                             AnchorY = 1.0f * Height;
072                     break;
073
074                     //Anchor is set to top-middle
075                     case AnchorPoint.TopMiddle:
076                             AnchorX = 0.5f * Width;
077                             AnchorY = 1.0f * Height;
078                     break;
079
080                     //Anchor is set to top-right
081                     case AnchorPoint.TopRight:
082                             AnchorX = 1.0f * Width;
083                             AnchorY = 1.0f * Height;
084                     break;
085
086                     //Anchor is set to right-middle
087                     case AnchorPoint.RightMiddle:
088                             AnchorX = 1.0f * Width;
089                             AnchorY = 0.5f * Height;
090                     break;
091
092                     //Anchor is set to Bottom-Right
093                     case AnchorPoint.BottomRight:
094                             AnchorX = 1.0f * Width;
```

```
095                        AnchorY = 0.0f * Height;
096                 break;
097
098                 //Anchor is set to Bottom-Middle
099                 case AnchorPoint.BottomMiddle:
100                        AnchorX = 0.5f * Width;
101                        AnchorY = 0.0f * Height;
102                 break;
103
104                 //Anchor is set to Bottom-Left
105                 case AnchorPoint.BottomLeft:
106                        AnchorX = 0.0f * Width;
107                        AnchorY = 0.0f * Height;
108                 break;
109
110                 //Anchor is set to Left-Middle
111                 case AnchorPoint.LeftMiddle:
112                        AnchorX = 0.0f * Width;
113                        AnchorY = 0.5f * Height;
114                 break;
115
116                 //Anchor is set to center
117                 case AnchorPoint.Center:
118                        AnchorX = 0.5f * Width;
119                        AnchorY = 0.5f * Height;
120                 break;
121
122                 case AnchorPoint.Custom:
123                 default:
124                 break;
125          }
126    }
127    //-------------------------------------------------
128    //Function called when window is updated
129    void OnSelectionChange()
130    {
131          //Check user selection in editor
132    if (Selection.objects != null && Selection.objects.Length
       == 1)
133          {
134          //Get path from selected asset
135    AssetFolder = Path.GetDirectoryName(AssetDatabase.
       GetAssetPath(Selection.objects[0]));
```

```
136                 }
137         }
138     //-----------------------------------------------
139     //Function to create quad mesh
140     void OnWizardCreate()
141     {
142             //Create Vertices
143             Vector3[] Vertices = new Vector3[4];
144
145             //Create UVs
146             Vector2[] UVs = new Vector2[4];
147
148             //Two triangles of quad
149             int[] Triangles = new int[6];
150
151             //Assign vertices based on pivot
152
153             //Bottom-left
154             Vertices[0].x = -AnchorX;
155             Vertices[0].y = -AnchorY;
156
157             //Bottom-right
158             Vertices[1].x = Vertices[0].x+Width;
159             Vertices[1].y = Vertices[0].y;
160
161             //Top-left
162             Vertices[2].x = Vertices[0].x;
163             Vertices[2].y = Vertices[0].y+Height;
164
165             //Top-right
166             Vertices[3].x = Vertices[0].x+Width;
167             Vertices[3].y = Vertices[0].y+Height;
168
169             //Assign UVs
170             //Bottom-left
171             UVs[0].x=0.0f;
172             UVs[0].y=0.0f;
173
174             //Bottom-right
175             UVs[1].x=1.0f;
176             UVs[1].y=0.0f;
177
178             //Top-left
179             UVs[2].x=0.0f;
```

```
180              UVs[2].y=1.0f;
181

182              //Top-right
183              UVs[3].x=1.0f;
184              UVs[3].y=1.0f;
185

186              //Assign triangles
187              Triangles[0]=3;
188              Triangles[1]=1;
189              Triangles[2]=2;
190

191              Triangles[3]=2;
192              Triangles[4]=1;
193              Triangles[5]=0;
194

195              //Generate mesh
196              Mesh mesh = new Mesh();
197              mesh.name = MeshName;
198              mesh.vertices = Vertices;
199              mesh.uv = UVs;
200              mesh.triangles = Triangles;
201              mesh.RecalculateNormals();
202

203              //Create asset in database
204      AssetDatabase.CreateAsset(mesh,
         AssetDatabase.GenerateUniqueAssetPath(AssetFolder + "/" +
         MeshName) + ".asset");

205              AssetDatabase.SaveAssets();
206

207              //Create plane game object
208              GameObject plane = new GameObject(GameObjectName);

209      MeshFilter meshFilter =
         (MeshFilter)plane.AddComponent(typeof(MeshFilter);

210              plane.AddComponent(typeof(MeshRenderer));
211
```

```
212                    //Assign mesh to mesh filter
213                    meshFilter.sharedMesh = mesh;
214                    mesh.RecalculateBounds();
215
216                    //Add a box collider component
217                    plane.AddComponent(typeof(BoxCollider));
218        }
219
220        //-------------------------------------------------
221  }
```

The following are the comments for code sample 9-2:

- **Line 004**: This sample is coded as an editor plugin. As a result, the UnityEditor namespace is included. For more information on creating editor plugins, refer to *Chapter 8, Customizing the Unity Editor.*

- **Line 135**: The OnSelectionChanged event is called when the user changes their selection, with the mouse or keyboard, in the Unity Editor. Here, the GetAssetPath method is called to retrieve the currently open folder in the **Project** panel.

- **Line 140**: The OnWizardCreate function is called to generate a Quad mesh in script. This is created by filling a vertex and UV array and then populating that inside a Mesh object created in line 196.

- **Line 204**: Critically, the mesh itself is saved, not as an object in a specific scene, but as a general asset of the project from which many instances can be made as prefab objects. This is achieved with the AssetDatabase class. This is important to allow the mesh to be reusable across multiple scenes, if required, and also to allow its changes and details to be persistent across scenes.

 More information on the AssetDatabase class can be found online in the Unity documentation at http://docs.unity3d.com/ScriptReference/AssetDatabase.html.

Animating UVs – scrolling textures

Scrolling textures are a general purpose requirement for lots of games, and yet, they are not natively supported by Unity; that is, they require you to "get coding" for their implementation. Scrolling textures are useful for parallax effects; to move clouds, surfaces, and water; or to express motion or movement in the game. Typically, scrolling textures are seamless images whose pixels tile vertically and horizontally. This allows infinite scrolling and repetition, as shown here:

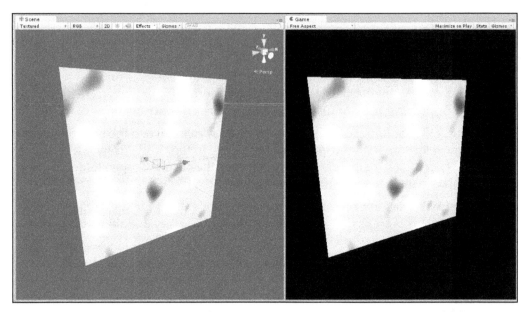

Scrolling texture on a Quad

When attached to a Quad, the following code sample 9-3 will animate its texture according to the horizontal and vertical speed:

```
01 //CLASS TO SCROLL TEXTURE ON PLANE. CAN BE USED FOR MOVING SKY
02 //------------------------------------------------
03 using UnityEngine;
04 using System.Collections;
05 //------------------------------------------------
06 [RequireComponent (typeof (MeshRenderer))]
07 public class MatScroller : MonoBehaviour
08 {
09 //Public variables
10 //------------------------------------------------
11 //Reference to Horizontal Scroll Speed
```

```
12 public float HorizSpeed = 1.0f;
13
14 //Reference to Vertical Scroll Speed
15 public float VertSpeed = 1.0f;
16
17 //Reference to Min and Max Horiz and vert
18 public float HorizUVMin = 1.0f;
19 public float HorizUVMax = 2.0f;
20
21 public float VertUVMin = 1.0f;
22 public float VertUVMax = 2.0f;
23
24 //Private variables
25 //---------------------------------------------
26 //Reference to Mesh Renderer Component
27 private MeshRenderer MeshR = null;
28
29 //Methods
30 //---------------------------------------------
31 // Use this for initialization
32 void Awake ()
33 {
34         //Get Mesh Renderer Component
35         MeshR = GetComponent<MeshRenderer>();
36 }
37 //---------------------------------------------
38 // Update is called once per frame
39 void Update ()
40 {
41         //Scrolls texture between min and max
42 Vector2 Offset = new
   Vector2((MeshR.material.mainTextureOffset.x > HorizUVMax) ?
   HorizUVMin : MeshR.material.mainTextureOffset.x + Time.deltaTime *
   HorizSpeed,
43 (MeshR.material.mainTextureOffset.y > VertUVMax) ? VertUVMin :
   MeshR.material.mainTextureOffset.y + Time.deltaTime * VertSpeed);

44
45         //Update UV coordinates
46         MeshR.material.mainTextureOffset = Offset;
47 }
48 //---------------------------------------------
49 }
50 //---------------------------------------------
```

The MatScroller class works with any MeshRenderer component and Quad object. A complete scrolling-texture project can be found in the book's companion files (code bundle).

Attach this script to your Quad object and tweak its scrolling speed to produce the results you need, as shown in the following screenshot. This will be useful to create animated sky backgrounds and backgrounds for side-scrolling shooter or platform games. It can also be useful to create flowing waterfalls and volumetric lighting when combined with transparency!

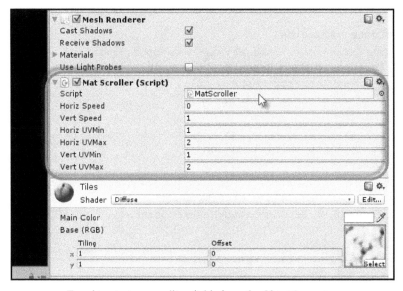

Tweaking texture-scrolling fields from the Object Inspector

Texture painting

There are many practical scenarios where it's necessary to paint pixels onto textures at runtime. Sometimes, the need itself will be trivial, such as displaying a decal texture (such as a foot print or written message) in front of another surface using alpha transparency. In these cases, you can simply workaround the issue with an alpha cut out plane positioned in front of another plane as the background. However, there are times when your needs are more complex, and you actually need to resort to true texture painting. For example, in a street-fighting game, blood splatters from punches and other attacks will fall to the ground and surrounding scenery, and you want to it remain as part of the environment texture. Another example might be a casual make-up artist game where the gamer must paint blusher or eye shadow onto a face mesh.

Here, you don't simply want to paint textured quads in front of the mesh as separate objects to create the appearance of textured decals. Instead, you really need to paint a source texture (such as a brush) onto a destination texture as applied to a mesh. Here, the painting does not just happen between two independent textures but with a mesh and its UV mapping intervening between them. In other words, a source texture must be applied or projected onto a mesh surface in the scene, and then, the brush pixels must be unprojected back onto the destination texture through the mesh UV mapping. This ensures that the brush pixels are painted to the correct place within the destination texture, as shown in the following screenshot. This method, therefore, allows any source texture of any size to be painted onto any 3D surface and its destination texture of any size via UV mapping.

In this section, we'll explore how this is achieved practically and effectively. Before getting started, however, it should be mentioned that texture painting in this way should be pursued as a last resort when alternative methods (such as cut out quads) are not adequate. This is because true texture painting is computationally expensive.

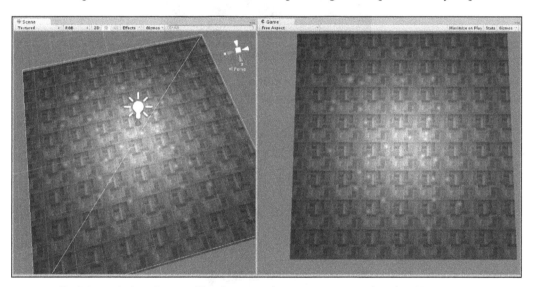

Real-time painting of textured brushes onto other textures via a mesh and its UV mapping

 A complete texture painting project can be found in the book's companion files (code bundle).

Step 1 – creating a texture blending shader

First, let's recognize the two-layer approach that's ideal here. First, we have the brush source texture itself, which will be painted onto a destination texture when the user clicks on a mesh in the scene, as shown here:

The brush texture, where black is transparent (alpha)

Then, we have the destination texture applied to the mesh onto which the brush strokes should be overlaid when painted, as shown in the following screenshot:

Destination texture onto which brushes should be painted

However, we don't usually want the painted brush strokes overwriting or changing the original destination texture during the paint operation. This is because the destination texture could be applied to multiple objects in the scene (at least in theory), and overwriting or changing the pixels of the original will result in its effects being propagated to all objects using the texture.

Instead, it'd be better to separate the paint effects onto a separate texture with a transparent background, which is layered over the destination texture via a custom material. This creates a true separation between the destination texture and the paint effects, even though in appearance, it appears as one consolidated texture. To achieve this effect, a custom shader must be written, as shown in the following code sample 9-4. This shader blends a top texture (with alpha transparency) on top of a background texture:

```
01 Shader "TextureBlender"
02 {
03     Properties
04     {
05     _Color ("Main Color", Color) = (1,1,1,1)
06     _MainTex ("Base (RGB) Trans (A)", 2D) = "white" {}
07     _BlendTex ("Blend (RGB)", 2D) = "white"
08     }
09
10     SubShader
11     {
12 Tags { "Queue"="Geometry-9" "IgnoreProjector"="True"
   "RenderType"="Transparent" }
13     Lighting Off
14     LOD 200
15     Blend SrcAlpha OneMinusSrcAlpha
16
17     CGPROGRAM
18             #pragma surface surf Lambert
19             uniform fixed4 _Color;
20             uniform sampler2D _MainTex;
21             uniform sampler2D _BlendTex;
22
23             struct Input
24             {
25                float2 uv_MainTex;
26             };
27
28             void surf (Input IN, inout SurfaceOutput o)
29             {
30                     fixed4 c1 = tex2D( _MainTex, IN.uv_MainTex );
31                     fixed4 c2 = tex2D( _BlendTex, IN.uv_MainTex );
32
```

```
33                    fixed4 main = c1.rgba * (1.0 - c2.a);
34                    fixed4 blendedoutput = c2.rgba * c2.a;
35
36 o.Albedo = (main.rgb + blendedoutput.rgb) * _Color;

37                    o.Alpha = main.a + blendedoutput.a;
38            }
39       ENDCG
40       }
41       Fallback "Transparent/VertexLit"
42 }
```

Once the shader is coded and saved, it appears as a selectable shader type for any material you create via the **Material** panel in the Object Inspector. This shader should be used for any object onto which details must be painted, as shown in the following screenshot. The _MainTex slot refers to the background texture onto which details must be overlaid but which must also be preserved from any true edits. The _BlendTex slot refers to the texture to be overlaid onto _MainTex, which preserves its alpha transparency. Typically, this slot will be populated at runtime from script by generating an alpha transparent texture to receive brush strokes, as we'll soon see.

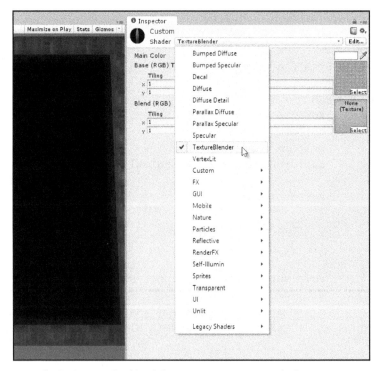

A custom shader is created to blend the top-most texture onto the bottom-most texture

Step 2 – creating a texture painting script

We've now created a shader that accepts two textures as input (the top and bottom textures) and blends the top over the bottom; this allows alpha transparency. This results in a Photoshop-layer style effect. This allows us to separate texture painting onto a top texture while preserving the pixels of the original background below it, as shown here:

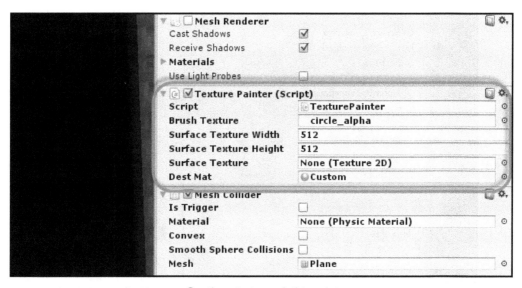

Creating a texture painting script

Before moving further, however, we must first edit the brush texture asset we plan on using via Object Inspector. Specifically, select the brush texture from the **Project** panel in the Unity Editor and change **Texture Type** to **Advanced**. Enable the checkbox for **Read/Write Enabled**; this allows the texture to be accessed using texture-editing functions.

In addition, enable **Alpha is Transparency** and disable **Generate Mip Maps**, as shown in the following screenshot:

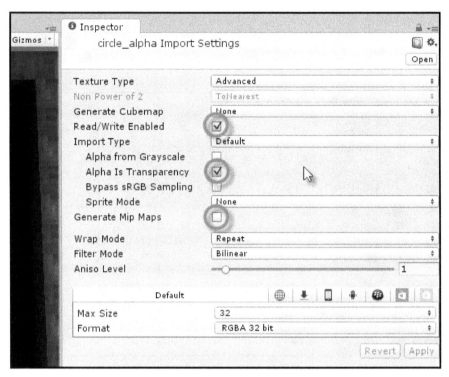

Configuring textures for texture painting

Now, we'll need to create a texture-painting script that allows us to paint the brush texture, using the mouse, onto a 3D object in the scene via its UV coordinates. The script is shown in the following code sample 9-5:

```
001 //------------------------------------------------------------
002 using UnityEngine;
003 using System.Collections;
004 //------------------------------------------------------------
005 public class TexturePainter : MonoBehaviour
006 {
007     //Square texture with alpha
008     public Texture2D BrushTexture = null;
009
010     //Width and height of destination texture
011     public int SurfaceTextureWidth = 512;
```

```
012        public int SurfaceTextureHeight = 512;
013
014    //Reference to painting surface texture
015     public Texture2D SurfaceTexture = null;
016
017    //Reference to material for destination texture
018    public Material DestMat = null;
019    //-----------------------------------------------
020    // Use this for initialization
021    void Start ()
022    {
023        //Create destination texture
024     SurfaceTexture = new Texture2D(SurfaceTextureWidth,
       SurfaceTextureHeight, TextureFormat.RGBA32, false);

025
026        //Fill with black pixels (transparent; alpha=0)
027        Color[] Pixels = SurfaceTexture.GetPixels();
028        for(int i=0; i<Pixels.Length; i++)
029            Pixels[i] = new Color(0,0,0,0);
030        SurfaceTexture.SetPixels(Pixels);
031        SurfaceTexture.Apply();
032
033        //Set as renderer main texture
034        renderer.material.mainTexture = SurfaceTexture;
035
036        //If destination material, set blend texture
037       //Used with custom shader
038         if(DestMat)
039    DestMat.SetTexture("_BlendTex", SurfaceTexture);
040    }
041    //-----------------------------------------------
042    // Update is called once per frame
043    void Update ()
044    {
045        //If mouse button down, then start painting
046        if(Input.GetMouseButtonDown(0))
047        {
048            //Get hit of mouse cursor
049            RaycastHit hit;
050
051            //Convert screen point to ray in scene
```

```
052        if (!Physics.Raycast(Camera.main.ScreenPointToRay(
           Input.mousePosition), out hit))
053                          return;
054
055             //Get hit collider
056             Renderer renderer = hit.collider.renderer;
057      MeshCollider Collide = hit.collider as MeshCollider;

058        if (renderer == null || renderer.sharedMaterial == null
           || renderer.sharedMaterial.mainTexture == null || Collide ==
           null)
059                          return;
060
061             //Get UV Coords of hit surface
062             Vector2 pixelUV = hit.textureCoord;
063      pixelUV.x *= renderer.material.mainTexture.width;
064      pixelUV.y *= renderer.material.mainTexture.height;
065
066      //Update coords to texture middle (align brush texture
         center to cursor)
067             pixelUV.x -= BrushTexture.width/2;
068             pixelUV.y -= BrushTexture.height/2;
069
070         //Clamp pixel values between 0 and width
071      pixelUV.x = Mathf.Clamp(pixelUV.x, 0,
         renderer.material.mainTexture.width);

072      pixelUV.y = Mathf.Clamp(pixelUV.y, 0,
         renderer.material.mainTexture.height);
073
074         //Paint onto destination texture
075      PaintSourceToDestTexture(BrushTexture,
         renderer.material.mainTexture as Texture2D, (int)pixelUV.x,
         (int)pixelUV.y);
076             }
077      }
078      //-------------------------------------------------
079      //Paint source text to destination
080      //Will paint a brush texture onto a destination texture
081      public static void PaintSourceToDestTexture(Texture2D
         Source, Texture2D Dest, int Left, int Top)
082       {
083           //Get source pixels
084           Color[] SourcePixels = Source.GetPixels();
085
```

```
086                     //Get dest pixels
087                     Color[] DestPixels = Dest.GetPixels();
088
089                     for(int x=0; x<Source.width; x++)
090                     {
091                             for(int y=0; y<Source.height; y++)
092                             {
093                                     //Get source pixel
094             Color Pixel = GetPixelFromArray(SourcePixels, x, y,
             Source.width);

095
096                                     //Get offset in destination
097                                     int DestOffsetX = Left + x;
098                                     int DestOffsetY = Top + y;
099
100             if(DestOffsetX < Dest.width && DestOffsetY < Dest.height)

101             SetPixelInArray(DestPixels, DestOffsetX, DestOffsetY,
             Dest.width, Pixel, true);
102                             }
103                     }
104
105             //Update destination texture
106             Dest.SetPixels(DestPixels);
107             Dest.Apply();
108     }
109     //------------------------------------------------------------
110     //Reads color from pixel array
111     public static Color GetPixelFromArray(Color[] Pixels,
        int X, int Y, int Width)
112     {
113             return Pixels[X+Y*Width];
114     }
115     //------------------------------------------------------------
116     //Sets color in pixel array
117      public static void SetPixelInArray(Color[] Pixels, int
         X, int Y, int Width, Color NewColor, bool Blending=false)
118     {
119             if(!Blending)
120                     Pixels[X+Y*Width] = NewColor;
121             else
122             {
```

```
123        //Here we blend the color onto existing surface,
           preserving alpha transparency

124        Color C = Pixels[X+Y*Width] * (1.0f - NewColor.a);

125                    Color Blend = NewColor * NewColor.a;
126
127                    Color Result = C + Blend;
128                     float Alpha = C.a + Blend.a;
129
130        Pixels[X+Y*Width] = new Color(Result.r, Result.g,
           Result.b, Alpha);

131                    }
132            }
133        //------------------------------------------------
134 }
135 //-------------------------------------------------------
```

The following are the comments for code sample 9-5:

- **Line 008**: The public variable in this line maintains a reference to a valid texture asset to be used as the brush graphic during paint operations. For each mouse click, this texture will be "laid down" or painted onto the variable `SurfaceTexture`.

- **Line 015**: `SurfaceTexture` will reference a dynamically generated texture filled, by default, with transparent pixels, which will reveal any texture layered beneath. This texture will accept all brush strokes during a paint operation. In short, this texture will be fed into the `TextureBlender` shader as the `_BlendTex` variable.

- **Lines 026-031**: A new texture is generated during the `Start` function. The texture is in the RGBA32 format, which supports an alpha channel. The `SetPixels` function is used to batch fill (flood fill) the texture with pixels of the same color. More information on the `GetPixels` and `SetPixels` functions are considered later.

- **Line 046**: In the `Update` function, mouse clicks are detected to initiate the texture-painting functionality.

- **Lines 048-059**: If a mouse button is pressed, the function should paint the brush texture onto the destination. `Physics.Raycast` is called in line 52 to determine several things, such as to see whether a mesh object in the scene was hit by the ray. For this to work properly, the object should feature a `Collider` component.

- **Lines 062-072**: If a collision was detected, the UV coordinates of the hit location should be retrieved through the `textureCoord` variable of the `RaycastHit` structure. More information on this variable can be found online in the Unity documentation at `http://docs.unity3d.com/ScriptReference/RaycastHit-textureCoord.html`. This member, is only valid if the intersected mesh has `MeshCollider`, as opposed to other collider types, such as `BoxCollider` or `CapsuleCollider`. However, this means that any object used as a texture-painting destination should feature a `MeshCollider` component, since it contains UV data. Lines 63–72 then convert the UV coordinates into absolute pixel positions, centering the brush source texture at the position of the cursor. The result of this code is to clearly identify a position on the source brush texture that should be the pivot or origin point, and to establish a pixel *x*, *y* coordinate location at which the source texture should be painted into the destination texture.

- **Line 075**: Finally, the `PaintSourceToDestTexture` function is called to perform the paint operation itself.

- **Line 081**: The `PaintSourceToDestTexture` function accepts four arguments: `Source`, `Dest`, `Left`, and `Top`. On the basis of these, the `Source` texture is painted onto the `Dest` at the positions `Left` and `Top`. This function is declared as static, which means that no instance of this class needs to be declared.

- **Lines 084-087**: The first step in the texture-painting process is to retrieve all pixels in both the `Source` and `Dest` textures. This is achieved using the `GetPixels` function. More information on `GetPixels` can be found online in the Unity documentation at `http://docs.unity3d.com/ScriptReference/Texture2D.GetPixels.html`. Now, although each image is visually a two-dimensional array of pixels, the returned array from `GetPixels` is in fact linear (one-dimensional). This is the reason for both the `GetPixelFromArray` and `SetPixelFromArray` functions, which convert pixel *x* and *y* positions into linear array indices.

- **Lines 89-101**: Here, each pixel is retrieved from the `Source` texture and painted onto the destination. This checks to ensure that the brush texture is painted with the destination bounds and allows clipping, if required. This is necessary because a brush mark could, in principle, be made close to the texture edge; in this case, only a part of the brush would actually be painted onto the destination, as some pixels would be "cut off". Pixels are retrieved from the `Source` texture with `GetPixelFromArray`, and destination pixels are set with `SetPixelInArray`.

- **Lines 106-107**: Finally, the destination pixels are pushed back to the destination texture buffer, and the `Apply` function is called to confirm the operation. Unity also supports a `SetPixel` function (singular) as opposed to `SetPixels` (plural). However, `SetPixels` results in better performance as it repeats the calling of `SetPixel`.

- **Lines 111-114**: The `GetPixelFromArray` function accepts an array of pixel data as well as the *x* and *y* coordinates of a pixel and the pixel width of the texture data. On the basis of this, it returns a linear index into the pixel array where you can find the pixel color value.

- **Lines 117-131**: The `SetPixelInArray` function changes the color of a pixel in a linear array. The method of change is determined by the argument `Blending`. If `Blending` is set to `false`, the source pixel would simply replace the destination pixel. If `Blending` is `true`, the source pixel would be blended or layered onto the destination pixel that preserves the alpha transparency. `Blending` should be set to `true` when painting alpha-transparent brushes onto the target texture to allow for the accumulation and blending of color values.

Step 3 – setting up texture painting

Now that we have a working shader, texture-painting script, and configured textures, we'll take a step-by-step run-through of configuring texture painting in Unity. Start from an empty project, including only our shader, texture painting script, and two configured textures: a background texture and a brush texture, as shown here:

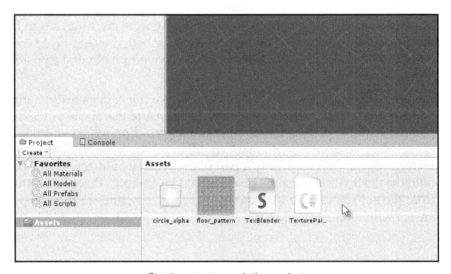

Starting a texture-painting project

Configure the brush texture from the **Project** panel to a small size (such as `32 x 32`) and set its **Format** to **RGBA 32 bit** for alpha transparency, as shown in the following screenshot:

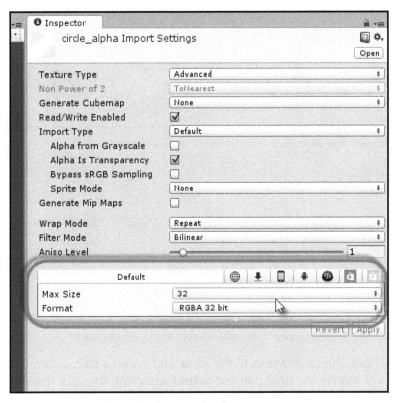

Configuring a brush texture

Create a new material using the **TextureBlender** shader and assign the background texture to the MainTexture slot, as shown here:

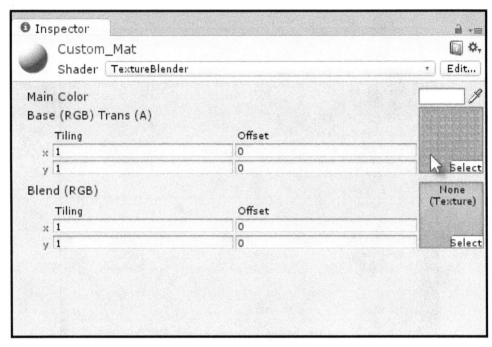

Creating a new material from our TextureBlender shader

Add a new **Quad**, **Plane**, or **Mesh** to the scene and remove its collider, if any. This object will receive the final painted output, although the click detection will occur on a duplicate mesh. I am keeping the final output mesh and the click-detection mesh separate to allow the destination mesh to have other collider types or components if required.

Once the Quad has been added, assign the custom material to it with the
TextureBlender shader, as shown here:

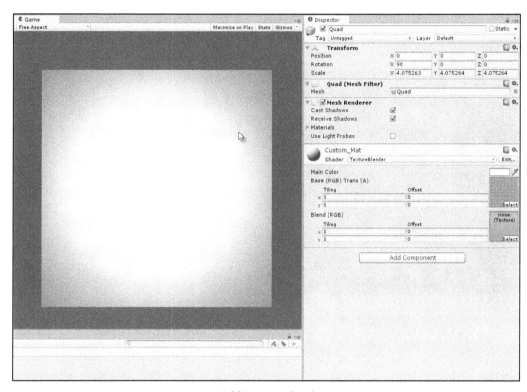

Adding a new Quad

Duplicate **Quad**, add **Mesh Collider**, disable **Mesh Renderer**, and assign an empty
diffuse material to it. This mesh will not render, but will detect mouse clicks and
perform the paint operation.

In addition, add the `TexturePainter` script to the object and assign the **Brush Texture** field to the brush texture itself and the **Dest Mat** field to the **Custom_Mat** material from the **Project** panel, as shown here:

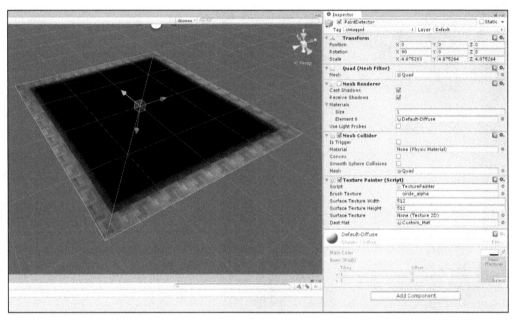

Creating a click detection quad

Now, run the application and start clicking on your mesh. When you do, paint strokes will be applied to the texture and display on the viewport, as shown in the following screenshot:

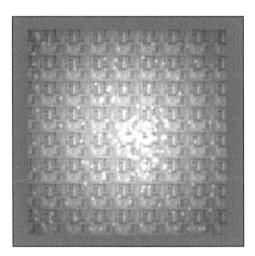

Texture painting completed

Summary

This chapter covered extensive ground under a general remit of "2D-ness". 2D was defined here not so much in the conventional sense of 2D games, but with a texture-based understanding that's critical to both 2D and 3D games more generally. The topics included the operations and ideas that pertain to the 2D plane and within the 2D space. Specifically, it explored how to create rotating Skybox backgrounds by building a manual Skybox, combined with the camera depth settings to create a layered render. Then, it explored how to generate procedural geometry such as planes. With the addition of Unity Quads as primitives, the generation of planes is more limited when taken alone, but the methods and concepts deployed to generate the Quad are more useful, allowing us to edit and tweak any mesh, whether it is a Quad or not. The real-time editing of meshes is important to create a wide range of effects, from shockwave explosions to jelly-based trampolines. Moving forward, we examined the animation of mesh UVs. They allowed us to scroll indefinitely across a 2D background Quad, with a tile-able texture, which is useful for parallax effects as well as for water and other motion-based illusions. Finally, we considered dynamic texture painting on a mesh, where, using the mouse, we can click on a mesh to paint a source texture onto the mesh texture that allows its UV coordinates and the alpha transparency to blend. This feature set is especially powerful and has wide applicability to create real-time decals, such as bullet holes, blood splatters, and player-based drawing. In the next chapter, we will consider a range of tips and techniques to work better with Unity projects.

10
Source Control and Other Tips

This chapter considers three main tips and tricks to script in C# or to work with scripts. These tips are themselves powerful and important but do not belong squarely in any of the previous chapters, which are divided mainly by subject matter. The tips are listed here in no particular order and their main justification for inclusion is based largely on their usefulness, and also because their documentation elsewhere is sparse and often inconclusive. Consequently, this chapter reads as a useful collection of did-you-know tips and tricks, which taken together, offer knowledge that is substantial and practical. The three tips cover:

- Git revision control
- Resource folders and externals files
- Loading and saving games

Git – source control

The term **source control** or **revision control** refers to any software aimed at making development in practice both simpler and safer for as many people as possible. In short, it allows you to track and undo changes to your files easily and quickly, as well as share these changes with others. Typically, software development (including game development) relies on two important facts or ingredients. First, it's a collective effort where multiple developers work together as part of a team, either at the same physical location (such as an office) or across distant locations but sharing a virtual space (such as a virtual office, forum, or even e-mail). Second, during development, developers will tweak, edit, and make improvements to the source code. From these two seemingly simple facts comes a range of important needs that revision control aims to satisfy.

These needs are as follows:

- **Collaboration**: When multiple developers work on coding the same project, they'll usually need to share source files. They can send them back and forth through e-mail or other manual methods, but this makes coding difficult on a large scale and on long-term projects. It quickly becomes difficult to monitor the code changes over time and integrate or merge two sets of changes into one file.

- **Reverting**: Sometimes, code changes and improvements turn out to be mistaken. A proposed edit or fix doesn't always have the intended outcome and must be undone or reverted to the earlier state. You can keep copies of the earlier files yourself, but maintaining potentially many copies over time will be tedious and unnecessarily confusing.

- **Tracking changes and histories**: Often, you'll need to keep track of who does what, especially when debugging. If someone makes a code edit, you'll want to know who changed the code, why, and when. Again, you could manually maintain a logfile, writing in comments and entries to document the changed process, but this would be tedious and time consuming.

Revision control aims to solve the three main problems of collaboration, reversion, and tracking changes. Revision control software includes Git, Perforce, Microsoft Team Foundation Server, and others. This chapter specifically considers Git; it is widely used, free, cross-platform, and open source. Using Git, you can begin by configuring a special database, known as a **repository**, which can be either local (on your computer) or remote (via a network). Then, once configured, you can track and maintain all and any changes to your Unity projects, allowing you to revert to the earlier states of your project, if needed, and to share or collaborate with others. Let's see how to configure Git for general use using a graphical user interface.

Step #1 – downloading

There are many ways to get up and running with Git for Unity projects. This chapter explores a combination of the official Git package alongside the frontend TortoiseGit. Using these two packages, developers can track and maintain all changes to their projects, whether working alone or in a team.

To get started, download and install the official Git software, which is available at `http://git-scm.com/`:

Downloading and installing Git

 Detailed information on using Git can be found in the free, online e-book, *Pro Git, Scott Chacon and Ben Straub, Apress,* available at `http://git-scm.com/book/en/v2`.

After Git is installed and downloaded, it's useful to get TortoiseGit. This is not part of the original Git package but is an optional frontend component for Windows, which it allows you to integrate Git with the Windows shell as well as interact with Git through a GUI rather than the command line.

To download and install TortoiseGit, go to `https://code.google.com/p/`
`tortoisegit/`:

Downloading and installing TortoiseGit

Step #2 – building a Unity project

The reason to install Git originally was to track and maintain changes to a
Unity project, allowing you to revert them if needed, acting as a backup version
in case anything happens to the original files, and to share changes with other
developers. This depends, therefore, on whether you already have a Unity project
to maintain. The next step, then, after installing both Git and TortoiseGit is to either
create a new Unity project or to find an existing one that should be tracked. The
following is the screenshot of the Unity project folder:

Viewing a Unity project folder

After finding a Unity project, open the project folder in Windows explorer to see the project files. If you don't know or don't remember the location of the folder, you could open it directly in explorer from the Unity Editor interface. To achieve this, right-click inside the Unity **Project** panel and select **Show in Explorer** from the context menu:

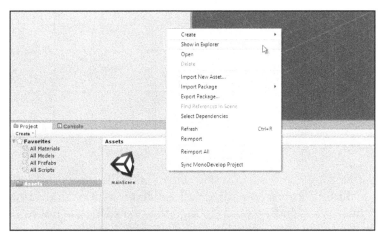

Accessing the project folder from the Unity interface

Step #3 – configuring Unity for source control

Git works with both binary and text files, but it works best with text files. When working with Unity, the editor generates many metadata files for your project and the assets you import. By default, these files are hidden and are in a binary form, and they exist inside the Unity project folder. Some of the generated metafiles are specific only to the instance of Unity that runs on your computer, such as interface preferences, while other files pertain to assets and data that are part of the project, such as meshes, textures, and script files. To get the best results from Git, you'll need to adjust Unity's default behavior by making metafiles visible in the **Project** explorer, and also using text-based formats as opposed to binary formats. To achieve this, go to **Edit | Project Settings | Editor** from the menu bar.

From here, use the object inspector to set the **Version Control** field to **Visible Meta Files** and the **Asset Serialization** field to **Force Text**:

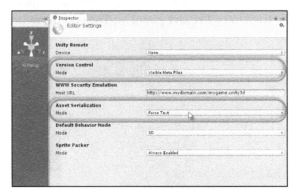

Configuring Unity for version control

When these settings are changed, you will see a `.meta` file associated with each project asset, including scenes. In addition, the metafile will be in a human-readable text format, which can even be edited (though manual editing is not recommended). Have a look at the following screenshot:

Viewing a scene asset (in text format) inside a text editor

Step #4 – creating a Git repository

The next phase, after creating and configuring a Unity project, is to create the Git database or repository itself that will track and maintain all changes to the Unity files. The repository can be either remote (hosted on a network or external computer) or local (hosted on the same computer). The repository will retain the original files and all the changes done to them over time, allowing you to revert to earlier versions of files, if required. The repository can also be shared and merged with other repositories for file sharing. This chapter considers only local repositories, so let's create one now. To do this, open the Unity project folder (the root folder) and then right-click to show the Windows context menu. From the menu, choose **Git Init Here**:

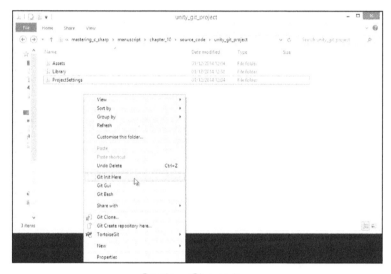

Creating a Git repository

Once created, a new and hidden folder named `.git` will be generated. This folder features all the repository files for the project. The icons for files and folders will change to default red symbols, indicating that the files inside the project folder have not yet been added to the repository, so Git cannot track changes made to them (we'll deal with this soon). This is shown in the following screenshot:

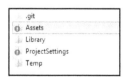

Folders highlighted in red contain files not included
in the Git repository

Step #5 – ignoring files

The Git repository is now created, ready to receive its first set of files (a *commit*). However, before adding them, there are some specific files and types that can safely be ignored. Unity features some project or system-specific files that are less project critical than user critical; that is, some files always contain only user interface preferences as well as read-only files, or temps, and other specific data that need not be added to the repository and can be safely ignored. To ignore these, we can create a .gitignore text file inside the project's root folder and list all the files and folders to be ignored, as shown here:

Creating a Git ignore file to exclude specific
file types from the repository

For Unity, this file (.gitignore) should look as follows. Be sure to put the file inside the root folder:

```
[Ll]ibrary/
[Tt]emp/
[Oo]bj/
[Bb]uild/
/*.csproj
/*.unityproj
/*.sln
/*.suo
/*.user
/*.userprefs
/*.pidb
/*.booproj
sysinfo.txt
```

Step #6 – creating the first commit

The repository is now configured to receive the first set of Unity project files. To add these, right-click inside the root folder window, and from the context menu, go to **Git Commit | Master**. In Git, files are typically submitted not one by one but in batches. The **Commit** window allows you to select all files to commit.

Click on the **All** button to select all files in the folder and then assign a description in the **Message** field to the commit. The message should allow any user to understand the files that the commit contains. When ready, click on **OK** to commit the files:

Submitting the original project files

When the commit is completed, the file icons will turn green to indicate a file match, that is, to indicate that the files in the project folder are identical to those in the repository:

Files are up to date with the repository

Step #7 – changing files

Git is supposed to be a complete file-tracking solution; this means that it should store not only your original files but all the subsequent changes and edits, allowing you to revert to any previous version.

If you now return to Unity and change your files, adding new assets or editing the existing ones, the file icons inside the Windows explorer change to red again, indicating a mismatch between the local files and the repository files:

Changing files

If you decide that your most recent changes were a mistake and you'd like to revert back to the changes made last, you can do this by right-clicking inside the project folder window and going to **TortoiseGit | Revert...** from the context menu:

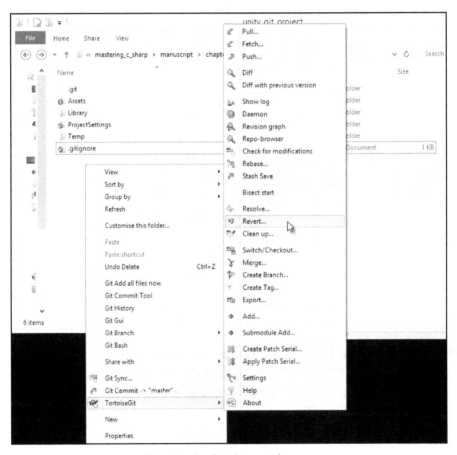

Reverting (undoing) recent changes

The **Revert** dialog will show, allowing you to select files for reversion. Select all the required files and then choose **OK**. Git will then restore all the selected files, overwriting the local versions with the latest versions from the repository:

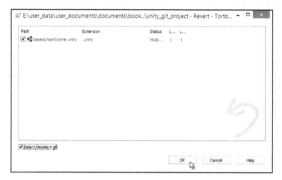

Select files to revert

On the other hand, you might not want to revert or undo the recent changes. Instead, you might have created a valid change; this should be added to the Git repo as the latest version of the files. If so, then simply recommit the files. Right-click inside the project folder window and, from the context menu, go to **Git Commit | Master**. Be sure to enter a new and descriptive message for the commit inside the **Message** field of the **Commit** dialog.

Step #8 – getting files from the repo

Once the original commit of all the files has been made, if you were to delete every file in the Unity folder either intentionally or accidentally, except for the `.git` and `.gitignore` files, you could still retrieve all the latest files again. This is because the Git repo contains the files.

You can retrieve deleted files
in the project folder from the Git repo

 Of course, if you are really following along with the book by deleting your own files, make sure to keep a manual backup of them, in case anything goes wrong during testing!

To achieve this, right-click inside the project folder window and navigate to **TortoiseGit | Switch/Checkout** from the context menu:

Using the Switch/Checkout option to retrieve the latest files from the repo

From the **Switch/Checkout** dialog, select the **Master** branch for the **Switch To** field.

You might also need to enable the **Force** check from the options (see the documentation for more details). Then, click on **OK** to retrieve the latest files. You will see the following screenshot once all the files are retrieved:

Retrieving the latest files with checkout

Alternatively, you might want to switch your project back to an earlier commit in the repo, retrieving not the latest files, but an earlier commit instead. To do this, first go to **Tortoise Git | Switch/Checkout** from the context menu to show the **Checkout** dialog. Then, from the **Switch To** group, enable the **Commit** radio box:

Enabling the Commit radio button to retrieve older commits

Click the browse button (**...**) next to the **Commit** field to display the repo commits available, and select the earlier version to switch to. Then, click on **OK** to exit the **Repo Commits** dialog, and click on **OK** again to confirm the checkout from the selected commit. The files from the selected commit will then be restored to the project folder. Remember that each commit has an author (for those working in teams), and this lets you get a picture of who has changed what:

Selecting older commits from the repo to restore

Step #9 – browsing the repo

Sometimes, you'll want to neither add nor retrieve files from the repository, but simply browse them to see what is there. You can do this quickly and easily using the Repo Browser tool, which is part of TortoiseGit. To access the tool, go to **TortoiseGit | Repo Browser** from the context menu:

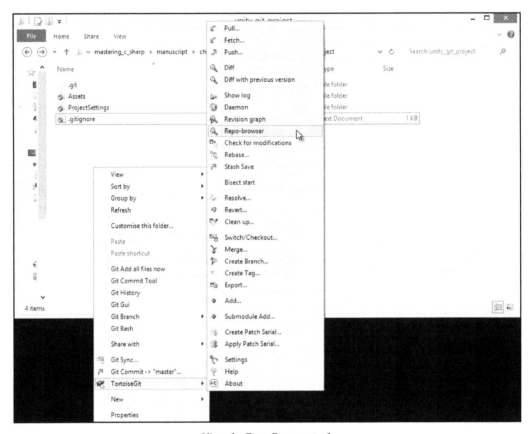

View the Repo Browser tool

The Repo Browser tool allows you to preview the files and hierarchy from a GUI window:

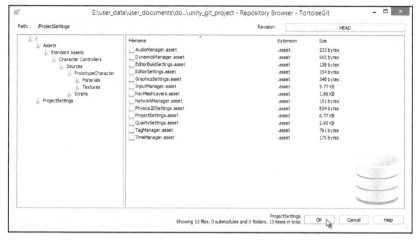

Examining the files inside the repo

Resources folder and external files

Your games will frequently rely on external data loaded from files such as XML files, perhaps, for subtitles, localization, or level serialization. Have a look at the following screenshot:

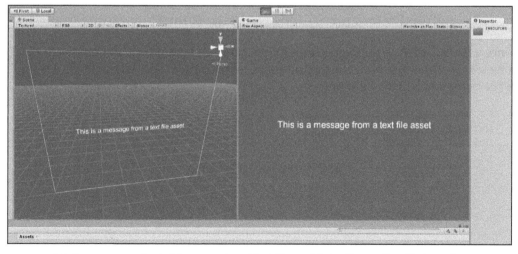

Printing a message loaded from an external text file asset that will compile with the project

In these cases, you want a specific range of abilities. The first one is the ability to dynamically load data from the file into memory in a way that Unity can parse and understand. The second is the ability to change and edit the file contents, even after importing it into Unity, and then have the effects of the changes update in the game without requiring code changes. The third is the ability to compile and distribute your standalone game with the file included as part of the main Unity build, rather than as a separate and editable file alongside the main executable. To elaborate further on the third point, you don't usually want to distribute your game as a standalone build alongside separate and external files, such as XML files, which can be opened and edited by the gamer. Instead, as the developer, you want to edit and change the files from the Unity Editor, and you want the files themselves to be compiled and built into your final Unity standalone project, like other assets. You can achieve this using resource folders.

To use resource folders, create a folder named `resources` in the Unity project. A project can feature none, one, or more `resources` folders. Inside the folder, add all assets, such as text files that can be loaded by Unity at runtime:

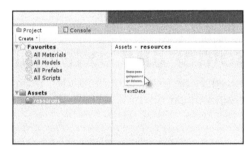

Adding external files to the resources folder

Once a file is added to the `resources` folder, you can load it into memory with the `Resources.Load` function. See the following code sample 10-1, which loads a sample text asset into a UI text component:

```
using UnityEngine;
using System.Collections;
using UnityEngine.UI;
//---------------------------------------------
public class LoadTextData : MonoBehaviour
{
    //Reference to UI Text Component
    private Text MyText = null;

    //Reference to text asset in resources folder
    private TextAsset TextData = null;
    //---------------------------------------------
    // Use this for initialization
```

```
void Awake () {
  //Get Text Component
  MyText = GetComponent<Text>();

  //Load text data from resources folder
  TextData = Resources.Load("TextData") as TextAsset;
}
//---------------------------------------------
// Update is called once per frame
void Update () {
  //Update text label component
  MyText.text = TextData.text;
}
//---------------------------------------------
}
//---------------------------------------------
```

 More information on resource folders and the `Resources` class is available in the online Unity documentation at `http://docs.unity3d.com/ScriptReference/Resources.html`.

AssetBundles and external files

If you're using Unity Pro and want to offer dynamic content to users, allowing gamers to **modify (mod)** game content, add their own assets, and add-ons, as well as support your own add-ons and plugins, then AssetBundles can be useful. AssetBundles let you package together many disparate Unity assets into a single, external file outside the main project, which can be loaded into any Unity project dynamically, either from a local file on disk or via the Internet:

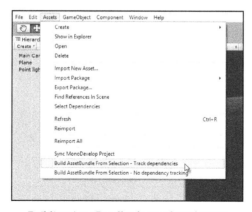

Building AssetBundles from selected assets

To get started, import the Unity asset bundle editor script to build AssetBundles easily from the **Project** panel. To do this, paste the following code sample 10-2 into a C# script file located inside an `Editor` folder in your project; otherwise, you can download the script from: `http://docs.unity3d.com/ScriptReference/` `BuildPipeline.BuildAssetBundle.html`:

```
// C# Example
// Builds an asset bundle from the selected objects in the
// project view.
// Once compiled go to "Menu" -> "Assets" and select one of the
// choices to build the Asset Bundle

using UnityEngine;
using UnityEditor;
public class ExportAssetBundles {
  [MenuItem("Assets/Build AssetBundle From Selection - Track
    dependencies")]
  static void ExportResource () {
    // Bring up save panel
    string path = EditorUtility.SaveFilePanel ("Save Resource",
      "", "New Resource", "unity3d");
    if (path.Length != 0) {
      // Build the resource file from the active selection.
      Object[] selection = Selection.GetFiltered(typeof(Object),
        SelectionMode.DeepAssets);
      BuildPipeline.BuildAssetBundle
        (Selection.activeObject, selection, path,
        BuildAssetBundleOptions.CollectDependencies |
        BuildAssetBundleOptions.CompleteAssets);
      Selection.objects = selection;
    }
  }
  [MenuItem("Assets/Build AssetBundle From Selection - No
    dependency tracking")]
  static void ExportResourceNoTrack () {
    // Bring up save panel
    string path = EditorUtility.SaveFilePanel
      ("Save Resource", "", "New Resource", "unity3d");
    if (path.Length != 0) {
      // Build the resource file from the active selection.
      BuildPipeline.BuildAssetBundle
        (Selection.activeObject, Selection.objects, path);
    }
  }
}
```

To make an AssetBundle, select all the assets in the **Project** panel to be included in the bundle and then go to **Assets | Build AssetBundle from Selection** from the menu bar. Once selected, choose a location on your computer where the bundle should be saved.

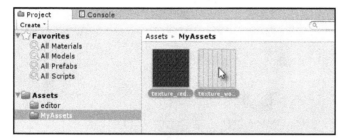

Selecting assets to be included in an AssetBundle

Then, to test the AssetBundle, create a new project or open a different project without the assets, and you can load them into your project at runtime using the WWW class. See the following code sample 10-3 for a sample script that downloads an AssetBundle from a local file, extracts a texture asset, and assigns it to the material of an attached mesh renderer component:

```
using UnityEngine;
using System.Collections;

public class LoadAssetBundle : MonoBehaviour
{
  //Mesh Renderer Reference
  private MeshRenderer MR = null;

  // Use this for initialization
  IEnumerator Start ()
  {
    //Get asset bundle file from local machine
    WWW www = new WWW (@"file:///c:\asset_textures.unity3d");

    //Wait until load is completed
    yield return www;

    //Retrieve texture from asset bundle
    Texture2D Tex = www.assetBundle.Load
    ("texture_wood",typeof(Texture2D)) as Texture2D;

    //Assign texture in bundle to mesh
    MR = GetComponent<MeshRenderer>();
    MR.material.mainTexture = Tex;
  }
}
```

This is how the texture asset will look:

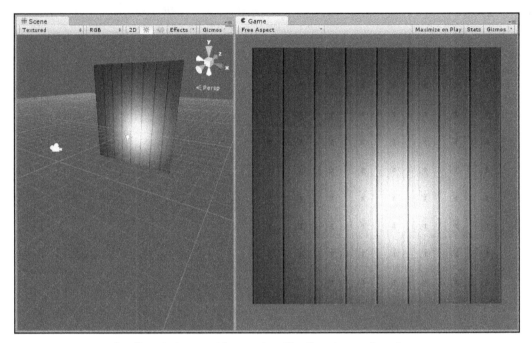

Loading a texture asset from an AssetBundle onto a mesh renderer

 More information on AssetBundles can be found in the online Unity documentation at http://docs.unity3d.com/Manual/ AssetBundlesIntro.html.

Persistent data and saved games

Allowing the gamer to save and load the state of their game is important for many games, especially longer duration games such as adventures, real-time strategies, and RPGs. In these cases, the game should allow the user to save and load game data to and from external files.

This is achieved in Unity using data serialization via either XML or binary files:

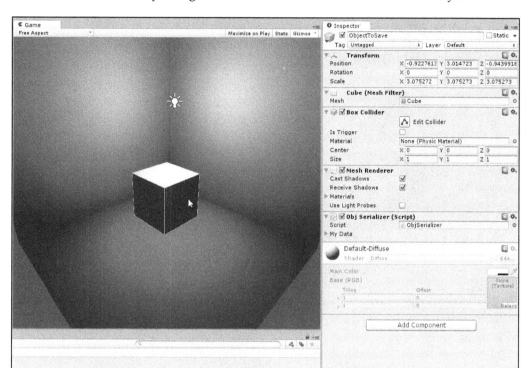

Saving the Transform properties of an object to an XML file

Serialization is the process of converting, or translating, data in memory (such as the state of a component on a `GameObject`) into a stream that can be written to a file and then loaded back from a file to recreate the component in memory, as it was when it was saved. The process of creating a save-game, therefore, is about first deciding which data must be saved and loaded (which is game specific) and then creating a new class to hold that data. Consider the following code sample 10-4 (`ObjSerializer.cs`) that can be attached to any `GameObject` to serialize its Transform component (Translation, Rotation, and Scale) to and from an external file, both in the XML and binary formats. To achieve this, the `XmlSerializer` class is used to convert an object in memory to XML, and the BinaryFormatter converts an object in memory to a binary file. XML files are human-readable text files, while binary files cannot normally be read or understood by humans:

```
001 //-----------------------------------------------
002 using UnityEngine;
003 using System.Collections;
```

```
004 using System.Collections.Generic;
005 using System.Xml;
006 using System.Xml.Serialization;
007 using System.Runtime.Serialization.Formatters.Binary;
008 using System.IO;
009 //-----------------------------------------------
010 public class ObjSerializer : MonoBehaviour
011 {
012   //Data to save to file XML or Binary
013   [System.Serializable]
014   [XmlRoot("GameData")]
015   public class MySaveData
016   {
017     //Transform data to save/load to and from file
018     //represents a conversion of a transform object
019     //into simpler values, like floats
020     [System.Serializable]
021     public struct DataTransform
022     {
023       public float X;
024       public float Y;
025       public float Z;
026       public float RotX;
027       public float RotY;
028       public float RotZ;
029       public float ScaleX;
030       public float ScaleY;
031       public float ScaleZ;
032     }
033
034     //Transform object to save
035     public DataTransform MyTransform = new DataTransform();

036   }
037
038   //My Save Data Object declared here
039   public MySaveData MyData = new MySaveData();
040   //-----------------------------------------------
041   //Populate structure MyData with transform data
042   //This is the data to be saved to a file
043   private void GetTransform()
044   {
```

```
045      //Get transform component on this object
046      Transform ThisTransform = transform;
047
048      //Got transform, now fill data structure
049      MyData.MyTransform.X = ThisTransform.position.x;
050      MyData.MyTransform.Y = ThisTransform.position.y;
051      MyData.MyTransform.Z = ThisTransform.position.z;
052      MyData.MyTransform.RotX =
            ThisTransform.localRotation.eulerAngles.x;

053      MyData.MyTransform.RotY =
            ThisTransform.localRotation.eulerAngles.y;

054      MyData.MyTransform.RotZ =
            ThisTransform.localRotation.eulerAngles.z;

055      MyData.MyTransform.ScaleX = ThisTransform.localScale.x;

056      MyData.MyTransform.ScaleY = ThisTransform.localScale.y;

057      MyData.MyTransform.ScaleZ = ThisTransform.localScale.z;
058      }
059      //------------------------------------------------
060      //Restore the transform component with loaded data
061      //Call this function after loading data back from a file
         // for restore
062      private void SetTransform()
063      {
064        //Get transform component on this object
065        Transform ThisTransform = transform;
066
067        //We got the transform component, now restore data
068        ThisTransform.position = new Vector3
              (MyData.MyTransform.X, MyData.MyTransform.Y,
              MyData.MyTransform.Z);

069        ThisTransform.rotation =
              Quaternion.Euler(MyData.MyTransform.RotX,
              MyData.MyTransform.RotY, MyData.MyTransform.RotZ);

070        ThisTransform.localScale = new
              Vector3(MyData.MyTransform.ScaleX,
              MyData.MyTransform.ScaleY, MyData.MyTransform.ScaleZ);
```

```
071      }
072   //------------------------------------------------
073   //Saves game data to XML file
074   //Call this function to save data to an XML file
075   //Call as Save
076   public void SaveXML(string FileName = "GameData.xml")
077   {
078      //Get transform data
079      GetTransform();
080
081      //Now save game data
082      XmlSerializer Serializer = new
            XmlSerializer(typeof(MySaveData));

083      FileStream Stream = new FileStream(FileName,
            FileMode.Create);

084      Serializer.Serialize(Stream, MyData);
085      Stream.Close();
086   }
087   //------------------------------------------------
088   //Load game data from XML file
089   //Call this function to load data from an XML file
090   //Call as Load
091   public void LoadXML(string FileName = "GameData.xml")
092   {
093      //If file doesn't exist, then exit
094      if(!File.Exists(FileName)) return;
095
096      XmlSerializer Serializer = new
            XmlSerializer(typeof(MySaveData));

097      FileStream Stream = new FileStream(FileName,
            FileMode.Open);

098      MyData = Serializer.Deserialize(Stream) as MySaveData;

099      Stream.Close();
100
101      //Set transform - load back from a file
```

```
102      SetTransform();
103    }
104    //------------------------------------------------
105    public void SaveBinary(string FileName = "GameData.sav")
106    {
107      //Get transform data
108      GetTransform();
109
110      BinaryFormatter bf = new BinaryFormatter();
111      FileStream Stream = File.Create(FileName);
112      bf.Serialize(Stream, MyData);
113      Stream.Close();
114    }
115    //------------------------------------------------
116    public void LoadBinary(string FileName = "GameData.sav")
117    {
118      //If file doesn't exist, then exit
119      if(!File.Exists(FileName)) return;
120
121      BinaryFormatter bf = new BinaryFormatter();
122    FileStream Stream = File.Open(FileName, FileMode.Open);
123      MyData = bf.Deserialize(Stream) as MySaveData;
124      Stream.Close();
125
126      //Set transform - load back from a file
127      SetTransform();
128    }
129    //------------------------------------------------
130 }
131 //------------------------------------------------
```

 A full example of loading and saving game data can be found in the book's companion files in the Chapter10/XML_and_Binary folder.

Summary

This final chapter considered three main tips of which, perhaps, the only underlying theme has been file management. The first tip considered Git version control, specifically, how the free and open source version control software allows us to track changes across a project as well as collaborate easily with other developers. The second tip concerned loading file data dynamically, first using internal project files inside a `resources` folder and then using AssetBundles. The latter options are especially useful for the creation of external assets that can be edited by both developers and gamers alike. The third and final tip demonstrated how in-game data can be saved to a file and then loaded back through serialization. Through serialization, users can save and restore game data, allowing them to resume playback at a later time.

Index

Symbols

#endregion directive
  used, for code folding in MonoDevelop 139
? operator 48
#region directive
  used, for code folding in MonoDevelop 139
@ symbol 216

A

active scene, Unity
  changing 118
AI
  about 223, 224
  games 224, 225
animation
  using, with camera 180
animation curves
  URL 186
Animator.StringToHash
  URL 241
arrays
  about 21-24
  URL 24
Artificial Intelligence. *See* **AI**
AssetBundles
  and external files 345-348
  URL 348
AssetDatabase class
  URL 307
Attack state
  creating 251
Awake function
  about 241
  versus Start 122
Axially Aligned Bounding Box (AABB) 163

B

Batch Rename tool 259
batch renaming functionality 259-264
bitwise operations
  URL 268
Blender
  URL 226
BroadcastMessage
  about 49-51
  online resources 51
  URL 50
BuildPipeline.BuildAssetBundle
  URL 346

C

C#
  about 8, 191
  Finite State Machines (FSMs) 240-242
  need for 8
  overview 7
  properties 42
  selecting 8
  URL 70
call stack 87, 88
camera
  camera shakes 178
  follow camera 180
  gizmos 156-158
  paths 186
  rendering 171-177
  using, with animation 180
  using, with curves 183-185
camera fly-throughs 180

PUBLISHING

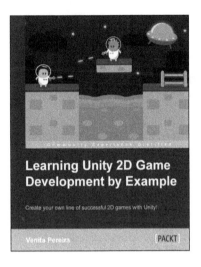

Learning Unity 2D Game
Development by Example

Venita Pereira

PACKT

Learning Unity 2D Game Development by Example

ISBN: 978-1-78355-904-6   Paperback: 266 pages

Create your own line of successful 2D games
with Unity!

1. Dive into 2D game development with no
   previous experience.

2. Learn how to use the new Unity 2D toolset.

3. Create and deploy your very own 2D game
   with confidence.

Unity Game Development
Blueprints

John P. Duran

PACKT

Unity Game Development Blueprints

ISBN: 978-1-78355-365-5   Paperback: 318 pages

Explore the various enticing features of Unity and
learn how to develop awesome games

1. Create a wide variety of projects with Unity in
   multiple genres and formats.

2. Complete art assets with clear step-by-step
   examples and instructions to complete all tasks
   using Unity, C#, and MonoDevelop.

3. Develop advanced internal and external
   environments for games in 2D and 3D.

Please check **www.PacktPub.com** for information on our titles

Mastering Unity 2D Game Development

ISBN: 978-1-84969-734-7   Paperback: 474 pages

Become an expert in Unity3D's new 2D system, and then join in the adventure to build an RPG game framework!

1. Learn the advanced features of Unity 2D to change and customize games to suit your needs.

2. Discover tips and tricks for Unity2D's new toolset.

3. Understand scripting, deployment, and platform integration with an example at each step.

Unity 4 Game Development HOTSHOT

ISBN: 978-1-84969-558-9   Paperback: 466 pages

Develop spectacular gaming content by exploring and utilizing Unity 4

1. Understand the new 2D Sprite and Immediate Mode GUI system (OnGUI()/GUI class) in Unity 4, and the difference between 2D and 3D worlds, with clear instruction and examples.

2. Learn about Mecanim System, AI programming, editor script, and Character Controller programming, including scripting and how to adapt it to your needs.

3. Create a menu for an RPG game – add powerups, weapons, and armor.

Please check **www.PacktPub.com** for information on our titles